# Praise for this book

This book is a must-read for all university leaders and senior managers to enable them to get a better insight into the numerous challenges facing academia in the new normal, where it is not only about academic excellence but also about the human dimension through the enhanced use of technology.
—Dhanjay Jhurry, Professor and Vice-Chancellor,
University of Mauritius, Mauritius

This thought-provoking book captures contemporary changes to higher education at the micro and macro level post-2020. Stakeholders across the sector will benefit from reading the research-driven chapters that are stimulating and insightful. The book interrogates and challenges ways in which internationalization and global mobility can be re-imagined.
—Dawn Joseph, Associate Professor,
Deakin University, Australia

This book shows a more intensive and multi-facetted response by the higher education community to the pandemic that one might have expected. Attention is paid notably to sustain international life on campus.
—Ulrich Teichler, Professor Emeritus,
International Centre for Higher Education Research,
University of Kassel, Germany

This volume is a welcome addition to the literature on international Higher Education produced during the COVID-19 era. With a sensitively chosen array of topics, it shows new thinking around internationalisation, which is encouraging for all, and is exactly what is needed.
—Amanda C. Murphy, Professor and Director,
Centre for Higher Education Internationalisation,
Università Cattolica del Sacro Cuore, Italy

With the COVID-19 pandemic seeing no end in sight and its effects on international higher education for students around the world yet unknown, the importance of this timely book cannot be overstated. At a time when we are literally awash in countless editorials prognosticating on *possible* implications of this health catastrophe, it is refreshing to get a carefully collected series of essays that step back, take a deep breath, and bring us back to the fundamental questions we need to be asking at this most dangerous time for humanity.

—Bernhard Streitwieser, IEP Program Director & Associate Professor of International Education & International Affairs, George Washington University, USA

This is a valuable addition to higher education for understanding the complexities that COVID-19 introduced into the academic landscape. This volume explores valuable topics and issues such as employability, research and mentoring, innovative teaching and learning, and emerging opportunities during the pandemic.

—Jane E. Gatewood, Vice Provost for Global Engagement, University of Rochester, USA

This timely book is much needed for practitioners, scholars, and policy makers who are grappling with the challenges created by the pandemic. The book is comprehensive given the depth and breath of topics. The human centric approach is refreshing.

—Fanta Aw, Vice President of Campus Life & Inclusive Excellence, American University, USA

# COVID-19 and Higher Education in the Global Context: Exploring Contemporary Issues and Challenges

*COVID-19 and Higher Education in the Global Context: Exploring Contemporary Issues and Challenges* addresses the lasting impact of the novel coronavirus (COVID-19) in the higher education sector and offers insights that inform policy and practice. Framed in a global context, this timely book captures a wide variety of topics, including student mobility, global partnerships and collaboration, student health and wellbeing, enrollment management, employability, and graduate education. It is designed to serve as a resource for scholar-practitioners, policymakers, and university administrators as they reimagine their work of comparative and international higher education in times of crisis. The collection of chapters assembled in this volume calls for a critical reflection on the opportunities and challenges that have emerged as a result of the global pandemic, and provides as a basis for how tertiary education systems around the world can learn from past experiences and shared viewpoints as institutions recalibrate operations, innovate programs, and manage change on their respective campuses.

**Ravichandran Ammigan, Ph.D.,** is the Associate Deputy Provost for International Programs and an Assistant Professor of Education at the University of Delaware, Delaware, USA.

**Roy Y. Chan, Ph.D.,** is an Assistant Professor of Education and the Director of the Doctor of Education (Ed.D.) program in Leadership and Professional Practice in the Helen DeVos College of Education at Lee University, Tennessee, USA.

**Krishna Bista, Ed.D.,** is a Professor of Higher Education in the Department of Advanced Studies, Leadership and Policy at Morgan State University, Maryland, USA.

# The STAR Scholars Network Titles

We seek to explore new ideas and best practices related to international and comparative education from the US and around the world, and from a wide range of academic fields, including leadership studies, technology, general education, and area and cultural studies. STAR Scholars publishes some titles in collaboration with Routledge, Palgrave MacMillan, Open Journals in Education, *Journal of International Students,* and other university presses. At STAR Scholars Network, we aim to amplify the voices of underrepresented scholars, epistemologies, and perspectives. We are committed to an inclusion of a diversity of racial, ethnic, and cultural backgrounds and are particularly interested in proposals from scholars who identify with countries in the Global South.

We value linguistic diversity. Although many of the volumes that we publish are written in English, we welcome proposals in any language. If you are proposing a book in another language besides English, please submit a version in the proposed language and a translated version in English, so we can send your proposal for peer review to scholars who may not speak the proposal's language but are able to review proposals in English. More information at https://starscholars.org/open-access/

**Recent Titles Include:**

**Global Higher Education During COVID-19: Policy, Society, and Technology**
*Edited by Joshua S. McKeown, Krishna Bista, and Roy Y. Chan*

**Home and Abroad: International Student Experiences and Graduate Employability**
*Edited by Xin (Skye) Zhao, Michael Kung, Yingyi Ma, and Krishna Bista*

**Cross-Cultural Narratives: Stories and Experiences of International Students**
*Edited by Ravichandran Ammigan*

# COVID-19 and Higher Education in the Global Context

Exploring Contemporary Issues and Challenges

**Edited by
Ravichandran Ammigan,
Roy Y. Chan, and Krishna Bista**

⭐ **STAR**SCHOLARS
N E T W O R K

**STAR**SCHOLARS
N E T W O R K

First Published 2022
by
STAR Scholars
In collaboration with
Open Journals in Education and
Journal of International Students

**Category**
Education/Higher Education

**Series**
Comparative and International
Education

Typeset in Garamond

*Series Editor*
Krishna Bista

*Project Advisor*
Chris R. Glass

*Copy Editor*
CodeMantra

*Cover Design*
Srdjan Marjanovic

Printed in the United States of America

**Editors**
Ravichandran Ammigan | Roy Y.
Chan | Krishna Bista

ISBN: 978-1-7364699-7-2

© STAR Scholars

**Library of Congress Control
Number**: 2021943758

COVID-19 and Higher Education
in the Global Context: Exploring
Contemporary Issues and Challenges
Subject: Education/Higher Education –
United States | International
Education | Student Mobility |
Comparative Education
Krishna Bista (series editor)

Library of Congress US Programs,
Law, and Literature Division

Cataloging in Publication Program
101 Independence Avenue, S.E.
Washington, DC 20540-4283

**In memory of those who lost their lives during the COVID-19 pandemic worldwide**

# Contents

# Tables

# Acknowledgments

We are extremely grateful to several teacher-scholars, practitioners, and policymakers who have supported our project since the COVID-19 global pandemic in January 2020. In particular, we are most grateful to our colleagues including Dr. Uttam Gaulee, Dr. Chris Glass, Dr. Darla Deardorff, Dr. Glenda Prime, Dr. Harvey Charles, Dr. Rajika Bhandari, Dr. Rosalind Latiner Raby, Dr. Shibao Guo, Dr. Stewart E. Sutin, Dr. Harry Bhandari, Dr. Don Jones, Dr. Sanoya Amienyi, Dr. Marvin Perry, and Dr. Eward J. Valeau at the Society of Transnational Academic Researchers (STAR) Scholars Network, Maryland. We also appreciate the support of colleagues whom we worked with over the years at the Open Journals in Education, a consortium of the professional journals and the *Journal of International Students*, as well as the Comparative and International Education Society's (CIES) Study Abroad and International Students (SAIS) SIG, and the Association for the Study of Higher Education (ASHE) Council on International Higher Education.

We would also like to acknowledge the help of all scholars and organizations who were involved in this project and, more specifically, Terra Dotta, LLC, who helped fund the publication of this book. We also acknowledge support from the authors and reviewers that took part in the review process. Without their support, this book would not have become a reality. At the University of Delaware, Dr. Ammigan would like to thank his colleagues at the Center for Global Programs & Services and the Office of the Provost for their support. At Lee University, Dr. Chan would like to thank his colleagues and Ed.D. students, who provided suggestions and feedback in this project. At Morgan State University, Dr. Bista would like to thank his colleagues for their encouragement and support including graduate students and graduate assistants in the Department of Advanced Studies, Leadership and Policy.

Special thanks to the following reviewers who assisted us in reviewing manuscripts received for this book. It could not be possible to finalize the selected chapters without their evaluations and constructive feedback.

## List of Chapter Reviewers

Adriana Medina, University of North Carolina Charlotte, USA
Ana Amaya, Pace University, USA
Barry Fass-Holmes, University of California, San Diego, USA
Charles Brown, Purdue University, USA
Chris Glass, Boston College Center for International Higher Education, USA
Darla K. Deardorff, Association of International Education Administrators, USA
Emily Schell, Stanford University, USA
Hatice Altun, Pamukkale University, Turkey
Jie Li, Rutgers University, USA
Kimberly Manturuk, Duke University, USA
Krishna Bista, Morgan State University, USA
Li Wang, Institute of Education Sciences, USA
Naif Daifullah Z Alsulami, Umm Al-Qura University, Saudi Arabia
Peggy Gesing, Eastern Virginia Medical School, USA
Ravichandran Ammigan, University of Delaware, USA
Roy Y. Chan, Lee University, USA
Ryan Allen, Chapman University, USA
Shawn Conner-Rondot, Indiana University, USA
Shytance Wren, Zayed University, Dubai, United Arab Emirates
Siyin Liang, University of Regina, Canada
William Harder, Goucher College, USA

We would like to thank the following colleagues for their feedback on the early draft of this book as well as for their endorsements:

- Amanda C. Murphy, Professor, Università Cattolica del Sacro Cuore, Italy
- Dawn Joseph, Associate Professor, Deakin University, Australia
- Dhanjay Jhurry, Professor and Vice-Chancellor, University of Mauritius, Mauritius
- Ulrich Teichler, Professor Emeritus, University of Kassel, Germany
- Bernhard Streitwieser, IEP Program Director & Associate Professor of International Education & International Affairs, George Washington University, USA
- Jane E. Gatewood, Vice Provost for Global Engagement, University of Rochester, USA
- Fanta Aw, Vice President of Campus Life & Inclusive Excellence, American University, USA
- Uttiyo Raychaudhuri, Vice Provost for Internationalization, University of Denver, USA

## About Terra Dotta

Terra Dotta is the trusted leader in global engagement solutions for higher education. Over 600 universities and colleges use Terra Dotta's global engagement platform to facilitate cross-cultural experiences for students, faculty and staff in more than 85 countries worldwide. The company's solutions help customers deliver end-to-end, accessible global engagement experiences that meet comprehensive safety and compliance requirements – from managing domestic and international travel to international student programs, virtual and global experiences and beyond. Terra Dotta is based in Chapel Hill, N.C. and can be found at http://www.terradotta.com.

terradotta.com

TERRΛDOTTΛ

Global Engagement Solutions for Higher Education

# Editors

**Ravichandran Ammigan** is the Associate Deputy Provost for International Programs and an Assistant Professor of Education at the University of Delaware. With over 20 years of experience in the field of international higher education, he has served in a number of leadership positions in international student and scholar services, education abroad, and admissions and recruitment. Dr. Ammigan's current research focuses on the international student experience at institutions of higher education globally, with a particular emphasis on student satisfaction and support services. He is the editor of the book *Cross-Cultural Narratives: Stories and Experiences of International Students* (STAR Scholars, 2021). Originally from the island of Mauritius, Dr. Ammigan first came to the United States as an international student himself and stayed to work as an expatriate. He holds a Ph.D. in Higher Education Internationalization from Università Cattolica del Sacro Cuore, Milan; an M.A. in Communication from Michigan State University; and a B.A. in Business from Kendall College. Email: rammigan@udel.edu

**Roy Y. Chan** is an Assistant Professor of Education and the Director of the Doctor of Education (Ed.D.) program in Leadership and Professional Practice in the Helen DeVos College of Education at Lee University. Previously, Dr. Chan served as the Director of TRIO Student Support Services (SSS), where he managed a budget of $1.3 million funded by the U.S. Department of Education. His research interest includes cross-border and transnational higher education, study abroad, global education policy, and educational philanthropy. Dr. Chan currently serves as Chair-Elect of the Comparative and International Education Society (CIES) Study Abroad and International Students (SAIS) Special Interest Group, and previously served as an advisor to the Forum on Education Abroad's Data Committee. His latest books include *Online Teaching and Learning in Higher Education during COVID-19: International Perspectives and Experiences* (Routledge, 2021); *The Future of Accessibility in International Higher Education* (IGI Global, 2017); and *Higher Education: A Worldwide Inventory of Research Centers, Academic Programs, Journals and Publications* (Lemmens Media, 2014). Dr. Chan holds a Ph.D. in History, Philosophy, and Policy in Education from Indiana University Bloomington, an M.A. in Higher Education Administration from Boston College, an M.Ed. in Comparative Higher Education from The University of Hong Kong, and a B.A. from the University of California, Irvine. Email: rchan@leeuniversity.edu

**Krishna Bista** is the Vice President of the STAR Scholars Network and a Professor of Higher Education in the Department of Advanced Studies, Leadership and Policy at Morgan State University, Maryland. Dr Bista is the Founding Editor of *Journal of International Students*. His research interests include comparative and international higher education issues, global student mobility, and innovative technology in teaching and learning. His recent books include *Online Teaching and Learning in Higher Education* (Routledge, w/Chan and Allen), *Global Perspectives on International Student Experiences* (Routledge), *Higher Education in Nepal* (Routledge, w/Raby and Sharma), *Rethinking Education Across Border* (Springer, w/Gaulee & Sharma), and *Inequalities in Study and Student Mobility* (Routledge, w/Kommers). Dr. Bista serves on the editorial review boards for *Kappa Delta Pi Record, Teachers College Record, Journal of Leadership and Organizational Studies,* and *International Journal of Leadership in Education*. Dr. Bista has organized more than 70 professional development workshops on a variety of topics related to college student experience, international student/faculty mobility, internationalization and exchange programs, and cross-cultural studies; has published 15 books, and more than 80 articles, book chapters, and review essays. He is the founding Chair of the Comparative and International Educational Society (CIES) Study Abroad and International Students SIG, and the editor of the Routledge Global Student Mobility Series. Previously, Dr. Bista served as the Director of Global Education at the University of Louisiana at Monroe, where he was also the Chase Endowed Professor of Education in the School of Education. He holds a doctoral degree in Educational Leadership/Higher Education, a specialist degree in Community College Teaching and Administration, both from Arkansas State University, and an M.S. in Postsecondary Education/ Higher Education from Troy University, Alabama. E-mail: krishna. bista@morgan.edu

# Foreword

*Darla K. Deardorff*

The COVID-19 pandemic has represented a unifying challenge globally, providing a defining era in human existence as the pandemic upended life as we know it. *COVID-19 and Higher Education in the Global Context: Exploring Contemporary Issues and Challenges*, edited by Ammigan, Chan, and Bista, delves into the pandemic's impact on higher education around the world. Such an exploration empowers "educators, administrators, practitioners, policy makers, and families" with ideas and guidance that not only can be applied in the current context but also in the post-COVID future.

As the world emerges from the COVID pandemic, it is good to remember the signs of hope that have been there all along from the small gestures of kindness to the heroic efforts of those on the frontlines, from strangers lifting their voices together in song across balconies as the pandemic began with the later Jerusalema dance challenge that swept around the world, even as the pandemic was raging. This pandemic has shown us that we are all truly interconnected, for better or for worse. Desmond Tutu reminds us that we are all in this together and that our humanity is bound up together. We are members of one human family, and when some members are hurting, we all are hurt. He goes on to say, "For us to engage in the practices that will ensure that we all prosper, we must come to know that each of us is linked in the chain of our common humanity."

As we move into the light of a new day, there is radical hope in truly embracing our shared humanity. Let's seek to see ourselves in others. Let's seek to see the whole picture through discovering others' perspectives beyond our own. Let's seek to see the invisible among us and to remember the power of being seen and heard. As we do so, we can reflect on some of the following questions:

- What do I know about my neighbors?
- Do I make an effort to learn more?
- What are others' perspectives and can I articulate those?
- What are the connections I see in others to my own experiences?
- How much do I really listen for understanding and seek first to understand?

Higher education provides opportunities for students to explore these and other questions, as universities seek to educate global citizens. As we have come to understand more poignantly over the last year that we are indeed part of one global community, we need to remember that education is more than employment or even graduating global citizens—in the end, it is about how we come together as neighbors both locally and globally, to build a better future together. We can make choices every day that help make the world better for all. As Tutu noted, "When we step into our neighborhoods, we can engage in the practices of good neighborliness or we can choose not to. The quality of life on our planet now and in the future will be determined by the small daily choices that we make as much as by the big decisions in the corridors of power." As we move forward into a post-pandemic era, we must remember that actions matter and what we do impacts others. What daily actions will we take to support the most vulnerable among us? To improve the quality of life for others? How will we uphold justice and dignity for all in the human family? In the end, how will we be good neighbors to each other?

Let us commit to taking action to address the racial injustices and inequities faced by our neighbors. Let us commit to being a good neighbor, as we live in authentic solidarity with each other, aspiring to be compassionate, generous, and kind, knowing that we can find our greatest joy in showing love to all and that in doing so, we are embracing the oneness of our humanity.

## Bio

Darla K. Deardorff is the Executive Director of the Association of International Education Administrators, a national professional organization based in Durham, North Carolina, USA. She is also a research scholar with the Social Science Research Institute at Duke University, where she has been an adjunct faculty member in the Program in Education and a faculty affiliate with International/Comparative Studies. In addition, she is an Adjunct Professor at North Carolina State University, a Visiting Research Professor at Nelson Mandela University in South Africa, and at Meiji University Research Institute of International Education (RIIE) in Japan as well as visiting faculty at Shanghai International Studies University (SISU) in China. Dr. Deardorff has served on faculty of Harvard University's Future of Learning Institute as well as Harvard University's Global Education Think Tank, in addition to being on faculty at the Summer Institute of Intercultural Communication in Portland, Oregon. She has also been an affiliated faculty at the University of North Carolina—Chapel Hill, and Leeds Beckett University (formerly Leeds Metropolitan) in the United Kingdom and taught at Thammasat University in Bangkok, Thailand. She receives numerous invitations from around the world (in over 30 countries including in Europe, Latin America, Africa, Australia, and Asia) to speak on her research and work on intercultural competence and international education assessment, and is a noted expert on these topics, being named a Senior Fulbright Specialist (to South Africa and to Japan).

Dr. Deardorff has published widely on topics in international education, global leadership, and intercultural learning/assessment, and has published eight books including as editor of *The SAGE Handbook of Intercultural Competence* (Sage, 2009) as well as lead editor of *The SAGE Handbook of International Higher Education* (Sage, 2012) with Hans de Wit, John Heyl and Tony Adams, *Building Cultural Competence* (Stylus, 2012) with Kate Berardo, and co-author of *Beneath the Tip of the Iceberg: Improving English and Understanding US American Cultural Patterns* (University of Michigan Press, 2011). She is also the author of the recently published book on *Demystifying Outcomes Assessment for International Educators: A Practical Approach* (Stylus, 2015) and co-editor of *Intercultural Competence in Higher Education: International Approaches, Assessment, Application* (Routledge, 2017) with Lily Arasaratnam-Smith. Her seventh book *Leading Internationalization* (Stylus, 2018) is with Harvey Charles, and her most recent book is *Manual on Developing Intercultural Competencies: Story Circles* (Routledge/UNESCO, 2019). E-mail: d.deardorff@duke.edu

# 1 The Impact of COVID-19 on Higher Education

## Challenges and Issues

*Ravichandran Ammigan, Roy Y. Chan, and Krishna Bista*

### Abstract

This chapter gives an overview of the novel coronavirus (COVID-19) in higher education and how colleges and universities have changed and adjusted along with new technology and challenges. In this book, we have tried to respond to the growing need for new insights and perspectives to improve higher education policy and practice in the era of COVID-19. The need to understand the impact of COVID-19 on higher education is more urgent as institutions seek to innovate and adapt during times of uncertainty.

**Keywords:**

higher education; COVID-19; issues and challenges; globalization

## Introduction

On March 11, 2020, the World Health Organization officially declared the novel coronavirus (COVID-19) a pandemic due to alarming levels of spread, severity, and inaction around the globe (Cucinotta & Vanelli, 2020). In an attempt to contain the virus, the United States and several other countries went into a state of public health emergency, imposing national lockdowns and bans on public gathering and travel (National Conference of State Legislatures, 2020). As the health crisis unfolded, educational institutions were forced to abruptly switch to remote and online learning after closing down their campuses and suspending in-person class instruction. Health and safety protocol had to be put in place and communicated to the campus community; large-scale, in-person events such as career fairs, orientation programs, and engagement activities were canceled; and the level of fear and public pressure had to be carefully managed with data-driven insights and guidance (Liguori & Winkler, 2020). Without question, the education sector continues to be one of the worst-hit by the pandemic, affecting opportunities for growth and development for over 1.5 billion students (or 91% of the world's school population) at all educational levels (UNESCO Global Education Coalition, 2021).

The COVID-19 outbreak has been characterized as the biggest test of resilience and relevance for higher education institutions in recent times, requiring innovative, risk-mitigating responses that ensure access to learning and the safety of all students (Fraser-Moleketi, 2021). With very little training and time to prepare for remote teaching, institutions scrambled to find different options of pedagogical approaches in synchronous or asynchronous environmental conditions as well as evaluation methods, all adding to the stresses and workloads of faculty and academic staff (Dhawan, 2020; Rapanta et al., 2020). The overwhelming challenges of e-learning faced by educators, administrators, and students alike can be broadly linked to issues around accessibility, affordability, flexibility, learning pedagogy, and educational policy (Pokhrel & Chhetri, 2021).

Over the past year, the landscape of higher education has changed dramatically. Substantial modifications in most aspects of teaching, learning, and campus life have eventually led to declines in student enrollment and net tuition, creating financial pressures and strained labor relations among faculty, staff, and administrators (Grawe, 2021). With the shutdown of residence halls and dining services, social and engagement facilities, conferences, and intercollegiate sports programs, among other in-person programs and businesses, the long-term financial impact from the loss of revenue has started to weigh in for many universities. The economic loss is estimated by the American Council on Education to exceed $120 billion for American colleges and universities, including furloughs, layoffs, and reductions in retirement benefits (Nietzel, 2020).

From a global learning and mobility standpoint, many study abroad programs came to a stop in 2020 due to restricted international travels and heightened health and safety risks. According to the Institute of International Education, most US institutions canceled travel for US students, both international (71%) and domestic (48%), with 93% of study abroad programs canceled entirely or in part last year (Martel, 2020). In the other direction, international student enrollment, which normally injects $44 billion and 460,000 jobs into the local US economy each year, dropped by 43% in fall 2019 due to travel bans, health and safety concerns, visa delays, and complex immigration policies (Baer & Martel, 2020). It remains unclear what the future of international education at colleges and universities will be, considering how critical global learning programs and student exchanges are to the competitiveness of American higher education.

For students, their college lives have been significantly upended. In addition to having to adapt to a new learning environment, factors such as fear about their safety and that of their loved ones, decreased social interactions, and disruptions to their academic performance and progress have contributed to increased levels of stress, anxiety, and depressive thoughts (Son et al., 2020). The long-lasting situation has also taken a financial toll on students, with many losing their on-campus jobs and others being impacted by the financial hardships experienced by their family (Lederer et al., 2021). Students who are already marginalized and discriminated against have sadly suffered the most from school closures and online instruction, considering that not all students have access to a computer, the internet, or a safe and quiet environment to study in (Arnove, 2020). In the United States, students of color, particularly Asian Americans and Asian international students, continue to face increased discrimination, stereotyping, and stigmatization during the pandemic, fueled partly by various social, political, and policy factors (Harper, 2020).

## The Current Situation

A year into the global pandemic, we are still uncertain as to how the COVID-19 crisis will reshape our society and drive innovation and advancement, especially in higher education (Kang, 2021). While some believe that the way in which higher education is delivered in the future will change permanently from face-to-face to a more aspirational online or hybrid mode of instruction, others have expressed a "renewed appreciation" for in-person classroom learning and expect institutions to revert back to their traditional academic model after the pandemic is contained (Ewing, 2021). In the meantime, however, policymakers and university administrators continue to invest time and resources into identifying effective information and communication technologies and virtual support services that enhance the e-learning experience of students, especially those who are underrepresented, vulnerable, and disadvantaged (Farnell et al., 2021). Balancing health and safety concerns with financial and enrollment considerations, institutions are actively developing plans to reopen their campuses as quickly and as securely as possible.

By the time this book is published, it is very likely that the world will be in a different place again—facing emerging challenges and finding answers in our fight against the virus. Regardless of whether regular classes and campus activities resume this coming fall, it is important that institutions consider a number of factors as they engage the university community in planning ahead. In keeping the health and safety of students, faculty, and staff as a priority, Lederer et al. (2021) offer four distinct recommendations to educational administrators as they continue to support students' experiences and success. First, survey the campus community about their experiences and use the assessment findings to identify institutional priorities and guide the decision-making process. Second, employ a holistic communication strategy via web, social media, and email to clearly and concisely disseminate reliable and scientifically based guidance and preventative measures about COVID-19 to the campus community. Third, prioritize and adapt student support services, such as health and counseling centers, wellness and engagement centers, academic support units, student affairs departments, multicultural centers, and international student offices, to increase access, reach a wider audience, and support the success of all students. And last, establish and implement student services and resources through a diversity, equity, and inclusion lens to ensure a welcoming and supportive campus climate for students and employees of all backgrounds, and especially those who are marginalized and underrepresented.

While there has been a heavy reliance on technology and information systems during the COVID-19 era, a new report from the World Council on Intercultural and Global Competence highlights the importance of ethical development in technology that promotes work and collaboration across cultures in order to solve the critical challenges that impact the world in a collective and equitable way (Veerasamy & Rasmussen, 2021). This points to a direct implication for institutions to provide adequate and intentional training for faculty and staff not only to increase proficiency in technology and evaluation methods but also toward intercultural and global competence in relation to course design. When institutions decide to fully resume their academic operations, evidence of faculty and staff preparedness in terms of professionalism, technical ability, and cultural awareness will be essential in what we expect to be a highly competitive environment to recruit and retain talented students (Rapanta et al., 2020). Humanizing the student experience at all levels of the institutional setting and building an engaged community among students and across cultures must remain a priority as we move forward, even when technology is driving the process (Liu & Ammigan, 2021).

## Themes and Structure of the Book

This book includes 14 chapters organized into three sections. The first section addresses some recent fundamental issues and challenges in higher education that educators have experienced as results of COVID-19 pandemic. In Chapter 1, editors Ammigan, Chan, and Bista give a general overview of the book projects, larger themes, and scope of the book, and present urgency of selected contributions in the volume. In Chapter 2, Silveus and Ekpe explore leadership styles that played significant roles during the COVID-19 at the institutions of higher education. In Chapter 3, Nguyen, Tran, and Tra focus on social responsibilities of universities in COVID-19 pandemic as a major component of institutional transformation. In Chapter 4, Muñiz and Borg discuss college admissions and enrollment issues that directly impact marginalized students, including students of color and students from low-income households, and how the concept of "Internationalization at Home" could be used to build inclusive practices in admissions and enrollment during and after the pandemic. In Chapter 5, Harry examines the financial ramifications of the coronavirus on athletic department operations, an important component of the higher education world .

In the second section, contributors bring academic issues such as graduate employability, research and mentoring, innovative teaching and learning, evolution in leadership, and emerging opportunities during and after the COVID-19. In Chapter 6, Kelly, Moore, and Lyons examine the relationship between exams and enhancing graduate employability through three key skills: problem-solving, creativity, and critical thinking during the COVID-19. In Chapter 7, Niño and Martínez II discuss how social distancing measures created new possible ways for graduate students to continue their research and publication using technology platforms during the pandemic. In Chapter 8, Armour reviews the accommodations and experiences of students with disabilities and students who are deaf or hard of hearing (DHOH) and called for considerations to disrupt the medical model of accommodations through Universal Design for Learning (UDL) in higher education. In Chapter 9, O'Shea, Zhang and Mou examine how this pandemic impacts international students' plan of study in Canada and the United States, with their concern for the expense and experience of online learning and their consideration of other alternative destination countries. In Chapter 10, Bai presents a case study documenting funding issues in higher education which has been public institutions to be more proactive to their diversity and inclusive missions.

The final section of the book brings together hope and prospect addressing public health and wellbeing, future global collaboration, and our academic relationships with dignity and humanity. In Chapter 11, Njoku highlights the need for public health curriculum to address racial and ethnic disparities in COVID-19 and to prepare and motivate a future healthcare workforce. In Chapter 12, Anzaldúa presents a trauma-informed human rights (TIHR) perspective to post-secondary education systems to maximize mental health and academic benefits for present and future college students.In Chapter 13, Minaeva and Marinoni present a strong case of how COVID-19 pandemic became an opportunity for global collaboration for seeking solutions to the virus at the same time when it is creating chaos and disorder in societies. In the final chapter, Liu and Ammigan present an exemplary case of how interactive and innovative use of information and communication technologies offer rewarding humanistic experiences to global learners during the pandemic.

## Guiding Questions

We anticipate that the chapters in this book will empower educators, administrators, practitioners, policymakers, and families with new ideas, principles, and advice that they can apply this academic year and beyond. To conclude, we leave our readers with a few guiding questions as they begin to peruse the book:

- How do we meet the needs of today's and tomorrow's students during the COVID-19 era?
- How do we rearticulate the value of global education after the COVID-19 pandemic?
- How do we innovate and develop effective curricula and co-curricular post-COVID-19?
- How do we foster collaboration and support in uncertain times?

- How do we handle health, safety, well-being, and crisis management during the COVID-19 restrictions?
- How do we articulate justice, equity, diversity, inclusion, and intercultural learning in the COVID-19 era?

## References

Arnove, R. F. (2020). Imagining what education can be post-COVID-19. *Prospects, 49*(1–2). https://doi.org/10.1007/s11125-020-09474-1

Baer, J., & Martel, M. (2020). *Fall 2020 international student enrollment snapshot.* Retrieved from https://www.iie.org/en/Research-and-Insights/Publications/Fall-2020-International-Student-Enrollment-Snapshot

Cucinotta, D., & Vanelli, M. (2020). WHO declares COVID-19 a pandemic. *Acta Biomedica, 91*(1), 157–160. https://doi.org/10.23750/abm.v91i1.9397

Dhawan, S. (2020). Online learning: A panacea in the time of COVID-19 crisis. *Journal of Educational Technology Systems, 49*(1). https://doi.org/10.1177/0047239520934018

Ewing, L.-A. (2021). Rethinking higher education post COVID-19. In J. Lee & S. H. Han (Eds.), *The future of service post-COVID-19 pandemic: Rapid adoption of digital service technology* (Volume 1, pp. 37–54). https://doi.org/10.1007/978-981-33-4126-5_3

Farnell, T., Skledar Matijević, A., & Šćukanec Schmidt, N. (2021). The impact of COVID-19 on higher education: A review of emerging evidence. In *NESET.* https://doi.org/10.2766/069216

Fraser-Moleketi, G. J. (2021, April 22). The impact of COVID-19 on higher education. Retrieved May 15, 2021, from ACCORD website: https://www.accord.org.za/analysis/the-impact-of-covid-19-on-higher-education/

Grawe, N. (2021, April 14). How have colleges fared during COVID-19? Retrieved May 16, 2021, from Econofact website: https://econofact.org/how-have-colleges-fared-during-covid-19

Harper, S. R. (2020). Covid-19 and the racial equity implications of reopening college and university campuses. *American Journal of Education, 127.* https://doi.org/10.1086/711095

Kang, B. (2021). How the COVID-19 pandemic is reshaping the education service. In J. Lee & S. H. Han (Eds.), *The future of service post-COVID-19 pandemic: Rapid adoption of digital service technology* (Volume 1, pp. 15–36). https://doi.org/10.1007/978-981-33-4126-5_2

Lederer, A. M., Hoban, M. T., Lipson, S. K., Zhou, S., & Eisenberg, D. (2021). More than inconvenienced: The unique needs of U.S. college students during the COVID-19 pandemic. *Health Education and Behavior, 48*(1). https://doi.org/10.1177/1090198120969372

Liguori, E., & Winkler, C. (2020). From offline to online: Challenges and opportunities for entrepreneurship education following the COVID-19 pandemic. *Entrepreneurship Education and Pedagogy, 3*(4). https://doi.org/10.1177/2515127420916738

Liu, C., & Ammigan, R. (2021). Humanizing the academic advising experience with technology: An integrative review. In R. Ammigan, R. Y. Chan, &

K. Bista (Eds.), *COVID-19 and higher education in the global context: Exploring contemporary issues and challenges* (pp. 185–202). STAR Scholars.

Martel, M. (2020). *COVID-19 effects on US higher education campuses.* Retrieved from https://www.iie.org/Research-and-Insights/Publications/COVID-19-Effects-on-US-Higher-Education-Campuses-Report-3

National Conference of State Legislatures. (2020). President Trump declares state of emergency for COVID-19. Retrieved May 15, 2021, from https://www.ncsl.org/ncsl-in-dc/publications-and-resources/president-trump-declares-state-of-emergency-for-covid-19.aspx

Nietzel, M. T. (2020, September 29). Pandemic's impact on higher education grows larger; now estimated to exceed $120 billion. Retrieved May 16, 2021, from Forbes website: https://www.forbes.com/sites/michaeltnietzel/2020/09/29/pandemics-impact-on-higher-education-grows-larger-now-estimated-to-exceed-120-billion/?sh=17716af422bd

Pokhrel, S., & Chhetri, R. (2021). A literature review on impact of COVID-19 pandemic on teaching and learning. *Higher Education for the Future, 8*(1). https://doi.org/10.1177/2347631120983481

Rapanta, C., Botturi, L., Goodyear, P., Guàrdia, L., & Koole, M. (2020). Online university teaching during and after the Covid-19 crisis: Refocusing teacher presence and learning activity. *Postdigital Science and Education, 2*(3). https://doi.org/10.1007/s42438-020-00155-y

Son, C., Hegde, S., Smith, A., Wang, X., & Sasangohar, F. (2020). Effects of COVID-19 on college students' mental health in the United States: Interview survey study. *Journal of Medical Internet Research, 22.* https://doi.org/10.2196/21279

UNESCO Global Education Coalition. (2021). *Supporting learning recovery one year into COVID-19: The global education coalition in action.* Retrieved from https://unesdoc.unesco.org/ark:/48223/pf0000376061

Veerasamy, Y. S., & Rasmussen, A. (2021). Futures of education: Learning to become initiative. In *World council on intercultural and global competence - UNESCO futures of education initiative.* Retrieved from https://iccglobal.org/downloads/

## Bios

**Ravichandran Ammigan, PhD,** is the Associate Deputy Provost for International Programs and an Assistant Professor of Education at the University of Delaware, Delaware, USA. rammigan@udel.edu

**Roy Y. Chan, PhD,** is an Assistant Professor of Education and Director of the Doctor of Education (EdD) program in Leadership and Professional Practice in the Helen DeVos College of Education at Lee University, Tennessee, USA. rchan@leeuniversity.edu

**Krishna Bista, EdD,** is a Professor of Higher Education in the Department of Advanced Studies, Leadership and Policy at Morgan State University, Maryland, USA. krishna.bista@morgan.edu

# Part I

# COVID-19 and Global Issues in Higher Education

# 2 The Evolution Revolution

The Application of a Leadership
Adaptation Continuum to
the Future of Global Higher
Education Post COVID-19

*Allison Silveus and Leslie Ekpe*

## Abstract

Viewing the COVID-19 crisis with the application of a leadership adaptation continuum provides insight into tracking systemic and environmental issues that could affect future educational sustainability. Leadership in higher education involves hedging in response to punctuated bursts that challenge educational stasis. Principles from the evolutionary theory of punctuated equilibrium illustrate leadership speciation that emerged during the fall of 2019 in Wuhan, China. Using an interdisciplinary phenomenological approach, the authors pulled concepts of evolutionary biology, business, and higher education leadership to understand the leaders' position on our leadership adaptation continuum model before and after the crisis, along with the association to varying leaders' response strategies; prevention-focused leadership, promotion-focused leadership, pragmatic leadership, and progressive leadership. By cross cutting our approach through different disciplines, new approaches to identifying future leaders that are adaptable and responsive can assist educators in surviving and succeeding during uncertain times.

## Keywords

COVID-19, leadership adaptation continuum, leadership

## Introduction

Punctuated bursts that produce a rapid evolution of leadership styles allow contemporary future leaders to be cognizant of how to navigate environmental pressures, such as the arrival of the novel coronavirus. On December 31, 2019, the World Health Organization (2020b) was notified of pneumonia-like cases in Wuhan City, Hubei Province, in China, later associated with the Huanan Seafood Market. The unexpected arrival of the novel virus produced a financial, psychological, and technological pandemic that led to massive leadership speciation. This speciation can be dissected through education, business, and science lenses, which can assist future leaders in understanding and preparing for a new form of higher education. Strategies adopted from leaders post-coronavirus disease-19 (COVID-19) represent various alignments or deviations from universities' visions, missions, and values as they attempt to grapple with a new reality.

### History of Coronavirus

A historical account of how the coronavirus arrived and spread across the globe provides the reader with an understanding of a unique setting, something that has been compared to the 1918 Spanish flu and the 2009 H1N1 Swine flu (Centers for Disease Control and Prevention, 2018, 2019). Following the notification of pneumonia-like symptoms in 2019, intensive investigations into the known causative agent of the infection disease occurred. By January 7, 2020, the health authorities in China had identified the novel coronavirus (nCoV) (World Health Organization, 2020a). Gardner (2020) reported by January 23, 2020, there were a little over 800 cases across about 20 regions in China, reflecting a vein-like connection among society. While the disease appeared isolated in China during January, arguments erupted in other countries. By January 19, 2020, the United States health officials reported the first case of a 35-year old man in Snohomish County, Washington, who had recently traveled to Wuhan, China (Holshue et al., 2020). He exhibited a prolonged cough and fever. This global spread presented a result of global mobility and reflected two facets of society: social networking as a mechanism to trace the disease and social connectedness among different cultures and people.

The progressive spread eventually created fear of the unknown and became a form of a global assessment of relative preparedness. Lotking (2020) referred to disaster preparedness and illustrated the desire for society to avoid disruption leading to a possible short-sighted adaptive mode, whereby the society will attempt to regain a sense of pre-COVID normalcy. Progressively, states mandated school closures, mask-wearing, and in-home grocery deliveries would shape a new form of routine. The word *normal* is a term that came to define the world without COVID and the world with COVID, with facets among society asking what normal would look like by fall 2020. As with any predictive model, it is grounded in evidence and impacted by values across society. The arrival of COVID-19 illustrated that the community was learning, adapting, and predicting all at once. However, as a leader, it is expected that answers are provided, and because of such a strong technological network, those answers are expected sooner rather than later. Therefore, leaders had the responsibility of being orators who had the solutions for the present moment and an unpredictable future.

Burke (2020) illustrated that predictive resurgence patterns over time will be influenced by overall immunity or cross-immunity and the transmission rates in warmer summer months. Cross-immunity, the ability to partially protect due to conserved antigens between other strains (Epstein & Price, 2010), can help understand how one can implement new strategies in education but is still one of many variables that impacts what the remaining years will look like. Factoring in vaccine production, vaccine adopters, and non-adopters adds challenges since a vaccine is only as good as the percentage of the population that agrees to be vaccinated. As evidence from public health officials poured in over time, it became apparent that no one could predict what the remaining part of 2020 would look like for higher education or what *normal* would mean.

## Leadership Speciation

Understanding of concepts related to evolution is challenging to comprehend and rarely as a learner can one witness the process. This lens, the researchers propose, is one in which the theory of punctuated equilibrium (Eldredge & Gould, 1972) can be applied to leadership style before COVID and after the arrival of COVID in the higher education system.

The concept of speciation arose through the work of Charles Darwin and Thomas Malthus, who, through observational scientific discovery, came to note that variation and similarities existed among species (Carroll, 2009). However, "Malthus proposed that there were checks-disease, famine, and death-upon the growth of populations that prevented them from increasing at an exponential rate" (p. 30). The theory of punctuated equilibrium explains that slow progressive change or stasis occurs with sudden bursts of fast progressive change, usually through some external force. The external pressure of COVID placed an unforgettable immediate hold on face-to-face social interaction, particularly as it relates to education. The educational structures exist as categories illustrating the vast diversity of the educational system ranging from community colleges, public and private colleges and universities, for-profit colleges, liberal arts colleges, research universities, religious colleges, and mission-driven colleges.

Online education threaded itself into some of these various structures and became a dominant form of knowledge in the spring of 2020 after the arrival of COVID. The sudden shift was a response to environmental change; a change Corning (2014) stated "can thus be expected to give rise to new needs (*besoins*) that in turn will stimulate the adoption of new '*habits*'" (p. 244). Rather than applying the punctuated equilibrium theory in biological terms, it can be used through a sociocultural lens. Kolondy et al. (2015) posited that in applying the punctuated equilibrium theory with computer simulations, cultural innovation views can be classified as lucky leap innovation, toolkit innovation, and innovative tool combination whereby change is not just about pure genius but also relies heavily on the contextualized environment. The environment is the fundamental foundation for this chapter in that leaders can avoid facing the disruption or they can use it as an opportunity to retool their organization. In applying the theory to university leadership, the ability to learn, adapt, survive, and thrive is mostly dependent on the culture that exists within the overall system. Under this model, it is assumed that leadership variation exists across all contexts, like how we can see genetic variation among humans. By recognizing this leadership variation, it is possible to predict a form of cultural innovation based on the differential distribution of traits such as knowledge, and the frequency of COVID resurgence as a form of environmental change to retool a new university. Kolondy et al. (2015) noted "the periods of little change are waiting times between occurrences of large leaps, and each of these rare occurrences brings about rapid change in the form of the invention of functionally related tools, functionally analogous tools, or innovative combinations" (p. E6767). Therefore, leadership variation pre-COVID-19 led to speciation and is dependent on organizational structure (i.e., differential knowledge), institutional structure, and the ability to take and support innovative risks that could reposition oneself ahead of other leaders. Thus, diverse thinking and discovery paves the way for the new *normal.*

This chapter should serve as a tool to assist current and future leaders in engaging in reflective practices as they grow a new university post COVID. While society may hope to attain a former view of the university prior to COVID, the researchers posit that evolutionary punctuation results in either persistence and growth in the university organization or progressive decline.

The research question the researchers sought to address was the following:

- How can a leadership adaptation continuum serve as a tool to prepare future global higher education leaders?

## Literature Review

An integral part of good leadership is a leader's capacity to adapt and grow from meeting significant crucibles. By committing to these best practices in direction, academic leaders will emerge from the crisis to rebuild with untarnished and perhaps enhanced credibility and branding. Many facets of the COVID-19 pandemic are unique, but it is unusual for university officials to contend with circumstances of this extent. Within this pandemic, universities are facing organizational change. Weick and Quinn (1999) perceived a shift in the organization as either continuous or episodic. The episodic difference is rare and radical at times, while constant change can be incremental, emergent, and endless. Possessing change management skills was related to bringing about effective organizational change. The lack of awareness of strategies for improvement in execution and the failure to adjust management style or organizational roles was cited as obstacles to progress (Bossidy & Charan, 2002; Gilley, 2005).

### *Global Higher Education*

While leadership practitioners in academia play a crucial role in their institution's response to crises, in fact, the position of campus leaders in developing a culture of confidence, cooperation, and shared leadership before a crisis can affect the institution's ability to withstand times of crisis more significantly (Kezar et al., 2018). The transition to online course delivery may require some stakeholders to make radical changes in attitude, values, and beliefs (Heifetz & Laurie, 2001). It may also entail drastic changes and innovative approaches.

The converse relationship between leadership and the COVID-19 virus is the extreme need for a balanced curriculum offering equal opportunities for the community it serves. Leaders' thoughts and abilities are reflected in attitudes, systems, and processes that promote or hinder progress, further reinforcing the link between their activities and efficacy in bringing about change. For those academic leaders who are goal-oriented, risk-takers, and long-term strategic thinkers, there is an opportunity to create a spiral of success and gain a competitive advantage in their redesigned educational environment.

## *Diversity of Leaders*

The work of Gulati et al. (2010) serves as a foundation for understanding four types of leadership before and after an evolutionary pandemic: prevention-focused leadership, promotion-focused leadership, pragmatic leadership, and progressive leadership. Leading change involves the use of a range of communication strategies to convey relevant communications, seek feedback, build preparation for moving forward with a sense of urgency, and inspire recipients to act. While Gulati et al. (2010) focused on companies, their definitions can be contextualized to the university leadership style.

In prevention-focused leaders, it is typical to adopt a defensive strategy after a disaster to avoid and minimize loss (Gulati et al., 2010). Leaders choose a static model where costs are immediately cut in the operating budget. Still, programs continue to operate, even though there might be fewer people and reduced quality. While prevention-focused leaders concentrate on the defensive, promotion-centered leaders develop offensive strategies that appear to benefit the overall system. Usually, the development-targeted leaders adopt a verbose mode of thinking that involves spending to get ahead of other networks, with a belief the university will become a superpower. Pragmatic leaders choose a combination of defensive and offensive strategies, where priorities become cutting from the budget and at the same time investing in new ways of conducting research. However, the critical element of investing after a crisis is that the investment is driven in response to the new needs from the crisis. Progressive leaders adopt the optimal balance between defensive and offensive strategies. By selecting the optimal balance where costs are cut using justified measurable data, the leadership can maintain support from the overall system. When the administration adopts more prevention-focused mechanisms and staff is let go as a response to the decline, it is more difficult for the leadership to achieve stability upon returning to normalcy. Thus, achieving a balance between cost-cutting and spending allows progressive leaders to survive and do well after the disaster. Leaders must understand that a professional re-articulation is necessary to convincingly redefine their position as invaluable in order not to be replaced.

## *Adversity of Leaders*

The variation within the structure of higher education, like the variation within society, provides an opportunity to understand risk aversion and risk tolerance in leaders. A fundamental trait necessary for campus presidents is being comfortable at taking risks. Leaders must realize that a professional re-articulation is inevitable to redefine their role convincingly as indispensable in order not to be replaced. Training programs need to be designed suitably for mobilizing faculty resources by providing them with a wide range of holistic solutions to the online teaching challenge that can be addressed and making them essential to higher education professionals (Gulati et al., 2010). Leaders should create multi-level structures to guide a campaign against the crisis. Established systems often do not have any support for crisis management. Because of a lack of creativity and foresight, leaders often forget that organizational structures are designed for purposes other than crisis management.

## *The Leadership Adaptation Continuum Framework*

Viewing leadership adaptation using a continuum (see Figure 2.1) allows educators and risk managers to analyze current and future preparedness as a model for identification of successful leadership. While all leaders possess a great deal of variability in traits, it is worth acknowledging one's own individual preparedness for events such as COVID-19. Lokting (2020) illustrated that after a 2016 Columbia University Disaster survey, 65% of households lacked plans for surviving a catastrophe, a concept that is related

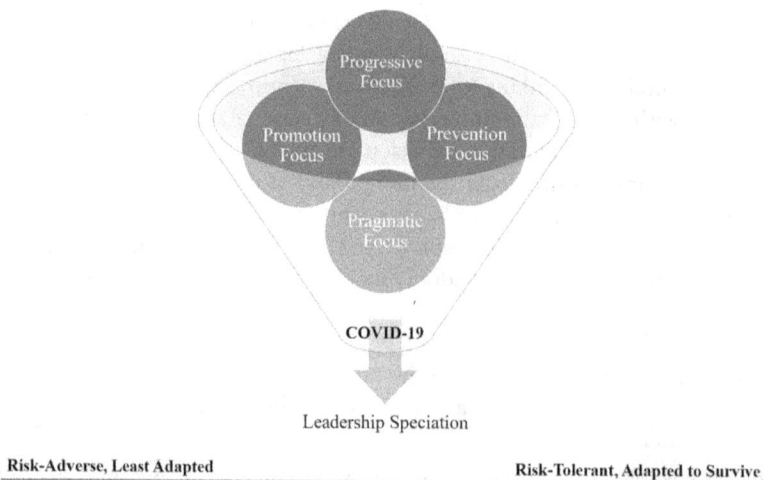

*Figure 2.1* Leadership adaptation continuum.

to our own innate individual level of preparedness. Individually, it is easy to assume that disasters will not impact us as the individual but are more likely to impact others.

## Research Method

The researchers sought to adopt a qualitative phenomenological approach to evaluating experiences within university leadership prior to and after the arrival of the novel 2019 coronavirus. Phenomenology, for the purpose of this work, refers to how society experienced and navigated the world, particularly in response to the pandemic.

The phenomenological approach, as explained by French philosopher Merleau-Ponty (1945), was used to seek understanding of how leaders navigated the pandemic from the researchers' point of view. The researchers assumed that individuals' truths emerged from what they directly were experiencing and thus could lead to internal desires central to their own identity (Byrne, 2001). In addition, research supported by Sohn et al. (2017) was used to illustrate how voices within a community may be interpreted with the Merleau-Ponty philosophy noting, "Human beings are not passive before the stimuli in the lifeworld; we take an intentional stance toward the objects and events in our conscious awareness" (p. 125). This approach was chosen not because the research was more dialogical but because the dialog created revolved around how people vocalized their realities about education needs through what they perceived from their own experience of the pandemic.

Secondly, the researchers also reflected on their own experiences to aid current leaders and new emerging leaders in higher education responses. To explore this, a proposed leadership adaptation continuum was adopted as a theoretical framework to which various leadership styles were critiqued.

### Sample

Leadership style was evaluated across two different university systems, each of which were renamed for the purpose of this research. The two university systems were different both in size and regarding the type of funding they receive. University A is a small private liberal arts college which depends on endowment funds and high tuition. University B is a large public, state school that serves a larger population and depends on state funding streams.

## Results

### University A Leadership

University A is a private four-year liberal arts college; the institution serves as an essential element in the higher education system today through increased educational opportunities. However, University A relies heavily on funding and has high institutional costs. University A administrators use a prevention leadership approach.

The pandemic exposed the ongoing mistrust between leaders of the academy and the communities they serve. The prevention leadership style highlighted the discrepancy between what is said and perceived and what derives from legitimate—and potentially productive—perspective variations (Gulati et al., 2010). Colleges and universities rely on outdated processes that have collapsed in this emergency period. How can we build lasting solutions rather than using band-aids to help us through the crisis? The academy is purposely made to look like a meritocracy that values diversity but is built down to its foundations to only support and value those of a specific subset of individuals. The preventative leadership style at University A ignores that the institution has a built-in system to continuously avoid the integration of oppressed and otherwise marginalized people in the academy, allowing for one group of privileged individuals to maintain power while providing crumbs to other communities. Leaders cannot separate capability through COVID-19, the campus discussion from the ongoing anti-racism violence by universities.

For University A, COVID-19 was and is an equity test, telling one who one might be if they respected equity as much as they think they do. Let leaders not hesitate until they have the next pandemic right. When leaders do hesitate, those who struggle will still be the ones who are suffering currently—the citizens who are really in need. Students recognize that the implementation of the Centers for Disease Control and Prevention's (2020) recommendations decreases the coronavirus spread, and the situation is continuously changing. Changes made regarding the upcoming semesters must be accompanied by clear information and instructions that are thoughtful and considerate of the difficulty students will face as they are implemented. With much uncertainty about the upcoming academic years, waiting for a new update or being directed to an empty website does not relieve the tension and anxiety that many students experience.

The lack of income that many students are facing will be at the top of their priority list. Many students have paid thousands of dollars in tuition to gain a sense of belonging on campuses. Many of whom must take out loans to cover these expenses. It is harsh and unreasonable to continue to pay for an on-campus experience within the current pandemic crisis. Administrators should recognize that students and parents are counting every penny that it takes to finance a college degree and be proactive in offering financial assistance and reimbursement when feasible. Leaders aim to make the numbers fit when carrying out their academic and educational missions. Transitioning into the *new norm* will require a different form of leadership (Gulati et al., 2010). Campus administrators need to ask, "How should academics and administrators concentrate on the potentially constructive aspect of their diverse viewpoints and stop becoming stuck in trench warfare despite the very complicated nature of the COVID 19 crisis?"

### University B Leadership

University B is a large public, state school, where survival requires bringing in revenue while acknowledging that the states must continue to balance their budget. The leadership within this institute responded to the pandemic using a progressive approach.

Prior to the pandemic, the leadership within this university focused on innovation as an alternative model for revenue streams. New models of revenue generation had been proposed, whereby faculty were perceived to be the authors of creative intellect. When new models such as the efforts to refit a university with a focus of intellectual property are utilized, there will be unintended consequences. This approach prior to the pandemic was associated with fear of change from the historical meaning and definition of tenure. Historically, the university structure has been grounded in traditional norms where faculty apply for promotion and rank through the journey of publication. However, when the paradigm shifts from publication to innovation, the system will attempt to resist this change. Gutsche (2009) refers to this resistance stating, "The 'old way of doing things' and fixed expectations are the enemies of adaptation" (p. 46). However, prior to the pandemic, this was a risk tolerant approach to generate revenue, specifically because it acknowledged the progressive decline in higher education funding.

During the transition to online coursework, the university leaders followed models that provided opportunity to continue measurement of effectiveness. While some areas saw cuts in the form of positions, the leadership within this university used the pandemic as a form of continued assessment. The sudden movement to online in March of 2020, proceeded with quick deployment of online coursework in conjunction with evaluation of cost savings for serving students online, versus face-to-face. Gulati et al. (2010) posited progressive companies stay close to the customer needs, and through this same lens, progressive leaders also stay close to the needs of their university. Examples of serving those needs involved contact with staff and faculty using wellness checks, whom at this point worked remotely, and deployment of new types of classes that now focused on emerging technologies in light of the technological revolution. The preparedness prior to the pandemic, shifting to alternate forms of revenue in the form of intellectual property and innovation and continued focus on people, allowed the entire system to persevere and evolve.

## Implications for Theory and Practice

We propose a leadership adaptation continuum that shows maximizing engagement in change allows leaders to reflect on how they inspire and engage in beneficiaries of change as agents of change. Inevitably, the dependent condition tends to divide higher education institutions:

1   Leaders who became paralyzed, cut costs, and saw no change following COVID, inevitably will struggle to catch up to the new societal needs that will drive education.
2   Leaders who overspent, saw only opportunity for growth and lacked appropriate evaluation of alignment of current program offerings to new potential programs, will likely struggle to catch up to competitors.
3   Leaders who cut costs with reduced manpower and increased revenue, will have difficulty offering quality education, even though they spent money to improve in other new areas.
4   Leaders, who anticipated financial decline, proposed new models for revenue generation prior to the pandemic, used both cost-cutting procedures that were not limited to cutting personnel, and incorporated innovative research models for revenue generation, will likely thrive in a new state of normalcy.

There is no such thing as a complete institutional leader, but those leaders with the versatility and flexible ability to grow and develop as a result of handling a crisis may be able to respond more quickly and with less commitment to potential problems and might well be the perfect allostatic leader for academic institutions going forward (Yarnell & Grunberg, 2017).

The pandemic induced changes needed in higher education. The online mode will remain as a modern standard. Leading in times of distress goes well beyond the organization's pure tolerance to it. Leaders need a clear people-first mentality, a willingness to communicate with others and not outshine them, the institution's reorganization to address the crisis firmly and robustly, and, above all, a dream that goes beyond crisis. In this chapter as a part of the modern transition sparked by the coronavirus pandemic, we focused on the topic of leadership in academia and higher education.

## Recommendations for Future Research

The questioning of the role of the university in educating the public has been debated for several years, producing evolutionary revolutions in how the university leadership responds to its changing environment. The education system is an example of a pluralistic organization that is constantly in a state of flux due to rising demands for measurable outcomes, response to unemployment rates, and societal need for instant gratification. This flux has produced a governing board not made up of trustees or faculty who make policy, but rather are market decisions acting as the governing board dictating every move the university leadership makes. While college education historically has been for the most elite social classes, the social shifts and the resistance by outsiders has produced a new generation of students who are women, minorities, and post-traditional students (Trow, 1989). Our desire for *lernfreiheit*, a student's right to decide their course of study (Kerr, 2001), along with the publication *Was College Worthwhile* by Tunis in 1936, gave way to a new generation of students (Horowitz, 1987). This new student is the post-traditional student who now needs to evolve to new societal needs, and our higher education system is still trying to grapple with how to define what this student looks like. Soares (2013) defined the post-traditional student:

> The term encompasses individuals with a range of education needs from high school graduates to high school dropouts and those with limited literacy and English language skills. Post-traditional learners also encompass many life stages and identities; they are single mothers, immigrants, veterans, and at-risk younger people looking for a second chance. (p. 2)

Applying this definition, one can understand the creation of the designer university one sees forming today in higher education as a response to *lernfreiheit* (Kerr, 2001), COVID-19, and an increased desire for accessibility to lifelong learning. It is by concerted and focused management intervention that universities successfully adopt success-fostering reform initiatives that target the needs of their students. Organizations and their members who do not understand the value of these talents will become another statistic in the history of reform failure.

## Discussion and Conclusion

The work presented by Gulati et al. (2010) assists in explaining the post-COVID results, particularly as it relates to their unexpected findings that post-recession winners were not always those cutting costs quick and deep. As science and technology grow, and new advances become ingrained as part of society, one will see the development of the designer university, like the creation of the designer gene. This will be a university not shaped by the administration, faculty, governing boards, but by the market itself. Lifelong knowledge, the commodity for which one will buy and sell, will come at a cost. Additionally, enrollment will be based on a desire to make one stand out as employable, marketable, and knowledgeable. Diversity today is one's own selling point, both in their own abilities and in institutions. One can even see this desire of uniqueness and measure it using social media *likes*. One can market themselves in the quest for lifelong learning and through their own design have selected and produced a university that is most compatible with the environment. Trow (1989) noted that the growth of older students, part-time students, minorities, and women in higher education is representative of how the power has shifted to the consumer, or what one refers to as the designer. This power of the consumer is illustrated in how students have demanded justification for high-cost tuition, considering the forced online coursework. The issue is a self-perpetuating problem, where a gap exists, and the university is slowly trying to tinker with how it accommodates these new diverse student needs.

In conclusion, the trouble with universities' leadership is their inability to understand what the students' needs are and how to design an environment to meet those needs. In higher education, leaders focus on teaching the importance of feedback and assessments but have missed one of the largest assessments of all. One would attribute this issue to biases on only seeing outcomes, usually measured quantitatively, or processes measured qualitatively, while failing to realize that both are valuable. Faculty are fragmented into camps grounded in Kuhn's (1970) paradigms of being either positivist or constructivist, negating that true value is based on the research question alone. Failure of higher education is not an outcome, nor should be a process, rather it should be approached by looking at it from the pragmatic lens. The university that dies will be the university that failed to change its approach.

## References

Bossidy, L., & Charan, R. (2002). *Execution: The discipline of getting things done.* Crown.

Burke, K. L. (2020). What might happen to COVID-19 over time? *American Scientist, 108*(3), 134. https://doi.org/10.1511/2020.108.3.134

Byrne, M. M. (2001). Understanding life experiences through a phenomenological approach to research. *AORN Journal, 73*(4), 830–832. https://doi.org/10.1016/s0001-2092(06)61812-7

Carroll, S. B. (2009). *Into the jungle.* Pearson Benjamin Cummings.

Centers for Disease Control and Prevention. (2018). *History of 1918 flu pandemic.* https://www.cdc.gov/flu/pandemic-resources/1918-commemoration/1918-pandemic-history.htm

Centers for Disease Control and Prevention. (2019). 2009 H1N1 Pandemic (N1N1pdm09 virus). https://www.cdc.gov/flu/pandemic-resources/2009-h1n1-pandemic.html

Centers for Disease Control and Prevention. (2020). *Guidance documents.* https://www.cdc.gov/coronavirus/2019-ncov/communication/guidance-list.html?Sort=Date%3A%3Adesc

Corning, P. A. (2014). Evolution "on purpose": How behaviour has shaped the evolutionary process. *Biological Journal of the Linnean Society, 112*(2), 242–260. https://doi.org/10.1111/bij.12061

Eldredge, N., & Gould, S. J. (1972). Punctuated equilibria: An alternative to phyletic gradualism. In T. J. M. Schopf (Ed.), *Models in paleobiology* (pp. 82–115). Freeman Cooper.

Epstein, S. L., & Price G. E. (2010). Cross protective immunity to influenza a viruses. *Expert Review of Vaccines, 9*(11), 1325–1341. https://doi.org/10.1586/erv.10.123

Gardner, L. (2020, January 23). *Mapping COVID-19.* Johns Hopkins University CSSE. https://systems.jhu.edu/research/public-health/ncov/

Gilley, A. (2005). *The manager as change leader.* Praeger.

Gulati, R., Nohria, N., & Wohlgezogen, F. (2010). Roaring out of recession. *Harvard Business Review*, 88(3), 62–69. https://hbr.org/2010/03/roaring-out-of-recession

Gutsche, J. (2009). *Exploiting chaos: 150 ways to spark innovation during times of change.* Gotham.

Heifetz, R., & Laurie, D. (2001). The work of leadership. *Harvard Business Review*, 37–48. http://www.kwli.org/wp-content/uploads/2015/01/Heifetz-Laurie-2001.pdf

Holshue, M. L., DeBolt, C., Lindquist, S., Lofy, K. H., Wiesman, J., Bruce, H., Spitters, C., Ericson, K., Wilkerson, S., Tural, A., Diaz, G., Cohn, A., Fox, L., Patel, A., Gerber, S. I., Kim, L., Tong, S., Lu, X., Lindstorm, S., ... & Diaz, G. (2020). First case of 2019 novel coronavirus in the United States. *New England Journal of Medicine*, *382*(10), 929–936. https://doi.org/10.1056/nejMoa2001191

Horowitz, H. L. (1987). *Campus life: Undergraduate cultures from the end of the eighteenth century to the present.* The University of Chicago Press

Kerr, C. (2001). *The uses of the university.* Harvard University Press.

Kezar, A., Gehrke, S., & Bernstein-Sierra, S. (2018). Communities of transformation: Creating changes to deeply entrenched issues. *The Journal of Higher Education*, *89*(6), 832–864. https://doi.org/10.1080/00221546.2018.1441108

Kolodny, O., Creanza, N., & Feldman, M. W. (2015). Evolution in leaps: The punctuated accumulation and loss of cultural innovations. *Proceedings of the National Academy of Sciences of the United States of America*, *112*(49), E6762–E6769. https://doi.org/10.1073/pnas.1520492112

Kuhn, T. S. (1970). *The structure of scientific revolutions.* University of Chicago Press.

Lokting, B. (2020). They were waiting for the big one. Then coronavirus arrived. *MIT Technology Review*, *123*(3), 64–69. https://www.technologyreview.com/2020/04/15/999514/oregon-preppers-the-big-one-coronavirus-disaster-preparedness/

Merleau-Ponty, M. (1945). *Phénoménologie de la perception.* Gallimard.

Soares, L. (2013). Post-traditional learners and the transformation of postsecondary education: A manifesto for college leaders. *American Council on Education*, 1–18. https://www.acenet.edu/Documents/Post-traditional-Learners.pdf

Sohn, B. K., Thomas, S. P., Greenberg, K. H., & Pollio, H. R. (2017). Hearing the voices of students and teachers: A phenomenological approach to educational research. *Qualitative Research in Education*, *6*(2), 121–148. https://doi.org/10.17583/qre.2017.2374

Trow, M. (1989). American higher education—past, present, and future. In J. Bess (Ed.), *Foundations of American higher education* (pp. 7–24). Ginn Press.

Tunis, J. R. (1936). *Was college worth while?* Harcourt Brace.

Weick, K. E., & Quinn, R. E. (1999). Organizational change and development. *Annual Review of Psychology*, *50*(1), 361–386. https://doi.org/10.1146/annurev.psych.50.1.361

World Health Organization. (2020a). *Novel coronavirus China.* https://www.who.int/csr/don/12-january-2020-novel-coronavirus-china/en/

World Health Organization. (2020b). *Pneumonia of unknown cause – China.* https://www.who.int/csr/don/05-january-2020-pneumonia-of-unkown-cause-china/en/

Yarnell, A. M., & Grunberg, N. E. (2017). *Developing "allostatic leaders": A psychobiosocial perspective.* In M. G. Clark & C. W. Gruber (Eds.), *Annals of theoretical psychology: Leader development deconstructed* (Vol, 15, pp. 23–50). Springer International Publishing. https://doi.org/10.1007/978-3-319-64740-1_2

## Bios

**Allison Silveus, EdD,** is an educational program manager for the University of North Texas Health Science Center, Texas College of Osteopathic Medicine Faculty Development Center. Prior to this role, she was a research assistant at UT Southwestern Medical Center, where she performed DNA typing. While at Texas Christian University (TCU), she had the privilege of being accepted for the TCU Global Outlooks Leadership program, publishing work on English Language Learners' use of hybrid language (2018), and presentation of research on in-group bias in a STEM program (2018). Allison is a member of the Golden Key International Honor Society and a reviewer for the *Journal for the American Board of Family Medicine.* She received her bachelor of science in biology (2005) and from University of Texas at Arlington, a master of science in forensic genetics at UNT Health Science Center (2007), and a doctorate in higher education leadership from Texas Christian University (2021). She co-founded Unbent Inc, which is a neurodiversity tool for assessing decision-making. https://orcid.org/0000-0003-2333-8920  E-mail: allison.silveus@unthsc.edu

**Leslie Ekpe** is a PhD student at Texas Christian University, where she is pursuing her degree in higher educational leadership. Her work aims to promote access for marginalized students at the K-12 and post-secondary education levels. Leslie holds a BS degree in Management from Alabama A&M University, an MA degree in Communication Management from the University of Alabama at Birmingham, and an MBA degree in Business Administration from Sam Houston State University. https://orcid.org/0000-0002-1353-5560 E-mail: l.ekpe@tcu.edu

# 3 Rethinking the Social Responsibilities of Universities in the Light of COVID-19 Pandemic

*Hằng Trần Thị, Quy Dinh Le Nguyen, and Luc-Diep Tra*

## Abstract

Universities should no longer be confined to their ivory tower. The ongoing revolution of higher education drives them to closely connect with outsiders to fulfill their vision, mission, and goals. The universities' social responsibilities have become of utmost importance during the COVID-19 pandemic. In fact, the pandemic leads to the critical transformation of higher education worldwide. Multiple initiatives have been introduced to keep students engaged with their education. These solutions themselves, unfortunately, also lead to some social problems. The main contribution of this chapter, thus, is to provide reflection on multiple perspectives of universities social responsibilities (USR) pre- and post-COVID 19.

## Keywords:

higher education, university social responsibilities, COVID-19, blended-learning

## Introduction

"Educating the mind without educating the heart is no education at all."
—Aristotle

The responsibilities of higher education institutions have long been well known as fostering high-quality graduates who possess critical, analytical thinking and can adapt quickly to the environment through their teaching and research (Nagy & Robb, 2008). From 1998, UNESCO highlighted that universities are also responsible for training young people who acquire sharp critical thinking and participate actively in solving the problems of society, who become ethical citizens to contribute to the construction of peace, and human rights (UNESCO, 1998, 2009, as cited in Chile & Black, 2015). Since then, the topic of universities' social responsibility (USR) has been widely discussed and significantly expanded, covering not only nurturing students' skills and knowledge to reach their full potential but also deepening their sense of social responsibilities and contributing to the development of society (Chile & Black, 2015).

The concept of USR originated from previous ideas of university-community engagement (Association of Commonwealth Universities, 2001, as cited in Esfijani, 2014) or scholarship of engagement (Boyer, 1996). University-community engagement (UCE), according to the Association of Commonwealth Universities (2001), is the collaboration and partnership between higher education institutions and their larger communities (local, regional/state, national, global). The purpose of UCE is to enrich scholarship, research, and creative activity; enhance curriculum, teaching, and learning; prepare educated, engaged citizens; strengthen democratic values and civic responsibility; address critical societal issues; and contribute to the public good. Moreover, UCE also contributes to addressing social disadvantage and exclusion, and focuses on "non-economically productive activity," promoting the idea of a fair society.

Scholarship of engagement (SOE) can be traced back to a study by Boyer (1996) who introduced four main patterns that scholarship can engage with the larger society: discovering, integrating, sharing, and linking knowledge to the real world. The underlying assumption of SOE is that scholarship only reaches their ultimate value when they contribute to the development of their communities (Boyer, 1996; Holland, 2005; Simpson, 2000, p. 12). To be more specific, SOE refers to academic functions such as teaching and research activities that can bridge the academic world and sponsoring the public on the basis of mutual benefits (Holland, 2005). Particularly, Sandmann (2008) advocated typical SOE practices such as participatory action research (PAR), service-learning, and community-based research by creating mutually beneficial and reciprocal relationships.

Based on the earlier work, the USR research area has been significantly extended. Until now, there has been a variety of USR conceptualization. For example, Harkavy (2006) defines USR as the actions that the universities go beyond their traditional duties to contribute to their communities (p. 13). In line with that, Kouatli (2019) divides the social impact of universities into four main categories: organizational impact, educational impact, cognitive impact, and social impact. First, the organizational impact emphasizes the lived and promoted values that are intentional or unintentional functions of work-related aspects, environment, and daily life habits. Second, the educational impact is defined as how the universities help develop students' skills and civic mindset to contribute to their surrounding community, encouraging them to acknowledge the effect of what they do in short and long term (Ayala-Rodríguez et al., 2019). In this regard, students are considered as the key agents of civic universities, who will transfer knowledge and contribute to the community. Third, the cognitive impact takes into account epistemology, deontology, theories, research, knowledge generalization, and diffusion process. Finally, social impact, which refers to the universities' external activities, and involvement in the sustainable development of the community, can be strengthened by maintaining and expanding the relationship between universities and their stakeholders (Benneworth & Jongbloed, 2010).

Recently, Larrán Jorge and Andrades Peña (2017) pinpoint that USR refers to the discretionary commitment of the universities to integrate social, environmental, and ethical issues into their main functions while considering their stakeholders' needs. In other words, to be socially responsible, a university needs to enact activities in educating, research, management, and community engagement activities (Larrán Jorge & Andrades Peña, 2017). Specifically, universities are expected to incorporate social responsibility and sustainability into their curricula, train instructors in USR approach (Valleys et al., 2009, as cited in Kouatli, 2019). Socially responsible universities also need to encourage interdisciplinary research to meet the needs of a variety of populations and to transfer knowledge to the community while they are expected to execute good practices of management to train students in a good civic environment (Larrán Jorge & Andrades Peña, 2017).

Although social responsibility has been proclaimed to be central to universities' mission, it is not always the case (Dey et al, 2009; Dey et al, 2010). One typical reason is that lacking financial resources, awareness and interest, the misconception about the issues, and the absence of quality control narrow the scope of USR implementation. Additionally, the exclusion of students who cannot afford extremely high tuition fees (everybody should get a chance of education) or even the lack of information for students and also parents about the possibilities also reduce the effects of USR effort. Regardless of these constraints, USR has evolved over time. In the following sections, we will discuss traditional and technology-based (or online) practices, challenges and recommendations in respect of USR, especially in the time of COVID-19. We end this chapter by reflecting on universities practices to promote their social responsibilities in the post COVID-19 Era.

## Traditional University Social Responsibility Practices

Responding to the increasing turbulence all over the world, an extensive body of research has urged for the significant role of universities in nurturing responsible citizens and leaders who will confront global and social problems (Ralph & Stubbs, 2014; Young & Nagpal, 2013). One of the early frameworks for USR practices was introduced by Kuh et al. (2005) which includes main elements such as: living mission and lived educational philosophy, unshakable focus on student learning, environments adapted for education enrichment, clearly marked pathways to student success, improvement-oriented ethos, and shared responsibility.

So far, the integration of social responsibility in pedagogies of higher education has been substantially progressed. For instance, the application of active learning approaches can make the incorporation of SR into business courses more effective by moving learners away from 'dependence on educators' approach toward a personal responsibility approach (MacVaugh & Norton, 2011). In other words, the principal responsibility of learners will not be to abide and be placed by the instructors, but to create true values to the society using their acquired knowledge and skills. Particularly, a wide range of active methods has been addressed to improve students' acknowledgment of social responsibilities, including using videos, team work, and group discussion, projects, Socratic method, role play, peer assessment, internship, case studies (Lambrechts et al., 2013).

However, the incorporation of USR into university curricula has encountered critical organizational, educational, cognitive and social obstacles. First, most USR initiatives have emerged from individual initiatives rather than an integrated program (Stubbs & Schapper, 2011) and different individuals have different interpretations of USR, further complicating the fulfillment process (Gaete Quezada 2011, as cited in Ayala-Rodríguez et al., 2019). Second, the traditional, teacher-centered educational approaches do not prioritize students' personal responsibilities, as students are encouraged to follow rules and expectations set by teachers. The traditional approaches are still embedded in the educational systems of many universities, and many universities do not change their approach out of resistance or lack of resources, resulting in low level of USR incorporation (Young & Nagpal, 2013). Third, universities themselves either may resist to change or do not have sufficient resources, resulting in low levels of USR incorporation (Young & Nagpal, 2013). Finally, even if universities and educators have devoted considerable effort and commitment to these courses, lacking experiences and knowledge about sustainability and USR reduces the effectiveness and efficiencies of the programs.

To address these challenges, USR researchers have figured out different ways to address these obstacles, among which is the execution of service-learning (MacVaugh & Norton, 2012). Based on the ideology of scholarship of engagement and university-community engagement as explained in previous literature review, service-learning pedagogy has been considered as the most effective method to engage universities to facilitate their mission in solving their community's problems (Bringle et al., 1999). Service-learning is defined as a pedagogical process that engages students in experiential education in order to promote student learning and development (Scott & Graham, 2015) and improve their civic responsibility and leadership to create positive changes to their community (Huda et al., 2018). Peric (2012) suggests that service-learning programs consist of five main components, namely reflective and experiential pedagogy, a combination of academic knowledge and community service, mutual cooperation between universities and community, enhancing learning as a purpose, and reflection.

Service-learning strategy has been paid increasingly considerable attention by universities as it has proved the effectiveness in academic and personal aspects for students (Hebert & Hauf, 2015; Lovat & Clement, 2016). Participants in service-learning courses advocate that the effects of those practices can last for life. First of all, this type of learning has a chronic effect on student's academic performance (Madsen & Turnbull, 2006) through developing specific skills, including communication skills, problem-solving, decision making, and leadership skills (Lai, 2009; Levesque-Bristol et al., 2011; Osiemo, 2012). Furthermore, it enables students to develop the ability to connect their thinking in theories and real life, thereby developing new knowledge and thinking (Colby et al., 2009). Besides, service learning contributes to increasing practices of social responsibility and equality among graduates (Chapdelaine et al., 2005; Compact, 2016; Kuh, 2009). Through service-learning courses, participants have an inclination to care more about societal problems, develop civic skills, increase mutual understanding (Lovat and Clement, 2016), and increase empathy (Brown, 2011; Levesque-Bristol et al., 2011).

Still, as service-learning directly affects any communities the programs target, improper application can hamper the development of said communities and damage the connection between them and students (Crabtree, 2013). Even if the programs are carried out properly, there are some unintended consequences, for instance a sense of absence and a sense of dependence from the helped communities (Crabtree, 2013). In addition, students might view activities in service-learning programs as forced volunteerism and thus, do their jobs superficially and/or purely for credits; or they can over glorify their deeds, doing services that have no long-term impacts besides a sense of self-satisfaction (Mitchell, 2008). It should be noted, however, the overall benefits of service-learning outweigh its issues; and these factors should be carefully considered to further improve service-learning programs, rather than be used to completely disregard them.

Apart from service-learning, the emergence of technology-based/virtual tools of USR practices can also enable universities to overcome some short-comings of traditional approaches. The application is discussed further in the next section.

## Online Learning as a Tool of University Social Responsibility

Given the above-mentioned drawbacks of traditional practices of USR, online learning has emerged to be a feasible strategy to provide benefits to underserved populations and to create an electronic communication (Stewart, 2004). Particularly, with electronic communication, it is much easier to implement collaboration among institutions and to unify social responsibility learning in institutional and societal levels, enabling students to expose to new experiences, new cultures, and foster positive social changes worldwide (Esfijani, 2014; Stewart, 2004).

Today, online pedagogy is not an option anymore, it is an inevitable trend for all higher education institutions, even less motivated institutions also consider online learning as a means to promote their reputation and image (Garde Sánchez et al., 2013). Especially, online education is of prominence under the serious influence of COVID-19 pandemic (Jung et al., 2021). Online learning, thanks to its own advantage in terms of accessibility, affordability, flexibility, and the advancement in learning pedagogy, has prominently dissolved a variety of problems and provided solution for demands of the society and building communities in the increasingly dynamic world (Dhawan, 2020; Stewart, 2004; Wheeler, 2002). Unfortunately, online learning has been paid much attention in the last decades in some aspects, namely, quality, content, and instructor training (Lozier et al., 2002) rather than the integration of social responsibility. Nevertheless, the higher education system in general, and their online learning in specific, cannot stay outside the frame of social responsibility (Vazquez et al., 2013). Online learning should be a part of universities' strategies to develop responsible citizens for the society in a transparent environment (Esfijani, 2014), at the same time, enhance universities' image and ethical values (Navarrete et al., 2012).

Responsible universities should go beyond their obligations to bring benefits to their students, employees, and their community by facilitating the quality of online teaching and learning (Esfijani, 2014). To do that, one of the key strategies for universities is to provide professional development training for their staff (Blair, 2011), which can be a step forward to enhance the quality of online education. However, one of the possible challenges for this might be the lack of trust and support from their stakeholders, including students and employers (Bower & Hardy, 2004), who can impose critical forces on online education (Chung & Ellis, 2003). For instance, students claim some challenges they have to face, including internet connectivity and lack of interaction with classmates and teachers (Bisht et al., 2020). Moreover, their performances can also be affected by economic and resource disparities, which lead to the uneven knowledge that students absorb (Adedoyin & Soykan, 2020).

It is clear, then, the application of impactful Higher Education via USR can only reach its full potential when carried out in tandem with the application of face-to-face learning and vice versa. For example, institutions should design courses with an emphasis on promoting USR, engagement, and deep comprehension and application of knowledge. These requirements stress not only the need for a separate department well-trained in providing students with online-supports (Fleck, 2012) but also the need for all members of the faculty being experienced with the online formats to some extent, for example delivering lectures online and dedicating face-to-face class times for teamwork, action learning, community-based learning, and so on (Fleck, 2012). Again, the process of blending should center around specific students' needs and interests and students' learning experience. The ultimate goal should be to build within students a sense of USR and the necessary knowledge and skills to fulfill it.

## Rethinking University Social Responsibilities in the Era of Post-COVID-19

Since early 2020, the COVID-19 pandemic has imposed critical effects on individuals' health, work, and life and on worldwide health, economy, social changes, and challenges (Ratten, 2020; Tian & Noel Jr, 2020). Specifically, the global education system has witnessed dramatic challenges, including the disruption of students' study and also the decrease of international student mobility (Mok et al., 2021). For example, more than 1.6 billion students, accounting for more than 91% of the worldwide student population were affected during April 2020 (DeVaney et al., 2020). The advent and spread of the pandemic have urged Higher Education Systems all over the world to transform all areas of their teaching, research, and service (Ratten, 2020). Particularly, USR should be proactively demonstrated during the time of this Pandemic (Tian & Noel Jr, 2020). As the global pandemic and uncertainty are still evolving while the previous normal will be replaced by the new normal (Cahapay, 2020), this chapter provides timely reflection on USR during and post COVID-19.

It is easily noticed that due to the threats of COVID-19, university campuses around the world have been closed during the quarantine time (Tian & Noel Jr, 2020). Alternatively, online learning has been applied worldwide to limit the spread of the virus while working toward educational goals (Cahapay, 2020; Ratten, 2020). Social responsibility of Higher Education Institutions in the online environment, hence, should be emphasized to bring benefits to students, staff, and society (Esfijani, 2014). Nevertheless, while little work has discussed multiple efforts of universities to support students and community overcoming this global crisis (Cahapay, 2020, Ratten, 2020; Tian & Noel Jr, 2020), less information is documented about policies to support faculty during this period (Cahapay, 2020).

Given the challenges that COVID-19 pandemic has brought, higher education and stakeholders need to rethink and plan for a sustainable education in the future (Ratten & Jones, 2021). During the pandemic and quarantine periods, Higher Education Institutions have introduced multiple initiatives to connect and facilitate students (Cahapay, 2020, Ratten, 2020; Tian & Noel Jr, 2020). For instance, faculty have successfully revised, redesigned, and transformed their curricular instruction and learning activities in the physical to virtual environment (Cahapay, 2020, Ratten, 2020; Tian & Noel Jr, 2020). Additionally, a virtual classroom not only provides students with required knowledge for their academic year but also engages them in a virtual community (Cahapay, 2020). Moreover, coronavirus has a drastic effect on students' mental health as they have had to adapt to a brand new virtual environment, social distancing and socioeconomic turbulence (Salimi et al., 2021). Given such conditions, online classroom has become a familiar space outside their family in which students can talk about their circumstances, can listen to their friends, and consult their faculty members for their daily issues. Moreover, by providing quality education during the crisis, universities cleverly and actively prepare their students for the hardest time in the future by building resilience, and a sense of preparedness. Students are also equipped with relevant workplace skills for the age of digitalization (Cahapay, 2020).

Higher Education Institutions not only focus on the benefits of their students but also proactively engage in solving social problems such as the health, economic and social demand of the community during the pandemic (Cahapay, 2020, Ratten, 2020; Tian & Noel Jr, 2020). For instance, in the area of public health and medicine, Medical Education Institutions need to perform multiple tasks: (1) eliminating the risks of transmitting Sars_Cov_2 to their students, (2), involving them in inter-professional teams in hospitals and the community, (3), equipping students with technological literacy, problem-solving and innovation competencies, and (4) preparing succession media workforce (Torda, 2020). These requirements ask medical universities to closely and creatively work with both students and the medical community via multiple online platforms. Initiatives of these universities provide medical students good chances to experience a variety of online learning and practicing approaches such as studying in a large-size class, discussing in small groups, collecting feedback from faculty members, and being "twinned" with junior medical officers (Torda, 2020).

In the area of Entrepreneurship Education, the operation of these universities can arise as business cases of time-compressed action, quick response to the crisis, deriving innovation from a crisis, and commercialization of research activities during the COVID-19 (Ratten, 2020). The global scale of these universities enables them to emotionally connect with worldwide students, teachers, alumni, and the community via digital platforms and immersive technologies, acting as the social fabric of community (Scott et al., 2019). In the area of Catholic Education, to remain relevant, Catholic universities have adopted e-service learning to support their students and community addressing such social issues emerging during the COVID-19 as health care, unemployment, poverty, racial discrimination, political corruption, the shortage of schools, and so on (Chick et al., 2020; Tian & Noel Jr., 2020). By applying e-service learning, Catholic university can approach the global community, raise global awareness, cultivate global citizens, and practice social inclusion. These institutions can reach students, their family members, people with special needs, introverted individuals, and the physically disabled population via economically digital devices, internet service, and/or cell phones (Tian & Noel Jr., 2020).

Technology-based practices of USR, however, are not free of limitation. Some major individual and contextual obstacles of universities' engagement with students and community during the turbulent time of pandemic are mentioned (Cahapay, 2020, Tian & Noel Jr, 2020). For instance, non-accessibility to computers/ laptops, digital devices, internet, and so on may prevent target participants from engaging in engagement activities. Family conditions including child/parent care responsibilities, family health, and financial uncertainty may be barriers for students and members of the community to closely connect with universities via a virtual environment (Cahapay, 2020). The nature of discipline also affects quality of online social responsibilities practices. In fact, practical classes and clinical experience are two major aspects that need to be conducted face-to-face in medical education (Torda, 2020). Besides, inattentive behaviors of students such as distraction, low attendance and engagement, indifference during class discussion, and turning of camera reduce quality of technology-based solutions (Cahapay, 2020). Furthermore, the hasty adoption of online learning has caused the dependence on commercial digital learning solutions that are problematic because of their dehumanizing structure and of their nature of profit-making through user data (Teräs et al., 2020).

The unforgettable experiences of Higher Education during COVID-19 has urged universities to critically evaluate their social responsibilities in the era of post COVID-19. For instance, faculty members, with their important roles of encouraging the independence in learning, promoting learning outcomes, initiating and engaging students in online activities (Paudel, 2021), should prepare effective teaching plans for online delivery of lecturing, action learning, community-based learning, teamworking, and so on (Fleck, 2012; Neuwirth et al., 2020). Additionally, the issue of equal access to learning resources and facilities should be carefully considered by University Top Management (Mann et al., 2020). The ideology of "a fair system for all students" may be achieved by sponsoring updated and comprehensive learning resources, providing low-income students with financial safeguards, and providing equipped working space for students. Besides, applying comprehensive methods to maintain good mental and physical health are critical (Mann et al., 2020). Last but not the least, designing pedagogical-driven virtual environments should be placed at the heart of USR Programmes. As the ultimate goal of education should be fostering holistic human growth, the digitalization process in Higher Education requires joined effort of multiple stakeholders to build virtually humanizing platforms (Teräs et al., 2020).

## References

Adedoyin, O. B., & Soykan, E. (2020). Covid-19 pandemic and online learning: The challenges and opportunities. *Interactive Learning Environments*, 1–13. https://doi.org/10.1080/10494820.2020.1813180

Ayala-Rodríguez, N., Barreto, I., Rozas Ossandón, G., Castro, A., & Moreno, S. (2019). Social transcultural representations about the concept of university social responsibility. *Studies in Higher Education*, *44*(2), 245–259. https://doi.org/10.1080/03075079.2017.1359248

Blair, K. (2011). Online learning and professional development. In M. A. Bowdon & R. G. Carpenter (Eds.), *Higher education, emerging technologies, and community partnerships: Concepts, models, and practices* (pp. 141–163). IGI Global. https://doi.org/10.4018/978-1-60960-623-7

Benneworth, P., & Jongbloed, B. W. (2010). Who matters to universities? A stakeholder perspective on humanities, arts and social sciences valorisation. *Higher Education*, *59*(5), 567–588. https://doi.org/10.1007/s10734-009-9265-2

Bisht, R. K., Jasola, S., & Bisht, I. P. (2020). Acceptability and challenges of online higher education in the era of COVID-19: A study of students' perspective. *Asian Education and Development Studies*. https://doi.org/10.1108/AEDS-05-2020-0119

Bower, B. L., & Hardy, K. P. (2004). From correspondence to cyberspace: Changes and challenges in distance education. *New Directions for Community Colleges, 128*, 5–12. https://doi.org/10.1002/cc.169

Boyer, E. (1996). The scholarship of engagement. *Bulletin of the American Academy of Arts and Sciences, 49*(7), 18–33. https://doi.org/10.2307/382445

Bringle, R. G., Games, R., & Malloy, E. A. (1999). *Colleges and universities as citizens*. Allyn and Bacon.

Brown, M. A. (2011). Learning from service: The effect of helping on helpers' social dominance orientation. *Journal of Applied Social Psychology, 41*(4), 850–871. https://doi.org/10.1111/j.1559-1816.2011.00738.x

Cahapay, M. B. (2020). Rethinking education in the new normal post-COVID-19 era: A curriculum studies perspective. *Aquademia, 4*(2), ep20018. https://www.aquademia-journal.com/article/rethinking-education-in-the-new-normal-post-covid-19-era-a-curriculum-studies-perspective-8315

Chapdelaine, A., Ruiz, A., Warchal, J., & Wells, C. (2005). *Service-learning code of ethics*. Anker Publishing.

Chick, R. C., Clifton, G. T., Peace, K. M., Propper, B. W., Hale, D. F., Alseidi, A. A., & Vreeland, T. J. (2020). Using technology to maintain the education of residents during the COVID-19 pandemic. *Journal of Surgical Education*. https://doi.org/10.1016/j.jsurg.2020.03.018

Chile, L. M., & Black, X. M. (2015). University–community engagement: Case study of university social responsibility. *Education, Citizenship and Social Justice, 10*(3), 234–253. https://doi.org/10.1177/1746197915607278

Chung, K. C., & Ellis, A. (2003, December). Online education: Understanding market acceptance in the higher education sector of Singapore. In *20th Annual Conference of the Australasian Society for Computers in Learning in Tertiary Education, Adelaide* (pp. 7–10).

Colby, S., Bercaw, L., Clark, A. M., & Galiardi, S. (2009). From community service to service-learning leadership: a program perspective. *New Horizons in Education, 57*(3), 20–31. https://eric.ed.gov/?id=EJ893701

Compact, C. (2016). Carnegie community engagement classification. Retrieved https://compact.org/initiatives/engaged-campus-initiative/carnegie-community-engagement-classification/why-apply-for-carnegie/

Crabtree, R. D. (2013). The intended and unintended consequences of international service-learning. *Journal of Higher Education Outreach and Engagement, 17*(2), 43–66. https://eric.ed.gov/?id=EJ1005304

DeVaney, J., Shimshon, G., Rascoff, M., & Maggioncalda, J. (2020). Higher ed needs a long-term plan for virtual learning. *Harvard Business Review*. https://hbr.org/2020/05/higher-ed-needs-a-long-term-plan-for-virtual-learning

Dey, E. L. (2009). *Civic responsibility: What is the campus climate for learning?* Association of American Colleges and Universities.

Dey, E. L., Antonaros, M., Ott, M. C., Barnhardt, C. L., & Holsapple, M. A. (2010). *Developing a moral compass: What is the campus climate for ethics and academic integrity*. Association of American Colleges and Universities.

Dhawan, S. (2020). Online learning: A panacea in the time of COVID-19 crisis. *Journal of Educational Technology Systems, 49*(1), 5–22. https://doi.org/10.1177/0047239520934018

Esfijani, A. (2014). *Methodology development for measuring virtual university social responsibility (VUSR)* [Doctoral dissertation, Curtin University]. https://espace. curtin.edu.au/bitstream/handle/20.500.11937/488/199910_Esfijani%20 2014.pdf?sequence=2&isAllowed=y

Fleck, J. (2012). Blended learning and learning communities: opportunities and challenges. *Journal of Management Development, 31*(4), 398–411. https://doi. org/10.1108/02621711211219059

Garde Sánchez, R., Rodríguez Bolívar, M. P., & López-Hernández, A. M. (2013). Online disclosure of university social responsibility: A comparative study of public and private US universities. *Environmental Education Research, 19*(6), 709–746.

Harkavy, I. (2006). The role of universities in advancing citizenship and social justice in the 21st century. *Education, Citizenship and Social Justice, 1*(1), 5–37. https://doi.org/10.1177/1746197906060711

Hebert, A., & Hauf, P. (2015). Student learning through service learning: Effects on academic development, civic responsibility, interpersonal skills and practical skills. *Active Learning in Higher Education, 16*(1), 37–49. https://doi. org/10.1177/1469787415573357

Holland, B. A. (2005, July). Scholarship and mission in the 21st century University: The role of engagement. *Proceedings of the Australian Universities Quality Forum*, 5, 11–17. https://www.academia.edu/download/45697763/ Industry_Engagement_Transforming_Good_In20160517-12353-3x64wf. pdf#page=25

Huda, M., Teh, K. S. M., Muhamad, N. H. N., & Nasir, B. M. (2018). Transmitting leadership based civic responsibility: Insights from service learning. *International Journal of Ethics and Systems*. https://doi.org/10.1108/IJOES-05-2017-0079

Jung, J., Horta, H., & Postiglione, G. A. (2021). Living in uncertainty: The COVID-19 pandemic and higher education in Hong Kong. *Studies in Higher Education, 46*(1), 107-120.

Kouatli, I. (2018). The contemporary definition of university social responsibility with quantifiable sustainability. *Social Responsibility Journal*. https://doi. org/10.1108/SRJ-10-2017-0210

Kuh, G. D., et al (2005). *Student success in college: Creating conditions that matter.* Jossey-Bass.

Kuh, G. D. (2009). What student affairs professionals need to know about student engagement. *Journal of College Student Development, 50*(6), 683–706. https://doi. org/10.1353/csd.0.0099

Lai, K. H. (2009). Developing leadership and cultural competency through service exposure attachment program. *New Horizons in Education, 57*(3), 105–118. https://files.eric.ed.gov/fulltext/EJ893708.pdf

Lambrechts, W., Mulà, I., Ceulemans, K., Molderez, I., & Gaeremynck, V. (2013). The integration of competences for sustainable development in higher education: an analysis of bachelor programs in management. *Journal of Cleaner Production, 48*, 65–73. https://doi.org/10.1016/j.jclepro.2011.12.034

Larrán Jorge, M., & Andrades Peña, F. J. (2017). Analysing the literature on university social responsibility: A review of selected higher education journals. *Higher Education Quarterly, 71*(4), 302–319. https://doi.org/10.1111/hequ.12122

Levesque-Bristol, C., Knapp, T. D., & Fisher, B. J. (2011). The effectiveness of service-learning: It's not always what you think. *Journal of Experiential Education, 33*(3), 208–224. https://doi.org/10.1177/105382590113300302

Lovat, T., & Clement, N. (2016). Service learning as holistic values pedagogy. *Journal of Experiential Education*, *39*(2), 115–129. https://doi.org/10.1177/1053825916628548

Lozier, G., Oblinger, D., & Choa, M. (2002). Organizational models for delivering distance learning. *EDUCAUSE Center for Applied Research, Research Bulletin*, (2), 1–11

Mann, S., Novintan, S., Hazemi-Jebelli, Y., & Faehndrich, D. (2020). Medical Students' Corner: Lessons From COVID-19 in Equity, Adaptability, and Community for the Future of Medical Education. JMIR Medical Education, *6*(2), e23604. https://doi.org/10.2196/23604

MacVaugh, J., & Norton, M. (2012). Introducing sustainability into business education contexts using active learning. *International Journal of Sustainability in Higher Education*, *13*(1), 72– 87. https://doi.org/10.1108/14676371211190326

Madsen, S. R., & Turnbull, O. (2006). Academic service learning experiences of compensation and benefit course students. *Journal of Management Education*, *30*(5), 724–742. https://doi.org/10.1177/1052562905283710

Mitchell, T. D. (2008). Traditional vs. critical service-learning: Engaging the literature to differentiate two models. *Michigan Journal of Community Service Learning*, *14*(2), 50–65.

Mok, K. H., Xiong, W., Ke, G., & Cheung, J. O. W. (2021). Impact of COVID-19 pandemic on international higher education and student mobility: Student perspectives from mainland China and Hong Kong. *International Journal of Educational Research*, *105*, 101718.

Nagy, J., & Robb, A. (2008). Can universities be good corporate citizens? *Critical Perspectives on Accounting*, *19*(8), 1414–1430. https://doi.org/10.1016/j.cpa.2007.10.001

Navarrete, E. E., Rojas, J. P. S., & Pantoja, J. I. A. (2012). Preliminary analysis of social responsibility inside Chilean universities. *African Journal of Business Management*, *6*(42), 10625–10633. https://doi.org/10.5897/AJBM11.3009

Neuwirth, L. S., Jović, S., & Mukherji, B. R. (2020). Reimagining higher education during and post-COVID-19: Challenges and opportunities. *Journal of Adult and Continuing Education*, 1477971420947738. https://doi.org/10.1177/1477971420947738

Osiemo, L. B. (2012). Developing responsible leaders: The university at the service of the person. *Journal of Business Ethics*, *108*(2), 131–143. https://doi.org/10.1007/s10551-011-1087-3

Peric, J. (2012). Development of universities' social responsibility through academic service-learning programs. *Economy of Eastern Croatia Yesterday, Today, Tomorrow*, *1*, 365–375. http://www.cepor.hr/App%207Social%20responsible%20universities_full%20paper_Julia%20Peric.pdf

Paudel, P. (2021). Online education: Benefits, challenges and strategies during and after COVID-19 in higher education. *International Journal on Studies in Education*, *3*(2), 70–85.

Ralph, M., & Stubbs, W. (2014). Integrating environmental sustainability into universities. *Higher Education*, *67*(1), 71–90. https://doi.org/10.1007/s10734-013-9641-9

Ratten, V. (2020). Coronavirus (Covid-19) and the entrepreneurship education community. *Journal of Enterprising Communities: People and Places in the Global Economy*. https://doi.org/10.1108/IJEBR-06-2020-0387

Ratten, V., & Jones, P. (2021). Covid-19 and entrepreneurship education: Implications for advancing research and practice. *The International Journal of Management Education, 19*(1), 100432.

Salimi, N., Gere, B., Talley, W., & Irioogbe, B. (2021). College students mental health challenges: Concerns and considerations in the COVID-19 pandemic. *Journal of College Student Psychotherapy.* https://doi.org/10.1080/87568225.2021.1890298

Sandmann, L. R. (2008). Conceptualization of the scholarship of engagement in higher education: A strategic review, 1996–2006. *Journal of Higher Education Outreach and Engagement, 12*(1), 91-104.

Scott K.E., & Graham J.A. (2015). Service-learning: Implications for empathy and community engagement in elementary school children. *Journal of Experiential Education, 38*(4), 354–372. https://doi.org/10.1177/1053825915592889

Scott, S., Hughes, M. & Kraus, S. (2019), Developing relationships in innovation clusters, *Entrepreneurship and Regional Development, 31*(1/2), 22–45. https://doi.org/10.1080/08985626.2018.1537145

Simpson, R. D. (2000). Toward a scholarship of outreach and engagement in higher education. *Journal of Higher Education Outreach and Engagement, 6*(1), 7–12. https://ojsprod.galib.uga.edu/jheoe/article/download/435/435

Stewart, B. L. (2004). Online learning: A strategy for social responsibility in educational access. *The Internet and Higher Education, 7*(4), 299–310. https://doi.org/10.1016/j.iheduc.2004.09.003

Stubbs, W., & Schapper, J. (2011). Two approaches to curriculum development for educating for sustainability and CSR. *International Journal of Sustainability in Higher Education.* https://doi.org/10.1108/14676371111148045

Teräs, M., Suoranta, J., Teräs, H., & Curcher, M. (2020). Post-Covid-19 education and education technology 'solutionism': A seller's market. *Postdigital Science and Education, 2*(3), 863–878. https://doi.org/10.1007/s42438-020-00164-x

Tian, Q., & Noel Jr, T. (2020). Service-learning in catholic higher education and alternative approaches facing the COVID-19 pandemic. *Journal of Catholic Education, 23*(1), 184–196. https://doi.org/10.15365/joce.2302142020

Torda, A. (2020). How COVID-19 has pushed us into a medical education revolution. *Internal Medicine Journal, 50*(9), 1150–1153. https://doi.org/10.1111/imj.14882

Vázquez, J. L., Lanero, A., García, M. P., & García, J. (2013). Altruism or strategy? A study of attributions of responsibility in business and its impact on the consumer decision making process. *Economics & Sociology, 6*(1), 108. https://doi.org/10.14254/2071-789X.2013/6-1/9

Wheeler, S. (2002). Student perceptions of learning support in distance education. *Quarterly Review of Distance Education 3*(4), 419–429

Young, S., & Nagpal, S. (2013). Meeting the growing demand for sustainability-focused management education: A case study of a PRME academic institution. *Higher Education Research & Development, 32*(3), 493–506. https://doi.org/10.1080/07294360.2012.695339

## Bios

**Hằng Trần Thị**, PhD, is a lecturer in the University of Economics, The University of Danang. Her major research interests lie in but not are not limited to the areas of talent management, work value, competencies-based training, career self-efficacy, career development, career-ecosystem, and higher education embedded in industry, national specific and glocal context. Email: tranthihang@due.edu.vn, hangtt@due.udn.vn

**Quy Dinh Le Nguyen** is a researcher of management science and development economics. His email address is: nldquy@gmail.com.

**Luc-Diep Tra,** MBA, is a lecturer in University of Economics, The University of Danang. Her major research interests lie in but are not limited to the areas of human resource management and organization behavior. Email: dieptl@due.udn.vn

# 4 "Internationalization at Home" in the United States

## Enhancing Admissions and Enrollment Practices for Marginalized Students during and after the COVID-19 Pandemic

*Raquel Muñiz and Natalie Borg*

### Abstract

The COVID-19 pandemic has had a disproportionate negative impact on Black, Brown, Indigenous and low-income communities, further marginalizing already marginalized students and their families. The marginalization has placed these students at a greater disadvantage when applying to college, unless admissions and enrollment practitioners account for these disadvantages in their practices. In this chapter, we discuss college admissions and enrollment issues that directly impact marginalized students, including students of color and students from low-income households, and how the concept of "Internationalization at Home" could be used to build inclusive practices in admissions and enrollment during and after the pandemic. In doing so, we provide examples to illustrate how admissions and enrollment officers can incorporate the concept into their practice.

### Keywords:

college admissions, college enrollment, COVID-19 pandemic, inclusivity, Internationalization at Home

## Introduction

The admissions and enrollment process in American higher education (HE) is a defining point that determines whether a student can enroll in college and access the benefits that come with a college degree. Critics have argued that these processes reproduce and reinforce social inequalities and inequities by limiting the proportion of marginalized students who can gain college access and improve their social mobility (AACRAO, n.d.; Form Your Future, n.d.). For example, admissions officers at HE institutions (HEIs) tend to focus recruitment efforts in wealthy, often White, high schools. A disproportionate number of Black and Brown high school students are concentrated in low-income high schools that lack resources, including college preparatory courses, classroom resources, and counseling services (Niu, 2015). Consequently, these students are less equipped for admission tests or to build a strong academic record that will help them in the admissions process (Clayton, 2019). Additionally, some states prohibit affirmative action policies in college admissions (Long & Bateman, 2020). Affirmative action policies would allow admissions officers to consider race and ethnicity and the unequal experiences of Black, Brown, and Indigenous students when admitting students. The COVID-19 pandemic and the consequent disruptions to HEIs' operations have only further complicated the admissions and enrollment process, in part, by wreaking havoc on the lives of students who will subsequently seek admission and enrollment at American HEIs. This reality requires a change in practices so that they are responsive to the realities of these students' lives.

The pandemic has had a disproportionately negative impact on Black, Brown, Indigenous, and low-income communities, further marginalizing already marginalized students and their families (Blanchard et al., 2020). For example, low-income families, who were already living paycheck to paycheck, experienced job losses and greater rates of COVID-19 cases (Rolland, 2020). Youth and college students in these communities lacked access to internet services or electronic devices necessary to access remote learning. Some families with youth in secondary schooling also lacked the resources to make additional beneficial educational arrangements, such as forming small learning communities of approximately three to ten students who learn together outside the classroom or enrolling their children in private schools with smaller student-teacher ratios that allowed schools to remain open during the pandemic (Kuhfeld et al., 2020). These resources greatly improve a student's ability to prepare for college. Thus, the lack of resources placed these marginalized students at a greater disadvantage when applying to and enrolling in college (e.g., inability to take admissions tests or complete classes), unless admissions and enrollment officers account for these disadvantages in their practices.

We argue that the concept of Internationalization at Home can help improve admissions and enrollment practices during and after the pandemic in service of marginalized student populations. No universal definition of the concept exists (Robson et al., 2018). However, we draw on core themes across prior definitions, which we describe below, and define the concept as follows:

> Internationalization at Home are the processes and practices that HEI agents can adopt across all institutional levels to be sensitive and responsive to the assets and the needs of international and marginalized students on campus.

Generally, Internationalization at Home can inform practices to account for the needs of marginalized students and thereby enhance inclusion and diversity on campus. The literature has extensively examined how the concept of Internationalization at Home can transform academic contexts and experiences. A smaller body of work has examined how Internationalization at Home can be applied to co-curricular contexts in the United States (Brown et al., 2016). We contribute to this growing body of work by examining how Internationalization at Home can apply to admissions and enrollment practices in American HE.

We begin with a discussion of the unique challenges and barriers marginalized students face in seeking admissions and enrollment during the pandemic. Next, we conceptualize Internationalization at Home. We conclude with a discussion on how practitioners can use the concept to inform their admissions and enrollment practices to enhance inclusion.

## Challenges and Barriers to Admissions and Enrollment in the COVID-19 Era

The COVID-19 pandemic and its deleterious effects have negatively affected already marginalized students and their families (Abedi et al., 2020; CDC, 2020), consequently, leaving some of them ill-prepared for college admissions. Marginalized communities have seen higher rates of significant illness and death related to COVID-19. Often living in areas where school districts lack resources, marginalized secondary education students were more likely than the non-marginalized to be enrolled in schools that lacked the resources to provide them the necessary support during the pandemic. The lack of support has a direct impact on students' college readiness and likelihood of gaining admission.

The pandemic has also disrupted the procedures involved in the admissions process and the operations at HEIs. For example, there have been significant disruptions to admissions testing, both domestically and globally due to COVID-19:

> spring and summer tests were canceled, seats are and will continue to be limited as testing sites are allowed to open, discussions about alternative formats for test administration accelerated, students have limited access to guidance on test taking, and test preparation is delivered in alternative formats.... It is also well-established that from an access and equity perspective, limited testing and retesting capacity will disparately affect students who are underrepresented, low-income, first-generation, or live in densely populated areas.

Moreover, fewer students completed the Free Application for Federal Student Aid (FAFSA), which directly impacts the amount of federal and state aid distributed to many low-income incoming students, and necessary for their college attendance (Form Your Future, n.d.). As of December 4, 2020, there was a −14% change in the number of completed FAFSA applications, nationally, when compared to the 2019–2020 academic year (Form Your Future, n.d.). The percent decrease at Title I eligible (i.e., low income) high schools (−17.2%) and high minority serving high schools (−19.5%) was greater than at Title I ineligible (−11.6%) and low minority-serving high schools

(–9.7%; Form Your Future, n.d.). Additionally, travel and gathering bans associated with COVID-19 interrupted or impeded campus gatherings such as tours, admissions events, and other valuable in-person practices that admissions officers use (Smalley, 2020).

The pandemic has also caused significant disruptions to the personal and academic pursuits of marginalized students enrolled in HE, and has caused considerable concerns for higher education leaders regarding enrollment during and after COVID-19 (Turk et al., 2020). The pandemic has exacerbated the pre-existing mental health concerns and stressors for marginalized students (Active Minds, 2020), impacting their experiences while enrolled in college. The COVID-19-related campus closures have also limited opportunities for marginalized students to live and work on campus, which can limit their access to affordable housing, healthcare, and food (Brown, 2020; Malee et al., 2020). These limitations can lead to disruptions in the students' educational trajectories toward graduation.

## Conceptualizing Internationalization at Home

In this section, we begin with a discussion of the multiple conceptualizations of Internationalization at Home. Next, we present a definition of Internationalization at Home for admissions and enrollment practices in the United States. We conclude this section with a discussion on why adopting the concept in admissions and enrollment practices would be useful to enhance the inclusion of international and marginalized students.

### *Multiple Conceptualizations of Internationalization at Home*

Internationalization at Home has evolved into multiple conceptualizations. A group of European scholars who saw a growing need to address the internationalization of HE in an increasingly global society developed the concept in 2000 (Crowther et al., 2000). Proponents of internationalization in HE defined internationalization as: "The process of integrating an international, intercultural, or global dimension into the purpose, functions or delivery of post-secondary education" (Knight, 2004, p. 11). In introducing the concept of Internationalization at Home, Crowther et al. (2000) provided a series of guiding questions for professionals interested in incorporating the concept in their practice:

- How much international vision do the people who finance, govern and manage the institution have, and how could this be improved, if necessary?
- How can one best internationalise the student body? Is one in a position to recruit internationally?
- How can one internationalise the curriculum and teaching methods?
- How can one promote the institution, its services and its graduates to an international community? (p. 39–40)

While these questions applied to three types of stakeholders which Crowther et al. (2000) deemed central to the implementation of Internationalization at Home (i.e., educational managers, academic, and administrative staff), the authors did not provide direct recommendations for the administrative staff. Those employees would be responsible for incorporating Internationalization at Home in the student admissions and enrollment processes. Nonetheless, Internationalization at Home has the capacity to be implemented in admissions and enrollment practices. The conceptualizations center institutional efforts to honor the cultures of international and marginalized students and to incorporate them into the university's campus culture. These efforts are similar to those of scholars who seek to enhance inclusion and support for marginalized students in the United States (Beelen & Jones, 2015; Crowther et al., 2000; Knight, 2003, 2004; Teekens, 2013).

Since its origin, several scholars have adapted the concept to fit different contexts. In 2013, Haneke Teekens, one of the scholars who originated the term, described Internationalization at Home as being "about inclusion, diversity and reciprocity in international education" (p. 1). Two years later, Beelen and Jones (2015) defined Internationalization at Home as the "purposeful integration of international and intercultural dimensions into the formal and informal curriculum for all students within domestic learning environments" (p. 76). Other scholars, such as Knight (2003), have adopted an expanded conceptualization of Internationalization at Home, defining the concept as "the process of integrating an international, intercultural, or global dimension into the purpose, functions or delivery of post-secondary education' (Knight, 2003, p. 2). Knight (2004) also adapted the concept more specifically to include activities and programs on campus, stating that Internationalization at Home featured the "creation of a culture or climate on campus that promotes and supports international/intercultural understanding and focuses on campus-based activities" (Knight, 2004, p. 20).

## *Internationalization at Home in Admissions and Enrollment in the United States*

While no single definition of the concept exists, the conceptualizations in the preceding section share certain themes in common. They have an orientation toward inclusion of international and oft-marginalized students, their cultures, and their assets and also encourage practitioners to center and remain responsive to the needs of international and marginalized students. Finally, the conceptualizations of Internationalization at Home include an acknowledgment that practitioners have the autonomy to adopt inclusive practices at all institutional levels at HEIs. Drawing on these core themes, we define Internationalization at Home as follows:

> Internationalization at Home are the processes and practices that HEI agents can adopt across all institutional levels to be sensitive and responsive to the assets and the needs of international and marginalized students on campus.

For purposes of our discussion, the HEI agents on whom we focus are admissions and enrollment officers at American HEIs. Accordingly, our discussion centers around their processes and practices, such as recruiting practices in the United States and internationally, training of employees on cultural sensitivity, and preparing recruitment materials for diverse student populations. Integrating Internationalization at Home at American HEIs requires modifications that account for the unique culture and context in the United States (de Wit, 2002). Thus, we define international students as those enrolled in post-secondary education in the United States and who intend to stay in the US temporarily. We do not adopt a purely legal definition of international student, because the definition is too narrow and lacks nuance. Under the legal definition, American HEIs categorize students who lack permanent residency or citizenship, including undocumented students, as international, even though these students consider the United States their home and do not intend on leaving the country. Finally, we recognize that different student populations experience marginalization in HE around the world. Given our focus on the US context, by "marginalized students" we mean students who have experienced systemic marginalization in the United States generally and in American HE specifically, including Black, Brown, and Indigenous students and low-income students.

## Enhancing Inclusivity of International and Marginalized Students

Why should admissions and enrollment practitioners at US HEIs adopt Internationalization at Home in their practices? Internationalization at Home has been effective in other contexts around the world and would be useful in the admissions and enrollment process in the United States, because it has the potential to increase the inclusivity of international and marginalized students. The concept has previously been used successfully to combat a rise in fascism and nationalism (Robson et al., 2018) and enhance inclusion for marginalized students via the curriculum and administrative processes (Kauffman, 2019). These are issues relevant to the US context. The Trump era saw a rise in nationalism, fascism, and xenophobia (Friedman, 2018), which were heightened during the pandemic (e.g., Mani, 2020; Ruiz et al., 2020; Serhan & McLaughlin, 2020).

Additionally, inclusion of marginalized students has been a topic of debate and the focus of many efforts in HE for decades, especially as the populations pursuing a college degree have increasingly become more diverse across racial, ethnic, gender, and national origin markers (Taylor & Cantwell, 2018). Given these trends, admissions and enrollment officers would benefit from learning about Internationalization at Home and incorporating the core themes of the concept into their practices. DeLaquil (2019) noted that Internationalization at Home has the capacity to enhance "inclusive internationalization, that is, global learning for all" (p. 3). Internationalization at Home is a fitting supplement to a common institutional goal in US HE: the development of global citizens (Horey et al., 2018; Lilley et al., 2017).

As well, scholars have championed for the internationalization of the curriculum (Leask, 2015). For example, many faculty and administrators have embraced the concept of "Internationalization of the Curriculum," which is "the incorporation of an international and intercultural dimension into the content of the curriculum as well as the teaching and learning arrangements and support services of a program of study" (Leask & Bridge, 2013, p. 81). Internationalization at Home builds on these prior efforts.

## Integrating Internationalization at Home in Admissions and Enrollment Practices at American HEIs

Given that admissions and enrollment officers have publicly declared their desire to enhance inclusion in their practices, integrating elements of Internationalization at Home into their processes could advance their goals and stymie the costs of COVID-19 experienced by international and marginalized communities. Before COVID-19, college admissions and enrollment organizations acknowledged the need to address inequities and enhance support for marginalized populations (AACRAO, n.d.; NACAC, 2016). The American Association of College Registrars and Admissions Officers (AACRAO), and the National Association for College Admissions Counseling (NACAC) included calls to action in support of marginalized students in their published strategic plans (NACAC, 2016), organizational values, and standards of professional practice (AACRAO, n.d.). In December 2020, the AACRAO updated their mission, vision, and goals, centering their support for a globally diverse community in their mission statement (AACRAO, 2020). Internationalization at Home has the potential to address their concerns, address the inequities and enhance the support for marginalized students.

We agree with Stuber's (2019) assertion that "colleges and universities are not neutral institutions but ones whose cultures, policies, and procedures systematically advantage some students and disadvantage others," (p. 1). Accordingly, institutions have the autonomy and responsibility to adjust their policies and practices to support their students, including international and marginalized populations, during and after the COVID-19 crisis. Below, we provide concrete examples of how practitioners working in admissions and enrollment can integrate Internationalization at Home. Scholars have recommended that Internationalization at Home should be integrated at all levels of the institutions, including "the overarching philosophy, mission, and curricula" of HEIs, and within the co-curricular "realms [which] builds strongly on students services and student associations" (Robson et al., 2018, p. 29). Accordingly, our examples range across different institutional levels; for example, the integration of Internationalization at Home in admissions and enrollment practices may reinforce the mission and philosophy of the HEI (Table 4.1).

*Table 4.1* Examples of How to Integrate Internationalization at Home in Practice during and after the Pandemic

| Barriers in admissions and enrollment (e.g.) | Tactic/Value/Potential for Integrating Internalization at Home |
| --- | --- |
| Lack of access to required standardized admissions tests | Reflect on undergraduate or graduate admissions requirements for standardized tests and consider making test scores optional in admissions. |
| Inaccessible campus visits (expectation or benefit of tours; on-campus orientation for students and parents) | Adapt current practices to account for students who are unable to physically visit campus or who cannot attend a satellite recruitment event. Work with external organizations and campus partners to develop recruitment videos, apps, and other remotely accessible information portals. |
| Hidden curriculum that is inaccessible to first-generation college students and other marginalized groups (immigrants, Black students, Brown students, Indigenous students) | Work with other student affairs professionals to identify what elements of the hidden curriculum exist in their office or practices which could be a barrier for these students. Internally, develop resources that can help students navigate these invisible barriers. Externally, work with campus partners to increase transparency for students. |
| English-only informational materials | Conduct annual assessments of the community to learn which languages students and their support networks use, and maintain a centralized, multilingual resource (or relationship with a transcription service) so information is readily accessible to students and their support networks. |
| Dependence upon federal or state financial aid supports for waiving test fees or issuing scholarships | Develop an institutional scholarship or a partnership with a local organization that could help supplement financial resources for low-income students. |
| Mental health concerns | Account for the unique challenges of marginalized students in admissions and enrollment practices and work with campus mental health resources to provide culturally competent counseling. Advertise these resources widely, across campus and effectively during recruitment events. |
| Low FAFSA Completion rates | Partner with high school counselors to provide informational sessions to students and their families regarding the function of the FAFSA application and how they can fill it out. Provide these sessions in multiple languages, as is possible. This could be addressed by national organizations of admissions and enrollment officers, regardless of institutional affiliation. |

Creating change in practices will require resources, including time and money. Well-resourced HEIs may find fewer obstacles to integrating Internationalization at Home than would HEIs with less resources. Institutional decision-makers can support Internationalization at Home in the admissions and enrollment process by allocating resources to train and support admissions and enrollment officers. Given its successful application in different contexts, allocating resources support offices as they incorporate the concept promises to be an investment that will help serve the needs of marginalized students (Kauffman, 2019; Robson et al., 2018). Even when HEIs are not able to allocate much in resources, admissions and enrollment officers can still adopt Internationalization at Home in their practices by being sensitive, attentive to the needs of students and modifying their current practices accordingly.

In conclusion, with its rich potential to positively influence all levels of an institution in service of marginalized students, Internationalization at Home can help practitioners adopt practices that are responsive to the needs of these students during and after the pandemic. Scholars who have advocated for the internationalization of HE have argued that Internationalization at Home aligns with HE's societal responsibility during crises and "with civil and human rights, social justice, and human dignity" (DeLaquil, 2019, p. 6). These ideals align with the goals of the work that practitioners in HE admissions and enrollment perform.

# References

American Association of Collegiate Registrars and Admissions Officers [AACRAO]. (n.d.). *Purpose, values, vision, and mission.* https://www.aacrao.org/who-we-are/mission-vision-values

American Association of Collegiate Registrars and Admissions Officers [AACRAO]. (2020, December). *Purpose, values, vision, and mission: Updated December 2020.* https://www.aacrao.org/who-we-are/mission-vision-values

Abedi, V., Olulana, O., Avula, V., Chaudhary, D., Khan, A., Shahjouei, S., Li, J., & Zand, R. (2020). Racial, economic, and health inequality and COVID-19 infection in the United States. *Journal of Racial and Ethnic Health Disparities*, 1–11. https://doi.org/10.1007/s40615-020-00833-4

Active Minds. (2020). *Recommendations for prioritizing student mental health and campus-wide healing and recovery during COVID-19.* https://www.activeminds.org/wp-content/uploads/2020/06/COVID-19-Position-Statement.pdf

Beelen, J., & Jones, E. (2015) Redefining internationalization at home. In A. Curaj, L. Matei, R. Pricopie, J. Salmi & P. Scott (Eds.), *The European higher education area.* Springer. https://doi-org.proxy.bc.edu/10.1007/978-3-319-20877-0_5

Blanchard, J., Haile-Mariam, T., Powell, N. N., Terry, A., Fair, M., Wilder, M., Nakitende, D., Lucas, J., Davis, G. L., Haywood, Y., & Kline, J. A. (2020). For us, COVID-19 is personal. *Academic Emergency Medicine, 27*(7), 642–643. https://doi.org/10.1111/acem.14016

Brown, S. (2020, March 25). When COVID-19 closed colleges, many students lost jobs they needed. Now campuses scramble to support them. *The Chronicle of Higher Education.* Retrieved from https://www.chronicle.com/article/When-Covid-19-Closed-Colleges/248345

Brown, P. M., Mak, A. S., & Neill, J. T. (2016). Internationalisation at home: Intercultural learning for social psychology students. *Psychology Teaching Review*, *22*(2), 30–40. https://search.proquest.com/docview/1969020483?accountid=9673

Centers for Disease Control and Prevention [CDC]. (2020, November, 30). *Hospitalization and death by race/ethnicity*. U.S. Department of Health and Human Services. https://www.cdc.gov/coronavirus/2019-ncov/covid-data/investigations-discovery/hospitalization-death-by-race-ethnicity.html

Clayton, A. B. (2019). Helping students navigate the college choice process: The experiences and practices of college advising professionals in public high schools. *Review of Higher Education*, *42*(4), 1401–1429. https://doi.org/10.1353/rhe.2019.0070

Crowther, P., Jories, M., Otten, M., Nilsson, B., Teekens, H., & Wächter, B. (2000). Internationalisation at home. A position paper. *European Association for International Education*. https://citeseerx.ist.psu.edu/viewdoc/download?doi=10.1.1.123.3826&rep=rep1&type=pdf

de Wit, H. (2002). *Internationalization of higher education in the United States of America and Europe: A historical, comparative, and conceptual analysis*. Greenwood Press.

DeLaquil, T. (2019). Inclusive internationalization is innovative internationalization: Purpose-driven higher education against inequity in society. In R. Schendel, H. de Wit, & T. DeLaquil (Eds.) *Inclusive and innovative internationalization of higher education proceedings of the WES-CIHE Summer Institute*. Boston College Center for International Higher Education. https://www.bc.edu/content/dam/bc1/schools/lsoe/sites/cihe/publication/Perspectives/Perspectives%20No%2014%20WES-CIHE%20UPDATED%20PDF%2002-18-2020.pdf

Form Your Future. (n.d.). *FAFSA Tracker*. https://formyourfuture.org/fafsa-tracker/

Friedman, J. Z. (2018). Everyday nationalism and elite research universities in the USA and England. *Higher Education*, *76*(2), 247–261. https://doi.org/10.1007/s10734-017-0206-1

Horey, D., Fortune, T., Nicolacopoulos, T., Kashima, E., & Mathisen, B. (2018). Global citizenship and higher education. *Journal of Studies in International Education*, *22*(5), 472–492. https://doi.org/10.1177/1028315318786443

Knight, J. (2003). Updated internationalization definition. *International Higher Education*, *33*, 2–3.

Knight, J. (2004). Internationalization remodeled: Definition, approaches, and rationales. *Journal of Studies in International Education*, *8*(1), 5–31. https://doi.org/10.1177/1028315303260832

Kuhfeld, M., Soland, J., Tarasawa, B., Johnson, A., Ruzek, E., & Liu, J. (2020). Projecting the potential impact of COVID-19 school closures on academic achievement. *Educational Researcher*, *49*(8), 549–565. https://doi.org/10.3102/0013189X20965918

Leask, B. (2015). *Internationalizing the curriculum*. Routledge. https://doi.org/10.4324/9781315716954

Leask, B., & Bridge, C. (2013). Comparing internationalisation of the curriculum in action across disciplines: Theoretical and practical perspectives. *Compare*, *43*(1), 79–101. https://doi.org/10.1080/03057925.2013.746566

Lilley, K., Barker, M., & Harris, N. (2017). The global citizen conceptualized. *Journal of Studies in International Education*, *21*(1), 6–21. https://doi.org/10.1177/1028315316637354

Long, M. C., & Bateman, N. A. (2020). Long-run changes in underrepresentation after affirmative action bans in public universities. *Educational Evaluation and Policy Analysis*, *42*(2), 188–207. https://doi.org/10.3102/0162373720904433

Malee Bassett, R., & Arnhold, N. (2020, April 30). COVID-19's immense impact on equity in tertiary education. *World Bank Blogs.* https://blogs.worldbank.org/education/covid-19s-immense-impact-equity-tertiary-education

Mani, B. V. (2020, May 14). Fighting the shadow andemic. *Inside Higher Ed.* https://www.insidehighered.com/views/2020/05/14/inclusive-teaching-needed-help-combat-xenophobia-racism-and-discrimination-brought

National Association for College Admission Counseling [NACAC]. (2016, November). *A framework for the future.* https://www.nacacnet.org/globalassets/documents/about/strategicplan2017-20.pdf

Niu, S. X. (2015). Leaving home state for college: Differences by race/ethnicity and parental education. *Research in Higher Education, 56*(4), 325–359. https://doi.org/10.1007/s11162-014-9350-y

Robson, S., Almeida, J., & Schartner, A. (2018). Internationalization at home: Time for review and development? *European Journal of Higher Education, 8*(1). https://doi.org/10.1080/21568235.2017.1376697

Rolland, J. S. (2020). COVID-19 pandemic: Applying a multisystemic lens. *Family Process, 59*(3), 922–936. https://doi.org/10.1111/famp.12584

Ruiz, N. G., Horowitz, J. M., & Tamis, C. (2020, July 1). Many Black and Asian Americans say they have experienced discrimination amid the COVID-19 outbreak. *Pew Social Trends.* https://www.pewsocialtrends.org/2020/07/01/many-black-and-asian-americans-say-they-have-experienced-discrimination-amid-the-covid-19-outbreak/

Serhan, Y., & McLaughlin, T. (2020, March 13). *The other problematic outbreak.* The Atlantic. https://www.theatlantic.com/international/archive/2020/03/coronavirus-covid19-xenophobia-racism/607816/

Smalley, A. (2020). Higher education responses to Coronavirus (COVID-19). *National Conference of State Legislatures.* https://www.ncsl.org/research/education/higher-education-responses-to-coronavirus-covid-19.aspx

Stuber, J. (2019). The elusiveness of inclusion in elite higher education [Review of The Elusiveness of Inclusion in Elite Higher Education]. *Contemporary Sociology: A Journal of Reviews, 49*(1), 10–14. SAGE Publications. https://doi.org/10.1177/0094306119889961a

Taylor, B., & Cantwell, B. (2018). Unequal higher education in the United States: Growing participation and shrinking opportunities. *Social Sciences (Basel), 7*(9), 167. https://doi.org/10.3390/socsci7090167

Teekens, H. (2013, June 15). Internationalisation at home - crossing other borders. *University World News.* https://www.universityworldnews.com/post.php?story=20130613084529186

Turk, J., Soler Salazar, M. C., & Vigil, D. (2020, April 23). *College and university presidents respond to COVID-19: April 2020 survey.* American Council on Education. https://www.acenet.edu/Research-Insights/Pages/Senior-Leaders/College-and-University-Presidents-Respond-to-COVID-19-April-2020.aspx

## Bios

**Raquel Muñiz, JD, PhD,** is an assistant professor of law and education policy at Boston College. Her research addresses the persistent educational inequities in American society using disciplinary tools of educational theory, policy, and law. She focuses on two lines of inquiry: (1) examining the role of law and policies in furthering educational equity; and (2) examining the use of research evidence in the legal system and public policy decision-making where such decision-making has implications for educational equity. Her research is particularly concerned with students who have experienced substantial adversity, systemic stressors that students face as a result of the nested systems of American laws, regulations, and accompanying social policies that shape their lived experiences and the school systems they attend. Email: raquel.munizcastro@bc.edu

**Natalie Borg, MEd,** is a doctoral candidate of higher education at Boston College, where she serves as a research assistant and teaching fellow. Natalie's research centers on the experiences of students and higher education professionals whose identities are marginalized by their respective systems of higher education. In this pursuit, Natalie focuses upon the role of law and policy to support or oppress these communities. Natalie's published works include comparative policy analyses of higher education systems outside of the United States, and their potential as support mechanisms for migrants and refugees. Prior to beginning her PhD at Boston College, Natalie worked in Housing and Residence Life at the University of North Texas, where she learned from a rich community of students and peers. Email: borgn@bc.edu

# 5 Financial Ramifications of Coronavirus on Division I Athletic Departments

*Molly Harry*

## Abstract

In the spring of 2020, safety and health concerns with COVID-19 shut down college sports. Most notably, the National Collegiate Athletic Association's basketball tournament, better known as March Madness, was canceled, costing the Association and its member institutions almost $1 billion. A common misconception concerning intercollegiate athletics is that most athletic departments generate revenue for their institutions. However, less than 30 of the 347 Division I athletic departments operate in the black. Thus, this loss of revenue has resulted in unprecedented financial issues and considerations, such as cutting sports, furloughing staff, and offering fewer support resources for athletes. Through the lens of resource dependence theory, this chapter offers a synthesis of the available literature and examines the financial ramifications of the coronavirus on Division I athletic department operations.

## Keywords:

COVID-19, Finance, Intercollegiate athletics

## Introduction

Athletic programs are often the "front porch" of many American institutions of higher education (Bass et al., 2015). Athletic department operations are managed by the Athletic Director (AD) who oversees coaches and senior level athletics employees such as administrators in the areas of athlete academics, compliance, event management, and finance, and reports to the institution president (Ott & Bates, 2015). Finances of athletic departments have received increased scrutiny as critics of college athletics argue that athletic departments are overly dependent on financial assistance in the form of subsidies from state governments and institutions (Cheslock & Knight, 2015). The average Division I athletic department competing at the highest level, often considered the Football Bowl Subdivision (FBS), receives 12% of its total revenues from state support and 7% from institutional subsidies and student fees. At the second highest level, the Football Championship Subdivision (FCS), the revenue from subsidies and student fees increases greatly: 51% of the operating budget comes from state support, while 19% comes from student fees (CAFI Database, n.d.). With massive media rights contracts with broadcasting companies and millions generated from football and men's basketball, many ask why athletics needs subsidizing in the first place (Cheslock & Knight, 2015). Despite these revenue streams, less than 30 of the 347 Division I programs in the National Collegiate Athletic Association (NCAA) operate in the black (NCAA Finances, n.d.). Expenditures from travel, facility management and capital projects, and athletic scholarships for hundreds of athletes and salaries and benefits for hundreds of department personnel consume most of the revenue generated.

Financial operations of Division I athletic departments were interrupted in March 2020 when health concerns stemming from a global pandemic sparked by the novel coronavirus (COVID-19) halted college sports. Through the lens of resource dependence theory (Bess & Dee, 2012), this chapter provides a synthesis of the available higher education and athletics literature to discuss the fiscal adjustments made by Division I athletic departments due to COVID-19.

## Literature Review

Resource dependence theory states that organizations depend on their environments for resources (Bess & Dee, 2012). Because organizations, such as athletic departments, cannot internally produce all of their required resources, they become reliant on external actors such as the NCAA (Pfeffer & Salancik, 1978). The NCAA, as the external actor, has power over athletic departments in two ways: (1) determining if departments receive resources and (2) deciding how athletic departments can spend or use said resources. Actions taken by the NCAA, and the resulting ramifications on athletic departments, demonstrate one way in which resource dependence is evident in college athletics in the wake of COVID-19. Given the novelty of COVID-19, fluctuating developments, limited scholarly publications concerning COVID-19 and athletics, and the unprecedented nature of the virus and its impact on sports, much of the literature examined in this chapter primarily comes from reputable online journalism platforms covering higher education and/or intercollegiate athletics. While less traditional than scholarly articles, using these sources ensures an up-to-date and informed presentation of the current state of college athletics affairs. Additionally, where applicable, these sources are complemented with journal articles covering both the college athletics environment pre-virus and during the pandemic. The articles chosen highlight the importance of resource dependence in the college sports landscape.

The first three sections focus on March Madness cancellation, expenditures associated with scholarships for returning athletes, and financial ramifications of administrator furloughs, terminations, and sports cuts. However, at the time of this writing, one vital area for Division I institutions remains uncertain: the truncated college football season. The fourth section offers a brief analysis of the financial advantages and disadvantages of playing or not playing football in the Fall 2020 semester.

### The NCAA & March Madness

Founded in 1906, the NCAA is a nonprofit governing organization for 102 athletic conferences and 1,098 institutions across the United States, with the primary purpose of maintaining athletics as an integral part of educational programs (Satterfiled, 2015). The Association is organized into Divisions I, II, and III, with Division I often considered more athletically elite due to generous scholarship offerings, larger athletic departments, and substantial budgets. Additionally, Division I houses 347 institutions, over 6,000 athletic teams, and more than one-third of the NCAA's total number of athletes (Grant et al., 2015). Division I institutions are the focus of this chapter due to size as well as importance of these departments to the Association, their ability to generate massive amounts of revenue, and the extensive literature and coverage of these schools during COVID-19.

In March 2020, due to health threats associated with COVID-19, the NCAA canceled all winter and spring championship events, most notably March Madness, the single-elimination men's basketball tournament in which 68 teams across Division I compete to be crowned the National Champion. March Madness is one of the biggest American sporting events, bringing in $867.5 million, over 80% of all the revenue generated by the NCAA in fiscal year 2017–2018 (NCAA, n.d.). Tournament revenue comes from two streams: sponsorships and TV media deals (Weight & Harry, 2019). The remaining portion of the NCAA's revenue comes from hosting other championship events and associated ticket sales, along with membership dues (NCAA, n.d.). However, the NCAA and its members are reliant on the tournament's revenue to subsidize the college athletics enterprise. This reliance on March Madness, along with dwindling contingency funds, created a host of fiscal issues, illustrating perhaps the greatest way in which resource dependence theory connects member institutions and the Association.

Prior to COVID-19, Division I athletic departments were expected to collectively receive $600 million in NCAA distributions. Post-March Madness cancellation, distributions were $225 million (NCAA, 2020). This highlights two important components to resource dependence theory: criticality, or importance of the resource, and scarcity, the availability of the resource (Bess & Dee, 2012). Because NCAA distributions are vital for the survival of these athletic departments, and because this money is scarce—there is not another supplier of such massive funds—departments are highly dependent on the NCAA. Thus, institutions and athletic departments needed to cut costs and develop innovative strategies to make up missing revenue, while also considering the safety of various stakeholders. For 2020, funds received from the NCAA are unrestricted, allowing conferences and schools to better support their athletes during the uncertainty surrounding the virus, such as offering eligibility extensions for spring sport athletes. The financial significance of the tournament can also be seen in 2021, as the NCAA hosted March Madness amid the pandemic and without requiring teams to be vaccinated.

### Athlete Eligibility Extension

Division I athletes are limited to four seasons of competition within a five-year span (NCAA Division I Manual, 2019). However, a few weeks after canceling all remaining championships, the NCAA released a statement allowing athletic departments to offer an additional year of athletic eligibility for spring sport athletes whose seasons were halted due to COVID-19. Given the continued uncertainty surrounding the virus, NCAA leadership also voted to allow schools to extend eligibility for athletes in fall and winter competitive seasons (Hosick, 2020a, 2020b).

While the NCAA offered this remedy to provide more support for athletes, it was up to individual departments to decide if and how to implement these changes. Thus, some programs, such as members of the Ivy League, decided not to offer additional eligibility (Associated Press, 2020), and others, depending on departmental financial resources, opted to increase or decrease the scholarships offered (Hosick, 2020a). For athletic programs that offered additional eligibility, projections indicated an increase in expenses from $500,000 to almost $1 million for athletes in just one competitive season (i.e., spring, fall, or winter) (Berkowitz & Myerberg, 2020). For Texas A&M University, the second most profitable college athletics program in the nation, bringing back 21 spring sport athletes who would have normally graduated, cost $550,000 (Brown, 2020). Indiana University, which ranks 25th on revenue-generation for Division I schools, estimated its expenses associated with returning spring athletes at $900,000 (Blau, 2020). For smaller athletic enterprises, such as Appalachian State University and Troy University, the cost to bring back spring senior athletes was expected to be $225,000 and $280,000, respectively (Berkowitz & Myerberg, 2020; Joyce, 2020). These eligibility expenses may be tripled, depending on how many fall and winter sport athletes return for another season.

The long-term implications of this extended eligibility remain unknown; however, this decision has already impacted recruitment and team rosters, and could affect scholarship allocation for athletes recruited in the coming years. Athletics leaders at national and institutional levels are considering how eligibility will be impacted and funded, as many Division I conferences postponed fall and some winter competition to spring 2021.

### Athletic Administrative & Sponsorship Cuts

Another financial consequence of COVID-19 and the cessation of college athletics came in the form of terminations, consolidations, hiring freezes, and furloughs. Salaries and benefits for athletic employees make up the majority of departmental expenses, with average percentage of total spending on employee compensation for FBS and FCS public athletic departments totaling 34.6% and 32.8%, respectively (Hirko & Sweitzer, 2015).

By the end of March 2020, the NCAA implemented its own pay reductions for executive members, along with a hiring freeze through the end of 2021 (Berkowitz, 2020a). Athletic departments across the United States quickly followed. The University of Arizona released a statement noting that the athletic director and the head coaches for baseball, football, and men's and women's basketball voluntarily cut their salaries by 20% as a means to help make up for a projected $7.5 million shortfall for fiscal year 2019–2020 (Cluff, 2020). This shortfall partially stemmed from the cancellation of the 2020 Pacific12 (Pac-12) men's basketball conference tournament and missing NCAA distributions, another example of the fiscal dependence of institutions on both their affiliate conferences and NCAA. This is not unlike budgetary actions taken by various other athletic departments across Division I (Cherney, 2020). In a more drastic case, the University of Maryland said its department's financial hit due to COVID-19 was expected to be roughly $40 million.

Other athletic departments instituted furloughs due to the lack of incoming revenue and the resulting economic downturn. The University of Louisville, facing a $15 million 2019–2020 fiscal year shortage, announced indefinite furloughs for almost 50 staff. The AD also eliminated 40 positions, approximately one third of the department, initiated executive employee salary cuts, and reduced all team operating budgets for the foreseeable future by 15% (O'Neil, 2020; Robinson, 2020). These and other similar athletic reductions accompanied institution-wide cutbacks at most universities (Kelderman, 2020).

For some Division I athletic units, administrative reductions did not balance the budget, and decisions were made to terminate teams (Swanson & Smith, 2020). Eliminating sports is viewed as a last resort due to implications for athletes, coaches, and the athletic department's reputation. Sport termination often involves teams that are classified as non-revenue-generating sports, which, in Division I, typically include all sports outside of football and men's basketball. Football and men's basketball are lucrative due to massive media rights deals with television networks and money from ticket sales (Clotfelter, 2019), which provide revenue that subsidizes other sports (Hirko & Sweitzer, 2015). However, with the uncertainty surrounding football and basketball seasons, leaders were concerned about the potential for having significantly less revenue to support all sports and associated expenses (Berkowitz & Myerberg, 2020). Thus, sport elimination is also touted as a way to save money by cutting expenses.

Old Dominion University (ODU) became the first Division I athletic department to cut sports: Three weeks after the NCAA canceled March Madness, ODU discontinued its 60-year-old wrestling program (Hays, 2020). In the hopes of saving money, a slew of other institutions followed:

the University of Cincinnati cut its men's soccer team (Nightengale, 2020), the University of Wisconsin-Green Bay ended its sponsorship of men's and women's tennis (Mizan, 2020), and the University of Akron terminated its men's cross country, men's golf, and women's tennis programs (Cobb, 2020). Most notably, Stanford University eliminated almost one-third of its sports when athletics and institutional leaders cut 11 of its 36 teams. This impacted 240 athletes, 22 coaches, and 20 support staff (Tessier-Lavigne et al., 2020).

Without these sports teams, departments may save money in the form of distributing fewer dollars to scholarships, paying fewer coaches' salaries and benefits, and decreasing costs associated with managing facilities used by these programs. Akron's AD announced that cutting the three sports, along with reductions in employee positions and salaries, is projected to save the department $4.4 million in current and future expenses (Williams, 2020). Similarly, Stanford's AD noted that prior to the pandemic, the department carried a $12 million deficit. However, due to COVID-19, that deficit was expected to increase to $25 million and potentially rise depending on the football season. Across all NCAA divisions, athletic departments have dropped almost 200 teams, with Division I constituting approximately half of those eliminations (Dittmore, n.d.). These elimination decisions are clearly linked to missing resources and departments' challenges to find external assistance, outside of NCAA distributions, to financially support the enterprise (Bess & Dee, 2012).

While potentially costly to an athletic department, non-revenue teams can bring in significant amounts of tuition revenue for institutions. Many athletes competing in non-revenue sports do not receive full athletics-based scholarships, and thus, still pay some or all of their tuition and other university expenses. Some scholars and members of the media have argued that if an institution were to begin a new non-revenue sport program and recruit students, particularly out-of-state or international students, on partial or no scholarship, that the institution could actually profit (Dittmore, n.d.; Hardwick-Day, 2008; Novy-Williams, 2020). Additionally, some critics of cutting sports note that rather than saving this money, it is reinvested in football programs (Weaver, 2020).

### Football & Coronavirus

Many scholars have noted that intercollegiate sports, particularly football, is the tail wagging the athletics dog (Clotfelter, 2019; Lopiano & Zimbalist, 2020). In fact, during the coronavirus pandemic, athletic directors have expressed strong sentiments about the need to have a football season, with the University of Florida's AD stating: "from a financial standpoint, if we're not playing football games in the fall, it will shake the foundation of college athletics. As everyone knows, football pays for the enterprise to go forward" (Bianchi, 2020). This quote highlights the criticality of media rights deals in sustaining athletic departments, another example of resource dependence in college sports. The keen emphasis on a football season grew from the foregone March Madness funds and decreased NCAA distributions, making the sport increasingly vital for Division I athletic departments' budgets.

On August 13, 2020, the NCAA officially canceled fall sport championships, including FCS football. While the NCAA has governance over FBS sports outside of football, because it does not provide a championship or bowl games for these programs—that is managed by the College Football Playoff—members of the FBS division have been more hesitant to postpone football and fall sports seasons. Citing too many unknowns about virus implications for athlete health along with liability concerns, the Mid-American Conference (MAC) became the first FBS conference to postpone fall sports until spring 2021 (Silverstein & Patterson, 2020). This was followed by presidents at the Big Ten and Pac-12 conferences opting to postpone their seasons until the following semester (Anderson, 2020).

Still, conferences such as the Atlantic Coast Conference (ACC), Big 12, and Southeastern Conference (SEC), remained steadfast in their determination to compete in the fall. Conferences that postponed fall sports, football in particular, were forgoing millions of dollars from media deals and ticket sales. Power Five programs operating without a football season were expected to lose an average of $78 million (Berkowitz, 2020b). Some of this lost income could be made up during a spring football season, but many institutional leaders noted the potential for no spring competitions if the virus gained momentum. As such, conferences who originally decided to not hold a football season (i.e., MAC, Big Ten, etc.), backtracked, including every FBS conference. Individual schools could decide to opt out, and out of the 130 FBS teams, only three did not compete in 2020. While athletic departments stated that the reason for a return was to provide sport opportunities for their athletes, critics argue such decisions are rooted in revenue dependence (Weaver, 2020).

Despite the varying decisions made across Division I, there were financial advantages and disadvantages of a fall football season. Football offers a host of benefits; mainly, a fall season ensured a revenue stream from the sport, albeit at a smaller level than the years before COVID-19. For programs who admitted fans, stadiums operated at a reduced capacity—depending on state and institution regulations anywhere from 20% to 50%— and revenue was generated from ticket sales, parking, and other auxiliary services. A football season may also have ensured continued donor support, as most athletics donors engage in philanthropy, such as buying premium football tickets (Stinson & Howard, 2010). Additionally, playing football and potentially other sports, enabled departments to continue charging students some athletics fees, a significant source of income for many programs.

However, the most significant financial benefit from a football season emerged from media rights deals conferences and institutions have with broadcasting companies. A recent inquiry by *ESPN* using 2018 tax filings by Power Five conferences—schools with the biggest athletic programs including the ACC, Big Ten, Big 12, Pac-12, and SEC—noted that TV and other media money generated anywhere from $237 million to $440 million for these conferences and their members. That funding is lost, or substantially reduced, without a football season. Media deals and ticket sales tied to football alone for the schools in the aforementioned five conferences, make up 60% of their athletics departments' combined operating revenues. Institutions competing in Division I outside of the Power Five would also lose millions. Undoubtedly, COVID-19 reinforced athletic departments' dependence on financial resources and commercialization (Weaver, 2020).

The pandemic also created significant costs associated with the football season, particularly regarding the health and safety of athletes, coaches, administrators, and staff. In fact, many scholars in higher education denounced athletic departments' and administrators' decision to return athletes to campus. Lopiano and Zimbalist (2020) argued steps to bring athletes back, especially football players, were disconcerting and neglected the safety of too many constituents to be rationalized. Indeed, they noted that higher education "lost its mind" (Lopiano & Zimbalist, 2020). Even athletes spoke out with one University of California, Los Angeles football player stating, "we're going to come to a point where a college player will literally have to die from COVID-19 for someone to understand what's going on" (Russell, 2020).

Given the uncertainty, increased testing and safety protocols for athletes, coaches, administrators, staff, and fans were a fiscal focal point for departments' expenses, both with and without football and other sport seasons. The financial considerations of testing consistently and effectively became the driving forces for leaders making health decisions. As athletes came back for workouts in June and July, athletic directors across Division I discussed budgetary impacts of testing, with some noting just testing the incoming athletes cost $500,000 to $2 million (Thamel, 2020). Additionally, throughout the 2020 season athletic departments faced expenses from COVID-19 team outbreaks. Outbreaks led to games being postponed or canceled depending on the conference, which influenced money received from TV deals. For example, each canceled PAC-12 football game cost the conference and its members $5 million (Wilner, 2020b). In addition, outbreaks required increased testing and quarantining, often in hotels, adding hundreds of thousands of dollars to these growing expenses. There were also expenses complementary to testing, stemming from increased materials such as hand sanitizer, gloves and masks, thermometers, and disinfectant fogger machines, and costs to train staff (LEAD1, 2020a). Similarly, more game day staff was needed to implement new health and safety regulations.

Litigation from an athlete or another constituent offered another potential expense. While some institutions drafted documents informing athletes of the risks associated with training and competing, others designed waivers that prevented athletes and others who may contract COVID-19 from suing (Dellenger, 2020; Pickman, 2020). However, the enforcement of such waivers depends on the state (Cotten, 2016; LEAD1, 2020b; Zagger, 2020).

Additionally, another trend involved the inclusion of a statement on the back or bottom of an event ticket stating that the institution was not liable if an attendee contracted the virus (LEAD1, 2020b). However, as with athlete waivers, fans remain a potential litigation source.

There are a multitude of financial measures that institutions also considered. These included honoring athlete scholarships across all remaining teams and paying coaches, administrators, and staff all or part of salaries and benefits. Some conferences, such as the Pac-12, implemented loan programs where conference members were eligible to receive up to an $83 million loan with 3.75% interest over the next ten years (Wilner, 2020a). Additionally, debt and rent payment for facilities, if applicable, remained an expense during the pandemic.

## Discussion and Conclusions

Regardless of how long the coronavirus pandemic lasts, there will be continued fallout from this period. Literature suggests there are at least three critical areas of future financial implications stemming from pandemic management: safety and training, media deals and ticket sales, and insurance and reserves. Researchers believe that even after the vaccine rollout for coronavirus, it is likely that some of the safety and health precautions implemented will remain, such as increased sanitization and monitoring of health conditions (LEAD1, 2020a; Parnell et al., 2020). The continuation of these practices is important for the well-being of all stakeholders but will add an expense line to budgets in the coming years.

With evidence demonstrating athletic departments' resource dependence on broadcasting deals, media rights deals are another area conferences and athletic departments will focus on even more. Prior to COVID-19, fan attendance at college sporting events was already decreasing (Clotfelter, 2019). With safety concerns associated with the virus, the number of fans who will remain at home to watch their teams compete, rather than trekking to arenas, could rise. This projected increase in at-home fans offers conferences and athletic programs leverage to seek more revenue from media deals. However, this increase in money from television and other media rights comes at the expense of ticket sales and perpetuates the reliance on media deals for revenue. Statistics from the College Athletics Financial Information Database show schools in the FBS, on average, receive 22% of their overall revenue from NCAA distributions and media rights and 19% from ticket sales. For Power Five athletic programs, those numbers jump to 30%–43% from distributions and media deals and 15%–24% from ticket sales. With changes in fan behavior, it is probable that percentages from the former will rise, while the latter will fall.

Finally, institutions and athletic departments must revisit the type of insurance they hold and whether or not they have the proper terms in place should another catastrophic event occur. Similarly, in the current model in which departments spend what they make, or even spend more than they make (Blue, 2019; Fort, 2015), further emphasis on bolstering departmental reserves would be fiscally responsible and assist in preserving the collegiate model for generations to come. Such actions would decrease dependence on NCAA distributions and media deals, limiting athletic departments' vulnerability to the potential scarcity of this income stream (Bess & Dee, 2012).

## Implications

It appears college athletics are "an essential business" during COVID-19, which speaks volumes about the connection of intercollegiate sports and higher education. It remains to be seen if the coronavirus may actually serve as a long-term positive influence on college sports. With reduced NCAA distributions, expenses associated with extended athlete eligibility, department furloughs and sport terminations, and the reduced football season, schools may be forced to consider new operating models that could result in fiscal conservatism and frugality for the years to come. In this way, athletic departments would engage in dependency-reduction strategies, creating a more financially stable athletics environment (Bess & Dee, 2012). Additionally, this could spark a financial reform in which athletic departments devote resources to areas critics say are neglected, such as academics, mental health, diversity and inclusion, and Title IX.

The pandemic has undoubtedly altered the relationship between education and athletics, and it is up to leaders across campus to understand how athletics financially fits with the institutional mission as intercollegiate sports moves forward post COVID-19.

## References

Anderson, G. (2020, August 12). Pulling the plug on fall sports. *Inside Higher Ed.* https://www.insidehighered.com/news/2020/08/12/big-ten-and-pac-12-postpone-2020-fall-sports?

Associated Press. (2020, April 2). Ivy League won't allow 5th year of eligibility for spring-sport athletes. *ESPN.* https://www.espn.com/espn/story/_/id/28987862/ivy-league-allow-5th-year-eligibility-spring-sport-athletes

Bass, J. R., Schaeperkoetter, C. C., & Bunds, K. S. (2015). The "front porch": Examining the increasing interconnection of university and athletic department funding. In K. Ward, L. E. Wolf-Wendel (Eds.), *ASHE Higher Education Report*, *41*(5), 1–62.

Berkowitz, S. (2020a, March 31). Top NCAA management to take pay cut amid lost revenue from coronavirus cancellations. *USA Today.* https://www.usatoday.com/story/sports/ncaab/2020/03/31/coronavirus-ncaa-president-mark-emmert-taking-20-percent-pay-cut/5094515002/

Berkowitz, S. (2020b, April 14). Major public college football programs could lose billions in revenue if no season is played. *USA Today.* https://www.usatoday.com/story/sports/ncaaf/2020/04/14/college-football-major-programs-could-see-billions-revenue-go-away/2989466001/

Berkowitz, S., & Myerberg, P. (2020, March 22). Giving NCAA athletes another year of eligibility for coronavirus cancellations is costly. *USA Today*. https://www.usatoday.com/story/sports/2020/03/22/coronavirus-giving-ncaa-athletes-back-missed-eligibility-costly/2872197001/

Bess, J. L., & Dee, J. R. (2012). *Understanding college and university organization: Theories for effective policy and practice*. Stylus.

Bianchi, M. (2020, March 21). Gators AD Scott Stricklin: Canceling football 'would shake financial foundation of college athletics. *The Orlando Sentinel*. https://www.orlandosentinel.com/coronavirus/os-sp-coronavirus-gators-ucf-fsu-orlando-magic-nba-20200322-r7reg4pqqzgarfqyy64kuxk4gm-story.html

Blau, J. (2020, June 5). Glass: Addition year for spring sport seniors will cost $900k. *Hoosier Sports Report*. https://www.hoosiersportsreport.com/2020/06/glass-additional-year-for-spring-sport-seniors-will-cost-900k/

Blue, K. (n.d.). Rising expenses in college athletics and the non-profit paradox. *ADU*. https://www.athleticdirectoru.com/articles/kevin-blue-rising-expenses-in-college-athletics-and-the-non-profit-paradox/

Brown, T. L. (2020, May 5). 21 Texas A&M seniors returning next year thanks to NCAA rule. *The Eagle*. https://www.theeagle.com/sports/21-texas-a-m-seniors-returning-next-year-thanks-to-ncaa-rule/article_bcea99c0-8f4b-11ea-8a54-9f23bd8ca764.html

CAFI Database. (n.d.). Explore where the money comes from. *The Knight Commission on Intercollegiate Athletics*. http://cafidatabase.knightcommission.org/reports/f8825701

Cherney, E. (2020, May 11). Northwestern University furloughs staff, cuts executive pay and taps endowment as it eyes 'significant shortfall' due to coronavirus pandemic. *The Chicago Tribune*. https://www.chicagotribune.com/coronavirus/ct-northwestern-university-finances-coronavirus-20200511-k4vv5mhkxnctdhtkjkaqqhrrxa-story.html

Cheslock, J. J., & Knight, D. B. (2015). Diverging revenues, cascading expenditures, and ensuing subsidies: The unbalanced and growing financial strain of intercollegiate athletics on universities and their students. *The Journal of Higher Education, 86*(3), 417–447. doi: 10.1080/00221546.2015.11777370

Clotfelter, C. T. (2019). *Big-time sports in American universities*. Cambridge University Press. doi: 10.1017/9781108366847

Cluff, J. (2020, May 6). Arizona Wildcats announce pay cuts for Dave Heeke, Sean Miller, Kevin Sumlin, others. *AZ Central*. https://www.azcentral.com/story/sports/college/ua/2020/05/06/arizona-wildcats-announce-pay-cuts-head-coaches-amid-coronavirus/5176722002/

Cobb, D. (2020, May 14). Akron eliminates three sports programs for financial reasons amid COVID-19 crisis. *CBS Sports*. https://www.cbssports.com/college-basketball/news/akron-eliminates-three-sports-programs-for-financial-reasons-amid-covid-19-crisis/

Cotten, D. J. (2016). Defenses against negligence. In D. J. Cotton & J. T. Wolohan (Eds.), *Law for recreation and sport managers* (pp. 78–129). Kendall Hunt Publishing.

Dellenger, R. (2020, June 17). Coronavirus liability waivers raise questions as college athletes return to campus. Sports Illustrated. https://www.si.com/college/2020/06/17/college-athletes-coronavirus-waivers-ohio-state-smu

Dittmore, S. (n.d.). Deciding what sports to add during a pandemic. *ADU*. https://athleticdirectoru.com/articles/deciding-what-sports-to-add-during-a-pandemic/

Fort, R. (2015). College sports spending decision and the academic mission. In E. Comeaux (Ed.), *Introduction to intercollegiate athletics* (pp. 135–146). Johns Hopkins University Press.

Grant, R., Leadley, J. C., & Zygmont, Z. X. (2015). *Economics of intercollegiate sports.* World Scientific Publishing.

Hardwick-Day (2008). *NCAA Division II Values Study.* Hardwick-Day. https://www.ncaa.org/sites/default/files/NCAA_DII_Values_Study_Jan_2008.pdf?division=d2

Hays, G. (2020, April 2). Old Dominion cuts wrestling, citing financial impact of coronavirus. *ESPN.* https://www.espn.com/college-sports/story/_/id/28988850/old-dominion-cuts-wrestling-citing-financial-impact-coronavirus

Hirko, S., & Sweitzer, K. V. (2015). The business model of intercollegiate sports: The haves and the have nots. In E. Comeaux (Ed.), *Introduction to intercollegiate athletics* (pp. 147–162). Johns Hopkins University Press.

Hosick, M. B. (2020a, March 30). Division I Council extends eligibility for student-athletes impacted by COVID-19. *NCAA.* http://www.ncaa.org/about/resources/media-center/news/division-i-council-extends-eligibility-student-athletes-impacted-covid-19

Hosick, M. B. (2020b, October 14). DI Council extends eligibility for winter sport student-athletes. *NCAA.* http://www.ncaa.org/about/resources/media-center/news/di-council-extends-eligibility-winter-sport-student-athletes

Joyce, E. (2020, May 8). The cost of App State's returning spring seniors, and how the athletic department plans to pay for it. *The Winston-Salem Journal.* https://www.journalnow.com/sports/college/asu/the-cost-of-app-states-returning-spring-seniors-and-how-the-athletic-department-plans-to/article_ff2454a9-abfa-5569-9fdb-019c5984705f.html

Kelderman, E. (2020, April 18). Major cost-cutting begins in response to Covid-19, with faculty and staff furloughs and pay cuts. *The Chronicle of Higher Education.* https://www.chronicle.com/article/Major-Cost-Cutting-Begins-in/248558

LEAD1. (2020a, June 10). *Back to business: What's it going to take to reopen your venues.* LEAD1 Association. https://lead1association.com/whats-it-going-to-take-to-reopen-your-venues/

LEAD1. (2020b, May 27). *Survive and advance: Understanding the legal and cultural impacts of COVID-19 on college sports.* LEAD1 Association. https://lead1association.com/survive-and-advance-webinar/

Lopiano, D., & Zimbalist, A. (2020, June 13). Has higher education lost its mind? *Forbes.* https://www.forbes.com/sites/andrewzimbalist/2020/06/13/has-higher-education-lost-its-mind/#17a32aa339c0

Mizan, N. (2020, April 24). University of Wisconsin-Green Bay to furlough 227 staff members from May 2–31; tennis teams suspended indefinitely. *The Green Bay Press Gazette.* https://www.greenbaypressgazette.com/story/news/2020/04/24/university-wisconsin-green-bay-announces-furloughs-187-staff-members-may-2-may-31/3019537001/

NCAA. (2020, March 26). NCAA presidents set revised financial distribution to support college athletes. *NCAA.* http://www.ncaa.org/about/resources/media-center/news/ncaa-presidents-set-revised-financial-distribution-support-college-athletes

NCAA. (n.d.). Where does the money go? *NCAA.* http://www.ncaa.org/about/where-does-money-go

NCAA Division I Manual (2019). *NCAA*. https://www.ncaapublications.com/p-4577-2019-2020-ncaa-division-i-manual-august-version-available-for-presell-now.aspx

NCAA Finances. (n.d.). *USA Today*. https://sports.usatoday.com/ncaa/finances/

Nightengale, B. (2020, April 14). UC AD John Cunningham: No other sports in danger after discontinuing men's soccer program. *The Enquirer*. https://www.cincinnati.com/story/sports/college/university-of-cincinnati/2020/04/14/university-cincinnati-discontinues-mens-soccer-program/2988656001/

Novey-Williams, E. (2020, July 2). Maybe colleges should be adding sports, not dropping them. *Sportico*. https://www.sportico.com/2020/leagues/college-sports/maybe-colleges-should-be-adding-sports-not-dropping-them-1234608297/

O'Neil, D. (2020, May 4). 'What do we really need here?' Colleges must revisit the way they spend money. *The Athletic*. https://theathletic.com/1791199/2020/05/04/what-do-we-really-need-here-colleges-must-revisit-the-way-they-spend-money/

Ott, M., & Bates, E. (2015). Leadership in intercollegiate athletics. In E. Comeaux (Ed.), *Introduction to intercollegiate athletics* (pp. 34–47). Johns Hopkins University Press.

Parnell, D., Widdop, P., Bond, A., & Wilson, R. (2020). COVID-19, networks and sport. *Managing Sport and Leisure*, 1–7. doi: 10.1080/23750472.2020.1750100

Pfeffer, J., & Salancik, G. (1978). *The external control of organizations: A resource dependence perspective*. Harper & Row.

Pickman, B. (2020, June 15). Report: Ohio State football players asked to sign waivers acknowledging COVID-19 risk. *Sports Illustrated*. https://www.si.com/college/2020/06/15/ohio-state-players-waiver-covid19

Robinson, C. T. (2020, April 22). Louisville athletics announces furloughs, position eliminations amid COVID-19 pandemic. *The Courier Journal*. https://www.courier-journal.com/story/sports/college/louisville/2020/04/22/u-l-athletics-announces-furloughs-pay-cuts-amid-coronavirus-pandemic/3003909001/

Russell, J. (2020, June 9). UCLA football players demand third-party oversight upon return to campus amid pandemic. *The Washington Post*. https://www.washingtonpost.com/sports/2020/06/19/ucla-football-players-demand-third-party-oversight-upon-return-campus-amid-pandemic/

Satterfiled, J. (2015). Organization and governance of the NCAA. In E. Comeaux (Ed.), *Introduction to intercollegiate athletics* (pp. 14–33). Johnes Hopkins University Press.

Silverstein, A., & Patterson, C. (2020, August 8). MAC becomes first FBS conference to cancel 2020 football season for the fall. *CBS Sports*. https://www.cbssports.com/college-football/news/mac-becomes-first-fbs-conference-to-cancel-2020-college-football-season-for-the-fall/

Stinson, J., & Howard, D. (2010). Athletic giving and academic giving: Exploring the value of split donors. *Journal of Sport Management*, *24*(6), 744–768. doi: 10.1123/jsm.24.6.744

Swanson, R., & Smith, A. B. (2020). COVID-19 and the cutting of college athletic teams. *Sport in Society*, *23*(11), 1724–1735.

Tessier-Lavigne, M., Drell, P., & Muir, B. (2020, July 8). An open letter to the Stanford community and the Stanford Athletics family. *Stanford News*. https://news.stanford.edu/2020/07/08/athletics/

Thamel, P. (2020, June 20). Will there be college football? A new flurry of pessimism has arrived. *Yahoo Sports*. https://sports.yahoo.com/

will-there-be-college-football-a-new-flurry-of-pessimism-has-arrived-222609082.html

Weaver, K. (2020, October 7). University of Minnesota, needing money for football, is set to drop four sports and 98 athletes. *Forbes.* https://www.forbes.com/sites/karenweaver/2020/10/05/minnesota-drops-98-athletes-from-program-while-spending-millions-on-testing-for-football/#3fe9ec668f5b

Weight, E. A., & Harry, M. (2019). The governance of college sport. In N. Lough & A. Guerin (Eds.), *Handbook of the business of women's sport* (pp. 329–340). Routledge.

Williams, L. (2020, May 14). Campus message from AD Larry Williams. *Go Zips.* https://gozips.com/news/2020/5/14/general-campus-message-from-ad-larry-williams.aspx

Wilner, J. (2020a, August 5). Pac-12 rescue operation: Coronavirus loan program would bail out athletic departments if football season is canceled. *The Mercury News.* https://www.mercurynews.com/2020/08/05/pac-12-rescue-operation-loan-program-would-bail-out-athletic-departments-if-football-is-canceled/

Wilner, J. (2020b, November 25). Stock report: Hope from the CDC but not the CFP; Utah's break and ASU's mess; and the rebirth of the Pac-12 Networks. *The Mercury News.* https://www.mercurynews.com/2020/11/25/stock-report-hope-from-the-cdc-but-not-the-cfp-utahs-break-and-asus-mess-and-the-rebirth-of-the-pac-12-networks/

Zagger, Z. (2020, June 19). NCAA teams' COVID-19 risk forms may fall flat in court. *Law 360.* https://www.law360.com/sports-and-betting/articles/1283174/ncaa-teams-covid-19-risk-forms-may-fall-flat-in-court?nl_pk=05b5d8bf-35ed-40b0-8c0a-6549fcee6ad4&utm_source=newsletter&utm_medium=email&utm_campaign=sports-and-betting

## Bio

**Molly Harry,** M.A., is a doctoral candidate at the University of Virginia in the School of Education and Human Development. Her research interests include education through athletics participation, academic reform for college athletics, the college athlete experience, and the collegiate sport business model. Email: mh4yf@virginia.edu

# Part II

# COVID-19 and Academic Issues in Higher Education

Special Topics and Themes

# 6 Traditional Exams, 21st Century Employability Skills and COVID-19

Disruptive Opportunities for
Rethinking Assessment Design
in Higher Education

*Andrew Kelly, Catherine Moore, and Emma Lyons*

## Abstract

High-stakes examinations have been a university tradition for nearly two centuries, due at least in part to a widespread perception that they offer validity, objectivity, and reliability in assessing learning. The disruptive COVID-19 crisis, however, has triggered shifts in thinking over whether university exams in an online environment hold the same rigor and authenticity—or even whether they still serve as a valid form of assessment for preparing students for post-graduate employment. This chapter examines those shifts against the backdrop of COVID-19 and examines the relationship between exams and enhancing graduate employability through three key skills: problem-solving, creativity, and critical thinking. Taking a global perspective, it reviews the current literature on these topics and considers alternative forms of assessment using practical examples that may provide more valid methods of improving post-graduate employability outcomes through more authentic real-world assessments. It ultimately argues that universities must seize the opportunities created by COVID-19 for widespread assessment reform and use this momentum for setting tasks that more closely reflect the types of skills needed for work in the post-pandemic world.

## Keywords

assessment, COVID-19, coronavirus, employability skills, exams, graduate employability, graduate outcomes

## Introduction

Four years before the global outbreak of the COVID-19 pandemic, the World Economic Forum's (WEF) *Future of Jobs Report* predicted the top ten employability skills for 2020. Through surveying senior executives in the world's largest employers, the report concluded that the top three desirable workplace skills at the start of the next decade would be "complex problem-solving, "critical thinking," and "creativity." "Emotional intelligence" and "cognitive flexibility" also featured 7th and 10th respectively on the 2020 list; both of which were not even listed as top priority skills in 2015 (World Economic Forum, 2016). While those surveyed certainly could not have predicted a pandemic such as COVID-19 would occur in 2020 and the significant disruption it would have on the global workforce, it is indeed telling that recent assessments of the key employability skills needed for a post-coronavirus world align closely with those earlier predicted skill demands (Bravery & Tomar, 2020; Marr, 2020). In short, the 2016 WEF predictions were largely correct: each of these employability skills have been incredibly important during a time of rapid change and instability worldwide.

During the global response to COVID-19, the role of universities in preparing graduates to develop these skills has become more critical than ever before. The 2016 WEF report had argued that educational institutions such as universities required a "skills evolution" because many of its continued "20th century practices" would not meet the needs of the future labor market (World Economic Forum, 2016). One of the most common forms of these ongoing practices are exams: an individual summative assessment that normally occurs in an invigilated face-to-face environment. High-stakes examinations have been a university tradition for nearly two centuries, due at least in part to a widespread perception that they offer validity, objectivity, and reliability in assessing learning. Yet, mandatory government social distancing requirements brought about by COVID-19 forced universities to either shift the facilitation of exams into an online environment or design alternative forms of assessment altogether (Watermeyer, Crick & Knight, 2020). These revisions have raised further questions over whether traditional university exams still serve as a valid form of assessment for preparing students for employment after graduation (Alexander, Cutrupi & Smout, 2019; Efu, 2019).

In the context of COVID-19 and the subsequent global demand for new employability skills, this chapter critically analyses university exams and their connection to post-graduate employability. Taking a global perspective, it reviews the current literature on exams and enhancing employability of graduates by focusing on the top three listed WEF report skills: problem-solving, creativity and critical thinking. It also considers alternative forms of assessment using practical examples that may provide more valid methods of improving graduate outcomes in an increasingly competitive and digital world. The chapter then focuses on how universities may be able to, and indeed already have, adapted assessments to develop the key aspects of an employability mindset that incorporates these skills. In short, this chapter explores the possibilities arising from this surge of disruptive innovation in higher education assessment. Through this exploration, it argues that universities must seize the opportunities created by COVID-19 for widespread assessment reform and use this momentum for setting tasks that more closely reflect the types of skills needed for work in the post-pandemic world.

## Employability in the COVID-19 World: Problem-Solving, Creativity and Critical Thinking

The COVID-19 pandemic had an unprecedented impact on global employment. Using a comparative population to employment ratio, there were significantly more jobs lost worldwide in early 2020 than the 1930s Great Depression (Coibion, Gorodnichenko & Webber, 2020). This recent job loss also occurred twenty times faster. For instance, an April 2020 poll showed that a third of workers in Canada and the United States reported that they had lost at least half of their income during the peak of the crisis. Similar trends occurred worldwide, with significant income loss reported by approximately one quarter of polled respondents in the United Kingdom and almost half of those polled in China (Bell & Blanchflower, 2020). Most job losses occurred in lower-skill roles such as those found in retail, tourism, and hospitality, while industries that were able to remain operational despite mandated government restrictions had to change work practices significantly. School classes, business meetings, and medical consultations all started occurring online at record rates.

By necessity, rapid response to this disruption required key employability skills such as problem-solving, creativity and critical thinking. These skills will be similarly crucial as the world continues to respond to the COVID-19 pandemic and its long-lasting impact on future work practices. As a result, it follows that those who develop these skills while at university and can apply them in practice will be best placed to find meaningful employment upon graduation. Many factors contribute to employability, which this chapter defines as the range of skills and personal attributes that recent graduates need to possess in order to find meaningful employment. It includes a strong foundation of discipline-specific knowledge and skills, and the cognitive, interpersonal and intrapersonal skills that facilitate productive working relationships. The categories often used to define skills for employability can be referred to as "hard skills" (including knowledge and technical proficiency) and "soft skills" (such as interpersonal skills and personal qualities; Sessanga & Mussisi, 2019). These latter traits are difficult to measure in traditional university assessments, yet they are essential components of an employability mindset. This mindset is also referred to in the literature as a "professional purpose mindset," characterized by the amalgamation of self-awareness, career management, confidence, and flexibility (Bates et al., 2019). It fosters adaptability in graduates to withstand the type of volatile labor market conditions that are predicted, and that can be extrapolated to a post-COVID-19 world.

Employers repeatedly express a preference for employees with a "can-do" attitude (Fraser et al., 2019; Osmani et al., 2019), referring to people that are confident and willing to respond constructively to new problems. The important role of universities in fostering an overall mindset for employability is crucial in framing assessment for employability. Bates et al. (2019, p. 7), for instance, contend that due to an increasingly dynamic future job market, universities should focus on fostering an employability mindset in students via four elements (curiosity, action, collaboration, growth) and three domains (self and social awareness, navigating the world of work, and building networks). Each of these elements and domains have clear links to problem-solving, creativity and critical thinking. For example, curiosity is a necessary precursor to thinking about creative ways to solve problems. Similarly, in order to think critically about a work-related problem, it requires an awareness of one's own social context and the impact of relationships that exist within professional networks.

Real-world problems such as COVID-19 are situated in an ever-changing environment, so solving them also requires an ability to anticipate potential difficulties and evaluate the impact of unforeseen events. Being able to work with ambiguity and uncertainty requires cognitive flexibility and resilience, which are both qualities highly valued by employers (Bridgstock, 2019; Seow, Pan & Koh, 2019). Solving real-world problems also requires a combination of critical and creative thinking, emotional intelligence, and cognitive flexibility to generate a range of potential solutions. Future graduates' success is heavily pinned on the ability to use problem-based learning in collaborative scenarios whereby "critical thinking, novel and adaptive thinking ... [and] social intelligence" combine to prepare students with transferable skills for the future (Tuffley, 2017, p.11). In other words, addressing real-world problems requires a willingness to engage with uncertainty and recognition that potential solutions will never be completely correct or incorrect. Adapting to such uncertainty and focusing on solving problems during critical moments was essential in responding to COVID-19 effectively. Leaders within organizations that successfully oversaw flexible changes to processes and practices based on government health restrictions were better placed to thrive in challenging circumstances.

Creativity is another valuable employability skill. Organizations are constantly seeking employees who display traits such as entrepreneurialism, initiative and innovativeness in order to create new products and improve services (Bridgstock, 2017). Employees that can demonstrate these types of traits were especially important at the height of the COVID-19 pandemic in early 2020, as the situation was largely unprecedented and required rapid responses to meet government health restrictions. For future students working in a post-COVID-19 world, this means that university learning activities need to develop higher-order thinking skills like creativity in order to be more competitive in the graduate labor market. Such activities teach students to embrace a range of possibilities, to become comfortable with uncertainty, and to remain open-minded and curious. In short, openness to questioning and idea sharing, as well as the flexibility to err and make corrections, will cultivate both creativity and professional resilience in students' future working lives (Sessanga & Mussisi, 2019). With these inclusions, students will learn to maintain an open mind and adapt to changing workplace practices, as well as be able to constantly analyze and reinterpret the world as the threat of COVID-19 gradually subsides.

Reframing and opening oneself to multiple viewpoints through cognitive flexibility not only cultivates creativity and innovation, but also allows learners to unbed and examine their own and others' assumptions. This ultimately leads to another core employability skill: critical thinking. Organizations seek employees that not only have interpersonal skills, but also the capacity to analyze problems from multiple perspectives critically (Hart Research Associates, 2015). Fields (2019) acknowledges the challenges in developing this kind of cognition amongst students in tertiary education, yet several strong employability traits can emerge through developing critical thinking skills. These include effective decision-making, communication, and investigative research skills. Moreover, the acceptance of ambiguity and a willingness to maintain an open mind whilst critically weighing up evidence will likely become increasingly important in order to discern credible information from a saturation of online content (Sessanga & Mussisi, 2019). This involves constant comparison, juxtaposition, and synthesis of incoming data (critical appraisal) in order to reframe issues and innovate (creatively problem solve). Therefore, the relationship between problem-solving, creativity, and critical thinking are inherently interconnected.

## COVID-19 and University Exams

When COVID-19 hit, universities were faced with the challenge of how to move traditional on-campus individual invigilated assessments to an online environment. Transferring exams to an online environment with access to limitless internet resources requires a change to the invigilation process or deployment of deterrent measures against cheating. Migration of traditional examinations to an online environment, however, can be much more complex and resource-intensive than often anticipated (Allan, 2020). Students need precise communication about preparation, such as clear instructions for accessing the exam itself and as well as technical support for any ad-hoc issues that may present during completion (Cramp et al., 2019). Despite these challenges, many universities still decided to move exams to an online environment at the height of the pandemic. In a survey of 312 higher education institutions worldwide, an Educause 'QuickPoll' found that 54% of respondents were using a form of online proctoring during early to mid-2020. It also found that another 23% of institutions were still considering using them for end of semester exams during that same period (Grajek, 2020).

In the higher education context, responses to the pandemic were not consistent globally. Growth rates of the COVID-19 infection were higher in some countries than others by mid-2020, and this necessitated varied approaches to teaching and learning practices depending on the context in which an institution was operating. Where the risk of COVID-19 was very low, some institutions did not need to respond significantly. In areas of high risk, however, universities and other higher education providers undertook rapid curriculum redesign in order to teach and assess in an entirely online environment. In a survey of 20 countries from the Americas, Europe, the Middle East and Asia, the move to online teaching and assessment during the first half of 2020 occurred most commonly in developed countries such as the United States, Germany, and Australia. However, despite these trends, there were still significant variations in the number of COVID-19 cases reported per one million population between these countries and others (Crawford et al., 2020). This suggests that the risk of the COVID-19 infection as well as the capacity in which an institution could deliver online teaching both contributed to whether face-to-face exams were replaced with alternative assessments during the initial response to the pandemic.

For some institutions, the unanticipated challenges of migrating traditional examinations to an online environment provided an impetus for universities to explore alternative forms of assessment. As Fuller et al. (2020) described, the disruption caused by COVID-19 presented genuine opportunities to explore different assessment designs that focused on higher order thinking. For instance, an Australasian Council on Open, Distance and e-Learning (ACODE) survey (Sankey, 2020) found that most institutions ran alternative forms of assessment to some of their exams and chose a range of solutions to run more formal examinations, either in a proctored or unproctored way. Some chose to manually proctor exams using internally employed tutors working through Zoom or similar platforms, whereas others used different measures such as test banks and keystroke information to improve the integrity of online tests (Clark et al., 2020). Another approach was to use alternative solutions such as assessment deferral, submission mode changes, online presentations, and virtual simulations. Despite these shifts occurring rapidly, alternative assessments such as presentations and simulations offered new opportunities for authentic work that can improve future employment prospects. Compared to writing answers individually during a timed and invigilated exam setting, students completed tasks that more closely resembled the type of work they might perform in the workplace after graduation.

By transforming traditional high stakes examinations into more authentic tasks, universities were unexpectedly able to drive learning behaviors that enhanced employability. To be sure, good assessment tasks must have integrity (validity and student identity verification) and authenticity (both relevant and rigorous). However, traditional high-stakes university assessment tasks have prioritized integrity over authenticity. In this context integrity prioritizes student identity verification by seeking to ensure that the work on which student achievement is judged and certified has been done by the individual purporting to have done it. The notion that traditional examinations in timed and invigilated settings offer the best assurance of integrity has led to a pre-dominance of this form of assessment. This is understandable as doubts cast on the integrity of university assessments threaten the reputation of universities and their graduates (Slade, Rowland & McGrath, 2019). Universities tend to pride themselves on the rigor of their assessment regimes, but authenticity in terms of relevance of assessments to students' current or future careers has been a lower priority (Care & Kim, 2018).

COVID-19 ultimately disrupted this status quo of traditional university assessment. Due to mandatory social distancing restrictions which prevented conducting on-campus invigilated exams, the pandemic prompted a proliferation of alternative authentic online teaching and assessment practices (Crawford et al., 2020). This transformation of assessment has required a concurrent reshaping of learning activities and may well change the landscape of university education. Boud (2020) suggests that previous conventional assessment practices cannot be assumed to continue to meet the needs of the present and encourages reflection on whether current assessments are promoting the type of learning behaviors that will support future success for our graduates. Traditional examinations may be suited to certifying discipline-specific knowledge, yet they are unlikely to be effective at evaluating key employability skills such as problem-solving, creativity and critical thinking. Even before COVID-19 hit, the question was already being asked: does current university assessment still pass muster (McKie, 2019)?

High stakes exams predominantly test students' ability to reproduce knowledge in the form of discrete facts, routine computational formulae and predetermined procedures. This is undoubtedly useful, as factual and procedural knowledge are necessary elements in the exercise of higher order skills. However, it is not sufficient for enhancing the capacity of graduates to solve complex problems, develop creative solutions, and to cultivate critical awareness around both these respective aspects. The proportionately heavy weighting of exams toward final grades also means that preparation for such exams becomes the default curriculum, even when other intended learning outcomes are stated. This problem of a narrow focus on factual and procedural knowledge is exacerbated when preparation for such exams shapes and pervades all teaching and learning activities. This influencing effect has been well documented as "the washback effects of high-stakes exams" (Tan, 2020). There is, indeed, a growing realization of the need to transform exams by including elements that reflect authentic "world of work" situations in order to ensure that assessment regimes enhance graduate employability. Online examinations can be tested via scenario-based or open-ended questions, simulations using discipline-specific professional software, and the use of multimedia, thus providing authentic assessments that prepare students for their working life.

## Exam Alternatives: Practical Examples

Traditional exams in timed and invigilated settings do not appropriately reflect the contexts that students will be performing tasks after leaving university. A more authentic alternative to these forms of exams is to design them as open book, in which students have either full or limited access to a range of resources such as websites and textbooks while completing an assessment. In this way, it more closely resembles real-world work tasks such as writing reports. In exploring open book exams as an alternative, Teodorczuk, Fraser and Rogers (2018) investigated the impact of medical teachers complaining about a full curriculum. Open book exams were trialled, and it was concluded that learners became less reliant on memorizing facts and achieved deeper learning of higher-level outcomes. The redesign also led to tasks that were more authentic to clinical practice where information is freely available during consultations. The nature of this assessment stress was closer to the inherent stressors that students would encounter in their future practice, thereby making the task more useful in developing resilience that would support students in future work.

A key challenge of simply migrating traditional face-to-face examinations to an online open book exam, however, is the extent to which academic integrity can be upheld. Although cheating also exists in the traditional assessment environment, it can be amplified in the online setting when the focus of the examination is demonstrating factual and procedural knowledge (Akimov & Malin, 2020). However, the move to online examinations can be used to transform examinations, testing higher-order skills via scenario-based or open-ended questions. Alternatively, exams can be reconceptualized as simulations that provide authentic assessment contexts whereby students apply the learnt content knowledge to theoretical case studies in a relevant work environment. It also offers opportunities for online oral examinations, in which students deliver a presentation or respond with applied knowledge to questions via videoconference or recording (Akimov & Malin, 2020). This approach improves assessment integrity and more appropriately reflects the type of skills graduates need to develop in the digitally competitive employment market.

How, then, can tertiary educators ensure graduates develop the "can-do" attitude that makes them confident and willing to deal with problems or new tasks? At least in part, building student confidence in solving complex problems creatively can be nurtured through setting clear expectations of assessment tasks and providing constructive feedback. In assessment, it is common practice to clearly define all task requirements and include clear marking guides that identify criteria and standards of performance against which work will be judged. Students now expect, even sometimes demand, such clarity in all assessments. While clearly defined assessments can be a useful exercise in applying knowledge and exercising critical and creative thinking in a study context, they only reflect a small dimension of the challenges that graduates will be expected to deal with once they enter the workplace (Boud et al., 2018). There are no marking criteria when completing tasks in a workplace. At times, even clear communication about expectations can be absent. This means that some tertiary learning activities and corresponding assessments also need to be designed to consider situations in which there is no obvious correct answer or the parameters of answering a question can change over time. Traditional exams are not well equipped to provide this sort of learning experience.

Engaging students in case studies that are real and ongoing (not resolved) offers a unique opportunity to develop critical thinking and innovative problem-solving skills. One practical example are dynamic case studies, in which the context and parameters of an assessed situation can change over time. This assessment model has been implemented with business students at an Australian university. Students are assigned a high profile Australian public company, and in groups they analyze their business, evaluate real scenarios, and engage in robust discussions to make predictions about the likely impact of key decisions (Moore & Chandra, 2019). As the semester develops, the context of these decisions changes as the companies' positions changes, and as a result, students need to conceptualize alternative forms of action. They also need to compare their recommendations against what the business actually did and reflect on the accuracy of their predictions. The course engages students in audit and risk assessment processes, and ethical decision making through contemporary cases. Unlike traditional case studies, students cannot "google" how the case unfolded at the time they need to make, and advocate for, their decisions.

Problem-solving requires both critical and creative thinking. Real-world problems are generally fuzzy and ill-defined, requiring an ability to first clearly define the problem before attempting to address it. Another interesting example of this type of alternative assessment approach is the International Mathematical Modelling Challenge (IMMC). In this annual competition, teams from around the world develop an original mathematical model that demonstrates how stores should arrange products during a flash sale in the most optimal way to minimize damage to merchandise. The challenge tests students' logical thinking and synthesis in a pressured real-world setting, as well as their collaboration and communication skills (Russell, 2020). While the IMMC is organized in secondary school settings, it could also be applied in a higher education context. The global challenge requires the application of mathematics to solve real-world situations and allows the use of freely available material from the internet. In contrast to recalling knowledge in an exam, the IMMC more closely resembles the types of tasks that future mathematicians, marketers and business analysts would be completing in a workplace situation.

Similar real-life examples can be found elsewhere, such as cases in which students solve problems in specific scientific domains that comprise of a few interconnected and complex variables. The enormous potential of this approach was recognized in the Programme for International Student Assessment (PISA) in 2012 (OECD, 2014; Scherer, 2015). In this example, students were presented with a system (i.e. the problem environment) that simulates a specific scientific concept (such as climate control). Their first task was to generate knowledge about this system of variables and their relations by testing how changes in the input variables affected the system. Students represented their mental model about these relationships in a path diagram. Their second task was to apply this knowledge in a problem situation which allowed for incorporating interactive, dynamic, and uncertain elements into the problem environment, but still provided sufficient psychometric characteristics in terms of reliability and validity (Greiff, Wüstenberg & Funke, 2012). Consequently, students needed to adaptively respond to dynamic changes in the problem environment and critically analyze whether proposed solutions are viable. In other words, students had to prepare for unexpected results and innovate alternative solutions as a response. This type of assessment is very difficult to create in a traditional exam environment.

## Future Possibilities

In the tertiary sector, the disruption and uncertainty brought about by COVID-19 has offered opportunities to rethink types of assessments and their role in developing employability skills. The restructuring of traditional high-stakes assessment formats into more collaborative and real-life case studies, such as the examples presented in this chapter, offers opportunities to build professional resilience in the face of future uncertainty. They also facilitate greater development of problem-solving, creativity and critical thinking; all of which were top projected employability skills in the 2016 WEF Report. COVID-19 and the resulting online adaptation and assessment reinvention at universities has inadvertently accelerated this shift toward enhancing the profile of flexible thinking styles and the aptitude for creative solutions.

Although COVID-19 has certainly changed life, learning, and work as they have been collectively known, its long-term impact may be characterized by the way it has accelerated some trends that were already underway. This includes increasing moves toward digital business operations and the transformation of university assessments to more authentic tasks (Grajek & Brooks, 2020). COVID-19 has unwittingly provided a view into the potential of online learning, teaching, and assessment to provide an employability-focused platform for students. Not only is there more potential for linkages to be created between assessment and work readiness in terms of the key skills discussed in this chapter, but there is also the opportunity to better equip students with the digital and information literacy needs of the future.

Universities now have an impetus to adopt alternative exam assessments beyond their forced introduction due to COVID-19. Given the unpredictability and need for adaptability during the pandemic, future employers will be looking for graduates that can adapt, think critically about problems, and find creative solutions. As this chapter explored, alternative assessments such as open book tasks, simulations, collaborative problem-based tasks, and dynamic case studies can provide more authentic ways for students to develop these skills and find meaningful employment upon graduation. Higher education institutions and their respective educators must seize the opportunities created by COVID-19 for widespread assessment reform and use this momentum for setting tasks that more closely reflect the types of skills needed for work in the world outside of academia. These assessment alternatives should not revert to their traditional counterparts once the world recovers from the impact of COVID-19. Instead, they should provide the way forward for rethinking the role of assessment in enhancing graduate employability in the post-pandemic world.

# References

Akimov, A., & Malin, M. (2020). When old becomes new: A case study of oral examination as an online assessment tool. *Assessment & Evaluation in Higher Education*, 1–17. https://doi.org/10.1080/02602938.2020.1730301

Alexander, S., Cutrupi, J., & Smout, B. (2019). Taking a whole of university approach to employability. In J. Higgs, W. Letts & G Crisp (Eds.), *Education for employability* (Volume 2): *Learning for future possibilities* (pp. 117–132). Brill. https://doi.org/10.1163/9789004418707_010

Allan, S. (2020). Migration and transformation: A sociomaterial analysis of practitioners' experiences with online exams. *Research in Learning Technology, 28*. https://doi.org/10.25304/rlt.v28.2279

Bates, G. W., Rixon, A., Carbone, A., & Pilgrim, C. (2019). Beyond employability skills: Developing professional purpose. *Journal of Teaching and Learning for Graduate Employability, 10*(1), 7–26.

Bell, D. N. F., & Blanchflower, D. G. (2020). US and UK labour markets before and during the COVID-19 crash. *National Institute Economic Review 252*. https://www.dartmouth.edu/~blnchflr/papers/BandB_CovidCrash.pdf

Boud, D. (2020). Challenges in reforming higher education assessment: A perspective from afar. *RELIEVE-Electronic Journal of Educational Research, Assessment and Evaluation, 26*(1), 1–15. https://doi.org/10.7203/relieve.26.1.17088

Boud, D., Ajjawi, R., Dawson, P., & Tai, J. (Eds.). (2018). *Developing evaluative judgement in higher education: Assessment for knowing and producing quality work*. Routledge.

Bravery, K., & Tomar, A. (2020). How companies and employees can make their best coronavirus comeback. *World Economic Forum*. https://www.weforum.org/agenda/2020/04/coronavirus-covid-business-resilience-preparedness-skills/

Bridgstock R. (2017). The university and the knowledge network: A new educational model for twenty-first century learning and employability. In L. Holmes & M. Tomlinson (Eds.), *Graduate employability in context: Theory, research and debate* (pp. 339–358). Palgrave Macmillan.

Bridgstock, R. (2019). Graduate employability 2.0: Learning for life and work in a socially networked world. In J. Higgs, G. Crisp & W. Letts (Eds.), *Education for employability (Volume 1): The employability agenda* (pp. 97–106). Brill.

Care, E., & Kim, H. (2018). Assessment of twenty-first century skills: The issue of authenticity. In E. Care, P. Griffin & M. Wilson (Eds.), *Assessment and teaching of 21st century skills: Research and application* (pp. 21–39). Springer, Cham.

Coibion, O., Gorodnichenko, Y., & Weber, M. (2020). Labor markets during the Covid-19 crisis: A preliminary view. *National Bureau of Economic Research*. https://www.econstor.eu/handle/10419/216634

Clark, T. M., Callam., C. S., Paul, N. M., Stoltzfus, M. W., & Turner, D. Testing in the time of COVID-19: A sudden transition to unproctored online exams. *Journal of Chemical Education, 97*, 3413–3417. https://dx.doi.org/10.1021/acs.jchemed.0c00546

Cramp, J., Medlin, J. F., Lake, P., & Sharp, C. (2019). Lessons learned from implementing remotely invigilated online exams. *Journal of University Teaching & Learning Practice, 16*(1), 10.

Crawford, J., Butler-Henderson, K., Rudoph, J., Malkawi, B., Glowatz, M., Burton, R., Magni, P. A., & Lam, S. COVID-19: 20 countries' higher education intra-period digital pedagogy responses. *Journal of Applied Learning & Teaching, 3*(1), 9–28. https://doi.org/10.37074/jalt.2020.3.1.7

Efu, S. I. (2019). Exams as learning tools: A comparison of traditional and collaborative assessment in higher education. *College Teaching, 67*(1), 73–83. https://doi.org/10.1080/87567555.2018.1531282

Fields, Z. (2019). Cognitive skills development at higher educational level in the fourth industrial revolution: A case for creativity. In Z. Fields, J. Bucher & A. Weller, (Eds.), *Imagination, creativity, and responsible management in the fourth industrial revolution* (pp. 126–157). IGI Global. https://doi.org/10.4018/978-1-5225-9188-7.ch005

Fraser, C. J., Duignan, G., Stewart, D., & Rodrigues, A. (2019). Overt and covert: Strategies for building employability skills of vocational education graduates. *Journal of Teaching and Learning for Graduate Employability, 10*(1), 157–172.

Fuller, R., Joynes, V., Cooper, J., Boursicot, K., & Roberts, T. Could COVID-19 be our 'there is no alternative' (TINA) opportunity to enhance assessment? *Medical Teacher, 42*(7), 781–786. https://doi.org/10.1080/0142159X.2020.1779206

Grajek, S. (2020). Educause COVID-19 QuickPoll results: Grading and proctoring. *Educause.* https://er.educause.edu/blogs/2020/4/educause-covid-19-quickpoll-results-grading-and-proctoring

Grajek, S., & Brooks, C. (2020). A grand strategy for grand challenges: A new approach through digital transformation. *Educause.* https://er.educause.edu/-/media/files/articles/2020/8/er20_3101.pdf

Greiff, S., Wüstenberg, S., & Funke, J. (2012). Dynamic problem solving: A new assessment perspective. *Applied Psychological Measurement, 36*(3), 189–213. https://doi.org/10.1177/0146621612439620

Hart Research Associates. (2015). Falling short? College learning and career success. *Association of American Colleges and Universities.* https://www.aacu.org/sites/default/files/files/LEAP/2015employerstudentsurvey.pdf

Marr, B. (2020). 8 job skills to succeed in a post-coronavirus world. *Forbes.* https://www.forbes.com/sites/bernardmarr/2020/04/17/8-job-skills-to-succeed-in-a-post-coronavirus-world/#456cf64c2096

McKie, A. (2019). Does university assessment still pass muster? *Times Higher Education.* https://www.timeshighereducation.com/features/does-university-assessment-still-pass-muster

Moore, C., & Chandra, A. (2019, June). *Dynamic assessment to prepare agile graduates to succeed in unpredictable future careers* [Conference session]. HEQN 2019 Assessment Conference, Melbourne, Australia. https://www.hes.edu.au/sites/default/files/uploaded-content/field_f_content_file/catherine_moore_heqn_2019.pdf

OECD (2014). *PISA 2012 results: Creative problem solving: Students' skills in tackling real-life Problems.* https://www.oecd.org/pisa/keyfindings/pisa-2012-results-volume-V.pdf

Osmani, M., Weerakkody, V., Hindi, N., & Eldabi, T. (2019). Graduates employability skills: A review of literature against market demand. *Journal of Education for Business, 94*(7), 423–432. https://doi.org/10.1080/08832323.2018.1545629

Russell, D. (2019). Challenging students in a collaborative maths competition. *Teacher Magazine.* https://www.teachermagazine.com.au/articles/challenging-students-in-a-collaborative-maths-competition?

Sankey, M. (2020). COVID-19 exam software survey. *ACODE Whitepaper.* https://www.acode.edu.au/pluginfile.php/8244/mod_resource/content/2/eExamsWhitepaper.pdf

Scherer, R. (2015). Is it time for a new measurement approach? A closer look at the assessment of cognitive adaptability in complex problem solving. *Frontiers in Psychology, 6*, 1664. https://doi.org/10.3389/fpsyg.2015.01664

Seow, P. S., Pan, G., & Koh, G. (2019). Examining an experiential learning approach to prepare students for the volatile, uncertain, complex and ambiguous (VUCA) work environment. *The International Journal of Management Education, 17*(1), 62–76.

Sessanga, J. B., & Musisi, B. (2019). The role of teacher education in developing employability skills in higher education. In Keengwe, J., & Byamukama, R. (Eds.), *Handbook of research on promoting higher-order skills and global competencies in life and work* (pp. 85–98). IGI Global. http://doi:10.4018/978-1-5225-6331-0.ch006

Slade, C., Rowland, S., & McGrath, D. (2019). Talking about contract cheating: Facilitating a forum for collaborative development of assessment practices to combat student dishonesty. *International Journal for Academic Development, 24*(1), 21–34.

Tan, C. (2020). Beyond high-stakes exam: A neo-Confucian educational programme and its contemporary implications. *Educational Philosophy and Theory, 52*(2), 137–148. https://doi.org/10.1080/00131857.2019.1605901

Teodorczuk, A., Fraser, J., & Rogers, G. D. (2018). Open book exams: A potential solution to the 'full curriculum'? *Medical teacher, 40*(5), 529–530. https://doi.org/10.1080/0142159X.2017.1412412

Tuffley, D. (2017). Can intelligent machines in the workforce lead to a net gain in the number of jobs? *Ecodate, 31*(1), 10–15.

Watermeyer, R., Crick, T., Knight, C.., & Goodall, J. (2020). COVID-19 and digital disruption in UK universities: Afflictions and affordances of emergency online migration. *Higher Education.* https://doi.org/10.1007/s10734-020-00561-y

World Economic Forum. (2016). Future of jobs report. https://reports.weforum.org/future-of-jobs-2016

## Bios

**Andrew Kelly, PhD** is the Manager, Learning Support, at Edith Cowan University. Dr Kelly's research interests include academic integrity, academic development, and online learning. Email: andrew.kelly@ecu.edu.au

**Catherine Moore, PhD** is the Division Secretary for the National Tertiary Education Union in Western Australia. Previously Dr Moore was a Senior Academic Developer at Edith Cowan University, specializing in assessment and moderation. Email: cmoore@nteu.org.au

**Emma Lyons** is a Senior Learning Designer at Edith Cowan University. She previously worked in learning adviser roles, specializing in English language teaching and development. Email: e.lyons@ecu.edu.au

# 7 From Hardships to Possibilities

## Dissertation Writing during the COVID-19 Pandemic

*Juan Manuel Niño and Onésimo M. Martínez II*

### Abstract

In an attempt to mitigate community spread of COVID-19, many universities canceled face-to-face sessions and shifted to online instruction. For advanced doctoral students, this sudden shift welcomed new hardships as they began to collect data for their qualitative dissertation studies. This change called for students and their supervising professor to revisit IRB (Institutional Research Board) protocols as interviews, focus groups and observations techniques were now impossible. In this chapter, we discuss how social distancing measures created new possible ways for students to gather rich, quality data from communication technology platforms. This new digital approach of engaging participants in meaningful discussions welcomed new possibilities for doctoral students to recruit participants for a more global context. This chapter will offer strengths, challenges, and new ways of knowing for future studies.

### Keywords

dissertation, education, interviews, qualitative studies, technology, social distancing

### Introduction

With the onset of Covid-19, new protocols for interactions between people were set in place as this virus increased in mortality rates. This novel virus forced the world to rethink how humans were to continue with their everyday lives. Unfortunately, there has been an unfamiliar shift in life due to the safe practices that were adopted because of the transmission of this virus. For the world, it invited us to be more creative in how we were going to continue living a life within the safety measures established by the World Health Organization and the Center for Disease Control. Much of their recommendations offered some hope to continue living a normal lifestyle, with some degree of physical distancing. For schools, this approach of learning was something new. A new practice that many schools would be needing to adjust in order to find ways to help students continue their learning experience. In higher education, more specifically, doctoral students seeking to begin a qualitative dissertation proposal, some adjustments would be needed to help them navigate the journey.

This chapter highlights the experiences of doctoral students who are in their final year of coursework as they develop their dissertation proposals in the Winter Garden program. A unique feature of this doctoral program is the notion of being an off-campus program offered by the Department of Educational Leadership and Policy Studies at The University of Texas at San Antonio. As such, this study highlights the experiences of students who matriculated in the program and are now preparing their proposal for collecting data for their qualitative dissertations.

A sense of belonging creates a form of social capital in that it highlights students' feelings about their connection with the college or university they attend (Nunez, 2009). The quality of social interactions within that community cannot be ignored. The impression that the faculty have taken an interest in students' growth and development is among the highest positive predictors of a sense of belonging, along with a "sense of obligation to community," and "engagement in community service activities" (Nunez, 2009). Latina(o) students who feel more connected with or engaged in their college or university are more likely to perceive an exclusionary environment (Nunez, 2009). Latina(o) students who have more familiarity with diversity issues, and report more academic connection and social engagement, are also more likely to experience an increased sense of belonging, even in hostile campus climates (Nunez, 2009).

Latinas(os) have experiences and understandings that have accumulated after years of family, school, work, and community roles (Wilson & Meyer, 2011). A doctoral program should insert into the curriculum an emphasis on diversity theories and research; use service-learning opportunities to make the theories real, and consciously use reflection to encourage acceptance of others who are different from us, and to self-understand (Wilson & Meyer, 2011). A doctoral program for all students can be a time and place to deepen, expand, and/or develop an understanding of social justice; where cultural awareness grows; where understanding and acceptance of others flourishes; and where equity and fairness are cultivated (Wilson & Meyer, 2011). In this study, participants have been asked to describe their personal and educational experiences during COVID times as they prepare their proposal for collecting data for their dissertation.

## Literature Review

Despite representing the largest racial/ethnic minority group in the United States, Latinas/os remain dramatically underrepresented in higher education (Ramirez, 2017). Although Latinas/os have recently experienced increasing rates of college attendance, they represented just 6.3% of all doctorates in 2011, whereas Whites accounted for 74% (Ramirez, 2017). Latinas/os are also the most underrepresented major racial/ethnic group among college/ university faculty (Ramirez, 2017).

A relatively small, albeit growing, body of empirical literature has documented the experiences of Latinas/os in doctoral programs, collectively stating that in addition to customary difficulties experienced by most doctoral students, Latinas/os experience barriers stemming from clashes with traditional academic cultures and/or institutionalized racism, sexism, and classism. Furthermore, attrition rates for women, first-generation, low-income, and historically underrepresented doctoral students are higher than for dominant group students.

Previous studies reveal that Latinas/os are influenced by several factors in their selection of a doctoral program, including: location (proximity to home), faculty influences, financial considerations, campus climate concerns, and circumscribed choices (Ramirez, 2013). In essence, Latinas/os' graduate school choice process is mediated by class, race, and gender inequalities (Ramirez, 2013). When focusing on Latinas specifically, of the 40,744 doctoral degrees conferred in 2001, Latinas represented 3.5% out of the 45% of women who graduated with doctorates (Gonzalez, 2006). Although students of color are holders and creators of knowledge, they often feel devalued, misinterpreted, and omitted from formal academic environments, especially when focusing on their histories, experiences, cultures, and languages (Delgado Bernal, 2002; Murakami-Ramalho et al., 2008). It has also revealed that researchers have found the academy to be conservative, restrictive, and racist toward Latinas/os (Murakami-Ramalho et al., 2008). Latinas/os have often experienced self-doubt, survivor guilt, imposter syndrome, and invisibility as they journeyed through their graduate process (Murakami-Ramalho et al., 2008; Solorzano & Yosso, 2002).

### Importance and Influence of Study

The majority of the population representing the Winter Garden are Latina/o. Although there is a misconception that Latinas/os only live in the city or urban areas, the participants in this study live in the Winter Garden. The majority of available jobs are within education, small business, and manual labor. This study can influence program development in other universities, which could lead to policies, practices, and programs becoming more student-centered, with the focus being on providing an authentic learning environment for their students, especially students of color.

Geography and place are among the most significant factors determining opportunity in America (Chetty et al., 2014; Hillman, 2016). For students of color who work full-time, have close social ties to their local communities, and/ or care for dependents, the proximity of home to college is an important factor in considering college attendance and in shaping educational opportunities (Hillman, 2016; Turley, 2009). Unfortunately, not all communities have access to colleges or universities nearby. Educational deserts, like the Winter Garden, are disproportionately allocated in the United States's poorest and most racially minoritized communities (Hillman, 2016). The location of colleges and universities is likely to be especially significant for socioeconomically disadvantaged families (Turley, 2009). Although socioeconomically disadvantaged families qualify for financial aid, tuition and fees have been rising at a significantly faster rate than financial aid or inflation, highlighting the fact that living at home would allow students to save money on rent, utilities, food, and travel (Turley, 2009).

Whether or not students choose to apply to and attend a given college depends in part on how close they live to it (Dache-Gerbino, 2016). The "predisposition mechanism" (visibility of local colleges) and the "convenience mechanism" (living close to college) increase students' likelihood of attending higher education institutions (Dache-Gerbino, 2016). Also, 82% of non-traditional older students both work and attend school at the same time, which emphasizes the impact distance plays in a students' decision to attend higher education institutions (Roszkowski & Reilly, 2006). Research projections have even stated that there will be three types of universities in the future: brick universities (traditional residential institutions), click universities (virtual universities), and brick and click universities (a combination of the two) (Roszkowski & Reilly, 2006; Terry, 2001). Because this research study focused on the educational experiences of the participants, we better understand their perspectives of the UTSA Winter Garden Doctoral Program. This doctoral program was travel-sensitive, with both faculty and students traveling almost equal distances. However, like many higher educational programs, COVID-19 forced changes to this program. As a result, no longer were students able to create a sense of community, and commute to the classroom ceased.

### Student Voice

The Winter Garden doctoral program focuses on social justice, equity, cultural awareness, and student voice (Niño et al., 2018). Student voice is imperative to the success of a truly authentic educational program (Monzo, 2016). Students need to feel welcomed, acknowledged, valued, respected, protected, and accepted (Niño et al., 2018). Latina/o students and their voices, individually and culturally, have historically been ignored (Monzo, 2016). Allowing the students to speak their truth will fundamentally alter the education landscape, which is why this study is important. It would be interesting to find out if this program was life-changing and/or transformational for its doctoral students.

### Transformative Learning

The theory of transformative learning was introduced to the field of adult education in the late 1970s (Ross-Gordon et al., 2015). Academic programs in higher institutions should include trust and support building, democratic decision-making, critical reflection, experimentation and risk-taking, inquiry, collaborative work, and ongoing dialogue (Ross-Gordon et al.,

2015). Implementation of transformative learning can also correlate with the recognition of student identity (Ross-Gordon et al., 2015).

## Research Method

For this chapter, data were collected from the perspectives of nine advanced doctoral students who are in their final year of academic work. The doctoral students are finalizing their proposal development on their intended topic of study. Through class reflection, class discussions via zoom, and students' journals, the voices of the students are shared and heard to highlight their struggles and new practices for completing their studies.

### *Participants*

The participants in this study were advanced Latina/o doctoral students from the Winter Garden area. The Winter Garden "forms a triangle that extends from San Antonio, west to Del Rio, south to Crystal City, and back to San Antonio" (Niño et al., 2018, p. 41). Along with Del Rio, Eagle Pass, and Uvalde, other major cities include Carrizo Springs, Crystal City, and Pearsall (Niño et al., 2018). Smaller communities include Asherton, Brackettville, Comstock, Cotulla, Dilley, Knippa, La Pryor, and Sabinal, along with others (Niño et al., 2018).

   While the cities of Eagle Pass, Del Rio, and Uvalde do offer a junior college (freshmen and sophomore coursework) and a two-year university (junior and senior coursework), the university does not offer a huge selection of bachelor and master degrees and fails to offer a doctoral program. The closest cities are Laredo and San Antonio. While San Antonio does offer multiple universities with many degree opportunities, it is two to three hours from the cities that represent the Winter Garden. Laredo, also two to three hours away, has one university but it only offers doctoral programs in business, education, and Hispanic studies.

## Results

There are many hidden opportunities to be found amidst this pandemic. Students are now forced to examine new ways for navigating the personal, professional, and collegiate lives. Due to the inability to safely conduct in-person interviews or on-site observations, students would have opportunities in their research that would have been unheard of before the pandemic.

   Now, interviews could be done virtually. Just this alone expands the potential participant pool exponentially. These interviews could be live via a teleconferencing platform, the interviews (with participant permission) could be recorded for further review and analysis. This is a blessing for someone who struggles with mobility.

   However, challenges and obstacles will always be present. A huge obstacle many students see is the lack of on-campus student interaction with the professors and classmates. Nonetheless, the students in this study were candid in expressing and sharing their thoughts on how they were navigating the dissertation process. The following themes were commonly shared and expressed by students as they completed their proposals.

### Challenges in Interviews and Observations

Most students shared an interest in conducting qualitative studies for their dissertations. Due to the pandemic, the traditional modes of data collection will be difficult to conduct.

Amand shared her concerns regarding her intended study,

> If students are learning remotely, it will be extremely difficult to observe leadership in action in the traditional setting. However, new opportunities have arisen to study leadership in unprecedented and non-traditional realities. Our school leaders are experiencing "never before" scenarios daily, and are having to make hard decisions in response. This pandemic provides each of us an opportunity to learn from this process.

However, Sam shared a different perspective,

> Research depends on analyzing social interactions and these methods typically involve proximity to human subjects which will be difficult to impossible under active social distancing. One of the concepts relating to social interactions is the value theory when discussing values, virtues, and character. These are the natural observations of character traits a researcher can collect during an in-person interview of observations. The social piece of the interviews becomes limited and less productive.

In a similar vein, Sandy shared her thinking,

> I think just getting access to traditional academic settings for observations or in-person interviews will be difficult as many campuses are closed to their staff and students much less additional visitors. I also think it will be difficult to get people who are willing to fully commit to participate simply because people are just exhausted from the stress COVID has brought about as well as fear of the virus spreading.

Ben shared how this new form of interacting with people, many times strangers, can be limiting to the authentic experience of collecting qualitative data. He expressed,

> With the onset of Covid-19 and new protocols for interactions between people, there has definitely been an unfamiliar shift in life. Some of the changes we may see to our qualitative studies could be the close personal interactions with participants. For example, if interviews are conducted virtually I feel people may be more guarded and less relatable.

For TJ, the pandemic has him questioning the relevancy of his study amid the pandemic. He was thinking about changing his topic due to the limited amount of data he might be able to collect due to the limited interaction.

> I have been debating the idea of changing my topic from the GPC process and student retention to analyzing the effectiveness of alternative certification programs because of the pandemic. I worried about the disruption in state testing, and related waiving of the retention of students, may make the study irrelevant or outdated by the time I got to the data collection process. Potentially I could be discussing a process with administrators they had not really dealt with for nearly two years. By contrast, the pandemic has forced a lot of teachers out of the field over concerns about personal health, and a wave of alt cert teachers often come in to fill that employment gap. Studying the lack of preparation in these programs would not be limited by COVID, and if anything, give me a large potential sample of participants to interview.

### Creative Approaches to Data Collection

In finding the challenges, students were looking forward to enacting creative practices as a way to seek participants and data for their dissertations. As the students shared in their reflections, many were optimistic in using COVID times to help them advance and reach larger pools of participants for their studies as traveling was minimal.

Amanda reflected on the effect of the pandemic and the possibilities for change in her practice and study. She shared,

> Due to the inability to safely conduct in-person interviews or on-site observations, I would have opportunities in my research that would have been unheard of prior to the pandemic. Now, interviews could be done virtually. Just this alone expands the potential participant pool exponentially. These interviews could be live via a teleconferencing platform, the interviews (with participant permission) could be recorded for further review and analysis. This is a blessing for someone who struggles with mobility.

TJ shared in his reflection, he was looking forward to using the virtual space as an opportunity so that participants would feel their contributions would be confidential.

> I think technology has given us an opportunity to still generally move forward with data collection. Regardless of my topic, I could still conduct interviews in person following social distancing guidelines, or better yet, via video conferencing. If I pursue the Alt Cert topic, the process of more "anonymous" interviews might be better. For example, after

screening potential participants to meet eligibility criteria for the study, I could arrange for online interviews that allowed for a higher level of anonymity which may allow the participants to speak more freely about their experiences and deficiencies in their respective programs.

In order to overcome some of the challenges that come with the new way of life, researchers will be forced to innovate. They will have to be creative in their methods and overcome the distance that is being put between human interactions. New methods may include virtual interviews. However, this may serve as an advantage in that the researcher may be able to interview a broader group of people who are further away.

Sandy shared,

> Data collection may have to take place primarily through virtual applications and platforms. This is definitely an area I have not really thought about but will need to have some sort of game plan to start with and then adjust as the following months progress.

Sam reflected,

> Qualitative research typically relies on face-to-face interaction for data collection through interviews and fieldwork. Creative approaches would be embracing the conference video resources such as Zoom or Microsoft Teams to coordinate live video conferencing.

For most students, these new COVID methods to collect data via zoom do provide convenience and flexibility depending on the individuals' schedule for work; however ethical guidelines and communication with the committee review board regarding approval for these methods must be taken into consideration. Aside from the video conferencing the other mediums that come to mind are social media, online forums, and pre-records speeches however I do speculate that concerns over validity from a research perspective may be an issue.

Eleazar shared his perspective in embracing new approaches during COVID as a way to embrace much of the learning concepts he had been introduced during his doctoral program. He credits the class format and the reflective nature of the learning process to help embrace the data collection journey.

> Building relationships for data entries will need to be established before any data can be collected. This is due to the required use of technology and the imitating forces and resource availability. The knowledge gained here I feel will help shape the way education is delivered and considered for the future that includes all levels of education from K through 12 through higher education. This data collected will highlight to the

forefront the importance of the data retrieved through these critical times in our society utilized to enhance education as it has been viewed in the past and delivered to students.

### Strengths and New Possibilities

While COVID has brought about many challenges, students think there are a number of topics that people will want to know about in the near future in regards to COVID. Some students shared ideas that researchers and doctoral students can focus on to better understand the COVID effect on schools.

Sandy shared some of the new research topics she has seen as a district administrator,

> Due to COVID, I have been thinking of the many topics to study such as adaptability of teachers in a hybrid teaching setting almost overnight; administrators adapting and leading down a path where no one has navigated previously, etc...and the list goes on. There are so many uncertainties of these times that will afford many learning opportunities in the near future.

For Larry, COVID has given him a sense of relaxation to conduct his dissertation study. He comments,

> Value theory provides the opportunity to use the approach that best fits the situation. It encourages and facilitates change and reform when current practices and habits have become obsolete and ineffective. The COVID environment has now forced us to transition and adapt to move beyond the standard practices. Live video provides many of the same benefits as in-person interviews, with the additional ability to switch between group and one-on-one interactions. Now, I can also use targeted social media recruiting to find harder-to-reach audiences.

In a similar context, Emily also shares how COVID and the use of the internet can be a helpful resource in conducting her dissertation. She shared,

> This is certainly an interesting time to be a doctoral student. I hadn't really thought about how the pandemic might affect my dissertation and research. I suppose it could be because a part of me is still in denial that the dissertation portion of this program is so near. I think interviews can be done by Zoom and Google Meets. COVID could allow for some innovative dissertation methods. I know a student from Cohort III utilized Twitter for their dissertation, perhaps that is just the tip of the iceberg? Even Facebook has group rooms where you can meet with specific people all together just invite them to that room. Our growing familiarity with technology is definitely a strength during and post COVID. Before, if you

were meeting with people in different areas, those interviews would be scheduled on different days. Now, they could be scheduled back-to-back and multiple interviews could take days as opposed to weeks.

TJ also shared the same sentiment with embracing technology to widen his scope of the study. He acknowledges the benefits of relying on technology to conduct interviews with participants. He expressed,

> With a likely shift in more qualitative studies having data collection being done through electronic means due to health concerns, does it matter where your participants are? For example, if I do interviews via Zoom, I would be able to interview not only Alt Cert teachers in the Winter Garden region but in other rural Texas areas, such as the Panhandle. This could add more unique perspectives while allowing a quicker turnaround time as there would be no traveling involved.

Larry, also shared the same positionality, "you can meet with someone you may have not been able to previously for a face-to-face due to scheduling, now you can meet in virtual space from the comfort of each person's home." In the same thinking, Ben looks forward to the new possibilities of conducting his study during COVID. He stated, "As I spoke of virtual interviews, that may be the preferred method at this time. This will reduce travel time, it may include recorded videos and the possibility of access to a greater number of sites." In the same way, he also shared how technology has made the learning process still accessible. Ben continued, "Some of the strengths in conducting research during COVID are having access to a broader range of participants. It may also reduce the cost of travel involved with research."

## Discussion and Conclusions

When schools were shut down, everyone understood there would be student regression and the learning experience would be slowed or perhaps even stopped. However, now more than ever qualitative studies can be beneficial in targeting and closing these academic gaps. However, the qualitative studies that provide insight into the how and why behind the numerical data we find will tell a much deeper story. Oftentimes, it is the feelings and emotions that are expressed in qualitative studies that help us to understand a situation more clearly in order to move forward constructively.

During the COVID period, the digital platform brings people from across the world into the comforts of our homes; therefore, we might be able to better understand communities and educational organizations at the macro level. Most communication for interviews is likely to be via video conference. Since the video interview captures and records participants' screens, the quality and integrity of the research process will continue. In most cases, the researcher can transcribe and note time-stamps within the video, making the data collection experience more authentic and meaningful for all.

Furthermore, aligning research activities with remotely conducted research methodology has the potential benefits of reducing time and cost for conducting the study, improving ease of participation for many individuals, enhancing the transferability of findings, and perhaps increasing the speed of publication of study findings, especially for students in rural areas where resource and populations may be a challenge.

## Implications

The Mexican-American population, particularly in the southwest, is the fastest-growing racial group with an estimated 33 million individuals (65% of the Latina/o population) (Hinojosa & Carney, 2016). While those numbers are encouraging, Mexican-Americans struggle to complete academic degrees, with Mexican-American women being underrepresented when compared with all other female doctoral recipients (Hinojosa & Carney, 2016). The perspectives of Mexican-American graduate students and faculty have not been fully studied, and more in-depth exploration is needed, especially perspectives of Mexican-American women in doctoral programs (Hinojosa & Carney, 2016).

Students of color, in rural communities, have unique perspectives of the world we live in. It is important to note that COVID, while bringing the world to a standstill, has the potential to create a new normal to reconnect the world virtually. It is through the perspectives of these students, as they engage in their dissertations, that we look forward to opportunities to revisit the dissertation experience through a different lens. No longer can we be conditioned to a one format, one size, one approach for master learning. As we continue to envision a new experience for the doctoral journey, this study can help other Latinas/os identify and/or create capital and space that will lead them to their versions of success and knowledge.

## Acknowledgements

We thank the Winter Garden PhD students for sharing their time and thoughts with us for this learning experience.

## References

Chetty, R., Hendren, N., Kline, P., & Saez, E. (2014). Where is the land of opportunity? The geography of intergenerational mobility in the United States. *The Quarterly Journal of Economics, 129*(4), 1553–1623.

Dache-Gerbino, A. (2016). College desert and oasis: A critical geographic analysis of local college access. *Journal of Diversity in Higher Education.* Advance online publication, 1–20. http://dx.doi.org/10.1037/dhe0000050

Delgado Bernal, D. (2002). Critical race theory, Latino critical theory, and critical race-gendered epistemologies: Recognizing students of color as holders and creators of knowledge. *Qualitative Inquiry, 8*(1), 105–126.

Gonzalez, J. C. (2006). Academic socialization experiences of Latina doctoral students. *Journal of Hispanic Higher Education, 5*(4), 347–365. http://dx.doi.org/10.1177/1538192706291141

Hillman, N. W. (2016). Geography of college opportunity: The case of educational deserts. *American Educational Research Journal, 53*(4), 987–1021. http://dx.doi.org/10.3102/0002831216653204

Hinojosa, T. J., & Carney, J. V. (2016). Mexican American women pursuing counselor education doctorates: A narrative inquiry. *Counselor Education & Supervision, 55*(3), 198–215. http://dx.doi.org/10.1002/ceas.12045

Monzo, L. D. (2016). "They don't know anything!": Latin immigrant students appropriating the oppressor's voice. *Anthropology & Education Quarterly, 47*(2), 148–166. http://dx.doi.org/10.1111/aeq.12146

Murakami-Ramalho, E., Piert, J., & Militello, M. (2008). The wanderer, the chameleon, and the warrior: Experiences of doctoral students of color developing a research identity in educational administration. *Qualitative Inquiry, 14*(5), 806–834. http://dx.doi.org/10.1177/1077800408318309

Niño, J. M., Garza, E., & Rodríguez, M. (2018). Making a Difference: Evidence from the field. In C. Rodríguez, M. Martinez & F. Valle (Eds.), *Latino educational leadership: Serving Latino communities and preparing Latina/o leaders across the P-20 pipeline* (pp. 39–56). Charlotte, NC: Information Age Publishing.

Nunez, A. (2009). Latino students' transitions to college: A social and intercultural capital perspective. *Harvard Educational Review, 79*(1), 22–48.

Ramirez, E. (2013). Examining Latinos/as' graduate school choice process: An intersectionality perspective. *Journal of Hispanic Higher Education, 12*(1), 23–36. http://dx.doi.org/10.1177/1538192712452147

Ramirez, E. (2017). Unequal socialization: Interrogating the Chicano/Latino(a) doctoral education experience. *Journal of Diversity in Higher Education, 10*(1), 25–38. http://dx.doi.org/10.1037/dhe0000028

Ross-Gordon, J., Gordon, S., Alston, G., Dawson, K., & Van Aacken, C. (2015). Efforts to transform learning and learners: The first decade of an innovative doctoral program. *Journal of Thought, 49*, 52–70.

Roszkowski, M. J., & Reilly, P. J. (2005). At the end of the day, I want to be close to home: Adult students' preferences for college proximity to work and home. *Journal of Marketing for Higher Education, 15*(1), 81–95. http://dx.doi.org/10.1300/J050v15n01_04

Solorzano, D. G., & Yosso, T. J. (2002). Critical race methodology: Counter-storytelling as an analytical framework for education research. *Qualitative Inquiry, 8*(1), 22–43.

Terry, N. P. (2001). Bricks plus bytes: How "click-and-brick" will define legal education space. *Villanova Law Review, 46*(1), 95–140.

Turley, R. N. L. (2009). College proximity: Mapping access to opportunity. *Sociology of Education, 82*(2), 126–146.

Wilson, J. L., & Meyer, K. A. (2011). A time and a place: Social justice in a doctoral program. *Journal of College Student Development, 52*(6), 753–759. https://doi.org/10.1353/csd.2011.0080

## Bios

**Juan Manuel Niño, Ph.D.** is an associate professor at the University of Texas at San Antonio in the Department of Educational Leadership and Policy Studies. He serves as Program Coordinator for PhD in Educational Leadership – K-12 Leadership, and co-coordinator of the Urban School Leaders Collaborative programs. Dr. Niño earned his PhD in School Improvement from Texas State University. His experiences as a scholar-practitioner are closely supported by a philosophy of preparing aspiring school leaders for social justice. Dr. Niño's research takes a critical perspective on the practice of education and leadership in multiple contexts, addresses issues of access, equity and excellence in education for diverse communities, and the Latin@ experiences that influence identity and advocacy. Email: juan.nino@utsa.edu

**Onésimo M. Martínez II, Ph.D.** is a psychology professor at Southwest Texas Junior College. He earned his PhD in Educational Leadership from the University of Texas at San Antonio. Dr. Martinez's current research interests center on the Latino experiences in post-secondary settings, equity and access, immigrants, and inclusive research. Email: ommartinezii@hotmail.com

# 8 Disrupting Accommodations through Universal Design for Learning in Higher Education

*Carly D. Armour*

## Abstract

While the world grappled with the COVID-19 pandemic, higher education institutions (HEI) decided to move classes to online modules. This interruption created issues for students with disabilities (SWDs) and students who are deaf or hard of hearing (DHH) who had to modify their accommodations. Ensuring equitable access to course content requires communication, problem-solving, and flexibility from faculty, service providers, and administrators—yet many students find the burden placed upon them. This is concerning because when students feel they are supported by their institutions, they are more likely to persist to graduate. How can we imagine a new system that is not fully dependent on students requesting accommodations in HEIs? This chapter reviews the accommodations and experiences of SWDs & DHH students and calls for considerations to disrupt the medical model of accommodations through Universal Design for Learning (UDL) in higher education.

## Keywords:

accommodations, disabilities, deaf, hard-of-hearing, universal design, COVID-19

## Introduction

While the world grappled with the COVID-19 pandemic, higher education institutions (HEIs) decided to move classes to online modules to reduce the risk of exposure to the virus and minimize the spread. College students were used to one set of instruction and then suddenly had to adjust to a new delivery platform (American College Health Association, 2020). This interruption especially created difficulties for students with disabilities and students who are deaf or hard of hearing who had to quickly adjust their accommodation needs (Anderson, 2020; Lederer et al., 2021). Before the arrival of the pandemic, undergraduate and graduate students with disabilities were already struggling with barriers that required them to request accommodations in order to access and learn course materials (Lederer et al., 2021). Ensuring equitable access to course content requires communication, problem-solving, and flexibility from faculty, service providers, and higher education administrators—yet Anderson (2020) discovered that many students with disabilities found the burden placed upon them. This issue is of concern because students who feel supported by their institutions are more likely to persist to graduate (Edman & Brazil, 2009; Tinto, 1993; Vaccaro et al., 2015).During a crisis, barriers are magnified when the "norm" is disrupted causing the necessity for accommodations for disabilities to be revisited and modified. The COVID-19 pandemic highlights a critical need for an examination of the current system of having students request disability-related accommodations in HEIs. How can we reimagine a higher education system that does not always require students with disabilities to ask for permission for inclusion? Through the lens of Freire's (1970) "practice of freedom," this chapter calls for considerations for HEIs to embrace Universal Design for Learning (UDL) as a practice of freedom and disrupt the current system of requesting disability-related accommodations.

## Deaf/HOH and Disability Context

Individuals who identify themselves as upper case "D" Deaf or DeafBlind and the few who identify as hard of hearing (HOH) consider themselves a cultural minoritized community and not "disabled" (Lane, 2002). Sometimes scholars, including myself, disaggregate Deaf/HOH from "disabilities" when discussing their research or argument. In this particular chapter, considering that the content is focused on accommodations, the term "disabilities" will include those who need accommodations on campus. Thus, "disabilities" will include those who need communication access (e.g. deaf, Deaf, hard of hearing, DeafBlind).

## Historical Context of Universal Design for Learning

Like a curb cut on the sidewalk that assists a person with reduced mobility or a worker pushing a food cart, inclusive designs are beneficial for everyone, not just those with disabilities. UDL is a proactive inclusive design that was introduced in the 1990s to serve as a framework for individuals to design instruction that reduces barriers and addresses learner variability in the classroom (Meyer et al., 2013). Scholars state that UDL prioritizes diversity and accessibility with a research-based set of principles to guide the design of learning environments that has the potential to be accessible and effective for more students (Black et al., 2015; Cook et al., 2009; Ketterlin-Geller & Johnstone, 2006; Meyer et al., 2013;). Evans and company emphasized the importance for higher education practitioners to "be aware of the necessity of, and strategies for, creating inclusive environments" (2017, p. 387). Lynn (2016) and Raue et al. (2011) accentuated the need for campuses to consider creating universally adaptable environments. UDL is praised for its inclusive, holistic approach that is integrated from the beginning.

## Disability Theoretical Frameworks

Scholars have given many theoretical perspectives on disabilities but there are two constructs of models often named in literature: medical and social. The medical model assumes that the problem stems with the *individual and their disability* and diverts solutions toward the correction or diminishing of the disability (Fisher & Goodley, 2007; Leake & Stodden, 2014; Shakespeare, 2012; Swain & French, 2000). Dolmage (2017) states that higher education institutions "often mandates that disability exist only as a negative, private, individual failure" (p. 56). I contend that the system of requiring students with disabilities (SWD) to obtain and use accommodations falls within the construct of the medical model since the student tends to be labeled as the one with the "problem" who require the pedagogy and/or environment to be retrofitted with accommodations to meet students' learning needs. This is troubling as scholars have found a disconnect between accommodations and the objective support for their implementations (Harrison et al., 2008; Kimball et al., 2016; Weis et al., 2014). Since the medical model focuses on individuals, it leads to stereotyping and defining people by a condition or their limitations. This shows the complexity of providing accommodations for SWDs who are encountering barriers and require various levels of support.

The social model of disability names the *environment* as the issue rather than the individual. In other words, disabilities only exist when the environment is constructed in a way that allows certain people to participate while excluding others. The social model calls for implementing inclusive learning strategies, such as the UDL principles (WHO, 2001), that include the strength of shifting the focus of the "issue" from the individual to the environment. The shortfall of the social model is that it does little to effectively *disrupt* systems of oppression and exclusion for students with disabilities. Without addressing this, students receive a message that accessibility is simply not valued. For example, a university can choose to remove specific inaccessible public videos online rather than captioning it if it is deemed as burdensome to the institution. While UDL is an inclusive design as a *noun*, Dolmage (2017) argues that UDL must be a *verb* with an emphasis on the *process* of designing instruction and campuses with the voices of SWDs included.

## Positionality

To provide suggestions for environmental shifts, Watt's (2015) Authentic, Action-Oriented, Framing for Environmental Shifts (AAFES) method encourages authenticity and a recognition of the researcher or scholar's own positionality. Thus, allow me to share a bit about myself. I am a student at a large research university who identifies as a White Deaf cis female. I worked as an Accommodations Coordinator for a disability services office at a large public research university for over a decade before becoming a full-time doctoral student. My journey includes personal experiences of exclusion in higher education as an undergraduate and graduate student as well as personally witnessing other students with disabilities and students who are d/Deaf or hard of hearing struggle to navigate the higher education's system to get their accommodations provided.

During the Spring 2020 term, because of the COVID-19 pandemic, all of the classes that I was enrolled in or teaching were abruptly shifted to synchronous online modules. Therefore, I spent several days working with the university's student disability services office to revisit and figure out which accommodations would successfully allow me to have effective communication access. A possible solution was found that included having an interpreter on a web conferencing platform (i.e. Zoom) on one side of my laptop screen and having a separate "virtual room" for classes on the other side of my screen. This worked well at first. Unfortunately, after three weeks of a world that was completely virtual—classes, research team meetings, papers, graduate assistantship work, assignments—like a computer in overdrive that suddenly crashes, I hit a wall. I found myself incapacitated with vertigo, motion sickness, and/or migraines each time I was online, which lasted through the following year. This was novel for me. The experiences that I and my d/Deaf and hard of hearing peers and those with disabilities encountered during this crisis brought me back to pondering questions about the practice of freedom, accommodations, and universal design.

## Legislation Historical Context

Before 1973 in the United States, students with disabilities were excluded from education. The passage of the Rehabilitation Act of 1973 and the Americans with Disabilities Act (ADA) of 1990 opened doors for students with disabilities by banning higher education institutions (HEIs) from preventing access for students with disabilities. As technology advanced, the ADA Amendments Act of 2008, the Higher Education Opportunity Act of 2008, and the Twenty-First Century Communications and Video Accessibility Act of 2010 were passed to serve as legislations to remove barriers in higher education for students with disabilities (Raue et al., 2011). However, researchers have found that HEI tend to only meet the minimal requirement of the law (Leake & Stodden, 2014; Lynn, 2016; Vaccaro et al., 2015). To elaborate on meeting such minimal requirement of the law, Dolmage (2017) explains:

> although laws like the ADA are supposed to have created a much more accessible Internet, research has shown that "the way disability rights laws currently stand allows the practices of private, non-profit, and public entities to undermine the overarching goals of the law in terms of accessible technology" (Wentz et al., 2011). In fact, "the law encourages the creation of inaccessible information and communication technologies that may eventually become accessible, but often do not. The current state of the law allows for separate but equal, but usually results in simply

unequal" (Wentz et al., 2011). This separation brings us a long way from the promise of the ADA, and reveals that in fact disability law can often be placed directly in the way of disability justice. (pp. 68–69)

Therefore, while disability-related laws exist to legislate against inequality, it should not be assumed that policy has become a substitute for action. I contend that disability-related laws are currently "performatives" since they depend on "how they get taken up" and is, thus, "unfinished" (Ahmed, 2012, p. 11) and are "diluted or not enforced" (Dolmage, 2017, p. 68). Laws and policies that are performative are discouraging for undergraduate and graduate students with disabilities as they face barriers to their education, often thwarting their persistence to graduate.

## Accommodations Process

In the United States, requests for disability-related accommodations must be "reasonable" as defined in the ADA (1990); thus, in the higher education realm, a "reasonable accommodation" is a modification or adjustment to the environment and materials for students with disabilities. As a result of the US Family Educational Rights and Privacy Act (FERPA), HEIs are not automatically informed that a current or incoming student needs accommodation nor does any accommodation plan automatically transfer to college after high school. FERPA serves as a double-edged sword since it allows students to at least have the choice to not to disclose their disability while also placing the burden on said student to self-disclose by having to register with the disability services office on campus if they need accommodations to alleviate barriers. The National Center for Education Statistics (NCES) reported in 2009 that half of students with disabilities do not disclose their disability to the campus disability service office. Various reasons include their wish to "blend in" and not disclose their disability (Harbour & Greenberg, 2017; Squires et al., 2018) for fear of stigmatization and discrimination (Hong, 2015; Squires et al., 2018). The other half who chooses (or feel forced) to disclose their disability find that the burden is placed on them to have barriers reduced or removed for their courses.

To understand how taxing it is for SWDs to obtain accommodations, one must understand the process. In the United States, students must first find the campus disability services office and figure out the steps that their specific higher education institution requires. Usually these steps include the following (AHEAD, n.d.):

1　**Complete an application form that requires**:

   a　naming their disability or disabilities;

   b　describing how the disability or disabilities impacts them academically; and,

   c　listing specific accommodations that may alleviate any barriers.

2   **Obtain and provide medical documentation from a licensed practitioner** who has diagnosed the disability or disabilities and listed recommendations for specific accommodations.

3   **Provide additional medical documentation(s)** if the student is not approved for services by the disability services office. During my experience of working for disabilities services, I found this decline of services a rare occurrence. It should be noted that if the student is approved for services, there is still no guarantee that all the accommodations they requested on their application will be approved. Depending on the documentation they submit, some accommodations may not be listed by their practitioner or the disability services office deem the request as not "reasonable," which is a thorn many find in the ADA.

4   **Complete intake:** Once approved for accommodations, the student is usually required to meet with a disability services staff member—such as the accommodations coordinator or disability advisor—to complete their intake. During this appointment, the student learns how they can obtain their accommodations form or letter that lists their approved accommodations for them to take to their instructors. To maintain confidentiality, this form or letter does not disclose the specific disability/disabilities.

5   **Provide letter of accommodations to instructor(s):** Once the intake is complete, the student (again) self-identifies as one with a disability by providing their letter/form from the student disability services office to each of their instructors. At that point, the responsibility is placed on the instructor to provide the accommodations and/or work with the disability services office to get the accommodations provided. Depending on the specific higher education institution, some disability services office require students to have the form signed by the instructor and returned while other institutions simply require the student to share the letter or form with their instructors.

6   **Notify student disability services office if there are any issues:** Students are instructed by the disability services office to contact their accommodations coordinator or disability advisor if they encounter any issues with getting their accommodations provided by the instructor.

7   **Repeat sharing letter of accommodations with new instructor(s) each academic term:** Students do not have to reapply for services each academic term. However, since there are new classes and instructors each term, the student has to repeat the process of getting their official accommodations letter or form from the disability services office and share with their instructors.

This process is not only common in the United States but also globally. Other countries may differentiate in their process with required steps for students with disabilities to receive accommodations. Nonetheless, the pattern remains the same that it is difficult for these students to receive accommodations and have barriers removed in higher education (Hurst, 2018; Kilpatrick et al.,

2015). This ordeal illuminates the exhausting process of asking for permission to receive disability-related accommodations in US HEIs as well as around the globe.

In addition to going through the lengthy process of requesting and obtaining accommodations, the weight also falls on the student to file a complaint with the office of equal opportunity and diversity at their higher education institution if their accommodations are not being provided. Some accommodations requested by students are seen as "beyond" what the ADA requires leaving the student excluded and with limited support, and at risk of not persisting to succeed. This underscores that the issue is in the environment, not the student.

## Examination of the Accommodations Process

Scholars state that "accommodations are an unresolved issue in higher education" (Ketterlin-Geller & Johnstone, 2006, p. 166). Accommodations listed on the accommodations letter or form from the disability services office often include a "laundry list" for instructors to check off. When HEIs provide accommodations for SWDs after the curriculum and pedagogy methods are already designed, the accommodations tend not to be appropriate for the student's specific needs. Dolmage (2017) argues that "accommodations can often increase what's broken" (p. 69), meaning that accommodations can actually do more harm by not addressing the root of the barrier. Thus, HEIs may want to consider being proactive to minimize the need for requesting accommodations. Integrating Universal Design for Learning, if used as a process that includes the voice of SWDs, can address such root of barriers and improve access for as many students as possible—not just the 50% who registered with their campus disability services office (Belch, 2004; Leake & Stodden, 2014).

## Understanding UDL

How can UDL be integrated into college courses? UDL is built on three core principles: representation, action and expression, and engagement (Meyer et al., 2013). This section explains each principle and discusses how to apply it to higher education.

### *Representation*

*Representation* promotes showing and communicating information in different ways. This is particularly critical for students with sensory or mental health disabilities who may be unable to take in information that is presented through a single form. For example, audio and video content present a barrier for those who are deaf or hard of hearing if it is not captioned. In some cases, instructors may mistakenly interpret the "cc" feature for online videos to mean that the video already has accurate captions embedded. I want to caution that certain platforms (i.e. YouTube) have a speech recognition tool that *guesses* what the audio is saying, often producing inappropriate and inaccurate captions. I suggest making it best practice to watch the entire video to see if it is appropriately captioned with correct grammar, spelling and terminology. If there are errors, the captions should be corrected or the video should have accurate captions embedded and appropriately synchronized. Automatically providing accurate transcripts for audio files and captions for videos is imperative for deaf and hard of hearing students. It also helps others who prefer to learn through reading or whose first language is not the same as the language of instruction. This is especially crucial during times of crisis, such as the COVID-19 pandemic.

### *Action and Expression*

The *action and expression* principle of UDL emphasizes providing multiple ways for students to interact with the material and show their knowledge. This helps students absorb information and make sense of what they observe. For example, a UDL approach for a final classroom presentation would mean offering alternatives such as students filming themselves and then sharing the video with class or allowing students to provide written deliverables. Another example is the choice for students to choose between having classes synchronously (having students in class online at the same time) or asynchronous (allowing students to watch lectures and do assignments at their own pace). Similar to the representation principle, applying the action and expression principle is especially critical during times of crises.

### *Engagement*

Student *engagement* means looking for a variety of ways to motivate and inspire learners to interact with the material. An example of this principle is offering different deliverables that is more rewarding for the student or providing different levels of challenge. Another example is the option for students to choose between a course letter grade (A-F) for the Pass/Nonpass for undergraduates or the Satisfactory/Unsatisfactory grade for graduate level students. As a result of this pandemic, many institutions offered this opportunity for students for their grades for Spring 2020 term. This principle is imperative because it allows students to demonstrate their skills and knowledge without barriers.

### Roots of Resistance of Implementing UDL

Some studies show that several instructors and faculty members are resistant to providing accommodations, feel limited with resources, or lack the knowledge of how to provide accommodations (Cook et al., 2009; Sniatecki et al., 2015; Vaccaro & Kimball, 2019). This has caused particular instructors and faculty to become resentful with having to do "extra work" to make changes for "that one student in the classroom." On the positive side, numerous disability services staff advocate UDL as a practical strategy for improving access to instructional resources for students with disabilities versus taking the route to retrofit materials for specific students (Singleton, 2017). Similarly, Wilson and company (2011) found that several faculty members and students have a general positive perspective and opinion on the implementation of UDL in the higher education courses. Research shows strong empirical evidence of UDL's beneficial effects (Black et al., 2015; Burgstahler, 2008; Ketterlin-Geller & Johnstone, 2006; Meyer et al., 2013). Thus, it leaves one wondering why UDL faces so much resistance and why it has yet to be fully implemented across HEIs around the globe. Only a few studies have explored the barriers and resistance behind the implementation of UDL principles and practices by higher education faculty (Lombardi & Murray, 2011; Meyer, 2010; Moriarty, 2007; Pliner & Johnson, 2004). These studies highlight the following as reasons for resistance: (1) institutional and faculty status quo and (2) the argument that it "costs too much."

### Institutional & Faculty Status Quo

HEIs have traditionally been resistant to change. This is evidenced by the fact that it was only as recent as 1973 that HEIs were no longer allowed, because of disability-related legislations, to exclude students with disabilities from their institution. Because of HEIs' status quo preservation, the creation of higher education environments that are accepting and supportive of students with different needs is often seen as a daunting process requiring a cultural transformation overhaul (Pliner & Johnson, 2004).

A study shows that certain faculty members remain resistant to integrating UDL principles because they prefer to maintain the status quo by providing accommodations instead ( Lombardi & Murray, 2011). Further, specific studies discovered that some faculty view UDL as a burden and too much work to implement (Cook et al., 2009; Hong & Himmel, 2009). Singleton (2017) notes that some fields of study "require rigid guidelines (e.g., nursing) or do not use particular formats (i.e., PowerPoint) and, thus, faculty in particular fields do not feel the need for certain types of UDL strategies" (p. 153). These examples of status quo preservations explain reasons for higher education's resistance to implementing UDL, which is unfortunate since it creates barriers for students with disabilities.

### "Costs Too Much"

"It costs too much." Professor Jal Mehta (2010) who teaches the *Introduction to Education Policy* course at Harvard Graduate School of Education explains that the first question asked regarding implementing Universal Design methods is "How much will it cost?" During my years working as an Accommodations

Coordinator, the question was frequently raised when discussing Universal Design or accessibility protocols. "The answer to these concerns is that UDL does not necessarily necessitate more resources; it is a way of organizing existing resources under a new pedagogical approach" (Ch. 3, Sec. "Funding for UDL"). While most universal design approaches require an adjustment in perspectives and pedagogy styles which requires energy and time, it does not tend to cost additional funds. While training may be required to assist faculty and staff with understanding how to implement UDL, there's often funding available that the institution can apply to receive. Mehta (2010) encourages institutions to seek federal and state funding available to assist students with disabilities and/or English language learners or technology for accessibility enhancements.

Singleton (2017) encourages for more research to be conducted on faculty attitude toward UDL implementation since there is not enough study on this topic. There's a need for more discussions on the barriers along with suggested solutions for implementing UDL in HEIs. In summary, the benefits of UDL as a wholistic proactive approach give reason to overcome the resistance of its implementations.

## Practice of Freedom—UDL as a Transformative Process

How can HEIs break through these resistances and have a transformative change? Schwanke and company (2001) share a theory that institutions ebb and flow through a three-phase developmental cycle required to achieve universal accessibility. They explain that there is a need for a consciousness raising of inequities (known as the advocacy stage). They also note that *Accommodations*, the second stage, is a response to the advocacy stage when environments and products are modified for individuals. Institutions then move toward *Accessibility*, the third stage, when equitable access is provided to everyone at the same time through a proactive design such as UDL. I have observed that most HEIs "stall" in the Accommodations phase, which is a systemic issue. Having access to education without barriers is a privileged construct that requires deconstructing systemic oppression.

To deconstruct systemic oppression, Watt (2015) calls to view multicultural initiatives as a "practice of freedom," a term from Freire's *Pedagogy of the Oppressed* (1970), that shift initiatives "toward an understanding that the dynamic social change process requires [a] complimentary multi-level transformative approach" (p. 15). It encourages the learning of new protocols and methods that are inclusive and emphasizes the importance of *process* versus outcomes. As mentioned in this chapter, there is strong empirical evidence of UDL's beneficial effects which I suggest are "practices of freedom."

With this in mind, it is important to consider Dolmage's (2017) caution for individuals to be aware that claiming UDL as beneficial for "everyone" has a danger of putting the needs of the majority over the needs of those who have been historically excluded—students with disabilities—and erasing their experiences. Thus, for UDL to be as effective as possible and as a practice of freedom, UDL should be prioritized as an evolving process and action of "becoming" that includes the voices of students with disabilities in the heart of the design phase rather than "a noun—a solid, clearly defined thing" (Dolmage, 2017, p. 155). This means when HEIs are going through changes and implementing Universal Design principles, their faculty and administration should host one-on-one interviews or focus groups with students with disabilities to gather their input. Implementing the three principles of UDL should include "multiple, overlapping strategies, not the delivery of single streams of information and not a blanket approach" (Dolmage, 2017, p. 131). Failing to do this means that UDL will have the threat of being empty promises and just another example of disappointing performance. Thus, I encourage HEIs to incorporate UDL assessments, training, and accountability across campus and ensure that UDL is consistently utilized. This will require a team of campus partners and possibly one or more new staff members. With this said, I highly encourage a representation of individuals with disabilities to be hired and included on these teams.

## Conclusion

This chapter explored how the system of accommodations currently burden students with disabilities in HEIs. Accommodations require that students ask for permission for barriers to be removed, which is far from an inclusive practice. Through the lens of Watt (2015) and Freire' (1970) practice of freedom and Dolmage's (2017) call for UDL to be a transformative process with the feedback of students with disabilities at the heart of the design, HEIs are asked to consider transforming their system toward inclusion by implementing UDL. Certain accommodations will still be needed such as requesting sign language interpreters; however, with UDL in place, when crises such as COVID-19 arise, less students around the globe will need to ask for accommodations. With UDL, students will have fewer burdens to navigate and be able to more easily access their course materials and demonstrate their skills and knowledge without barriers.

## References

Ahmed, S. (2012). *On being included*. Duke University Press.

American College Health Association. (2020). ACHA guidelines: Considerations for reopening institutions of higher education in the COVID-19 era. https://achatest.app.box.com/s/k202537ahi3w27b0w6cdhqxynr3vljif

Anderson, G. (2020, April 6). *Accessibility suffers during pandemic*. Inside of Higher Ed News. https://www.insidehighered.com/news/2020/04/06/remote-learning-shift-leaves-students-disabilities-behind

Association on Higher Education and Disability (AHEAD). (n.d.). Support accommodation requests: Guidance on documentation practices. https://www.ahead.org/professional-resources/accommodations/documentation.

Belch, H. A. (2004). Retention and students with disabilities. *Journal of College Student Retention: Research, Theory, & Practice, 6*(1), 3–22. https://doi.org/10.2190/MC5ADHRV-1GHM-N0CD

Black, R. D., Weinberg, L. A., & Brodwin, M. G. (2015). Universal design for learning and Instruction: Perspectives of students with disabilities in higher education. *Exceptionality Education International, 25*(2), 1–26. https://doi.org/10.5206/eei.v25i2.7723

Burgstahler, S. (2008). Universal design in higher education. In S. Burgstahler & R. Cory (Eds.), *Universal design in higher education: From principles to practice* (pp. 3–20). Harvard Education Press.

Cook, L., Rumrill, P. D., & Tankersley, M. (2009). Priorities and understanding of faculty members regarding college students with disabilities. *International Journal of Teaching and Learning in Higher Education, 21*, 84–96. https://eric.ed.gov/?id=EJ896246

Dolmage, J. T. (2017). *Academic ableism: Disability and higher education.* University of Michigan Press.

Edman, J. L. & Brazil, B. (2009). Perceptions of campus climate, academic efficacy and academic success among community college students: An ethnic comparison. *Social Psychology of Education, 12*(3), 371–383. https://doi.org/10.1007/s11218-008-9082-y

Evans, N. J., Broido, E. M., Brown, K. R., Wilke, A. K., & Herriott, T. K. (2017). *Disability in Higher Education: A Social Justice Approach.* San Francisco: Jossey-Bass.

Fisher, P., & Goodley, D. (2007). The linear medical model of disability: Mothers of disabled babies resist with counter-narratives. *Sociology of Health & Illness, 29*(1), 66–81. https://doi.org/10.1111/j.1467-9566.2007.00518.x

Freire, P. (1970). *Pedagogy of the oppressed.* Continuum.

Harbour, W. S., & Greenberg, D. (2017). Campus climate and students with disabilities. *National Center for College Students with Disabilities, 1*(2). https://eric.ed.gov/?id=ED577464

Harrison, A. G., Nichols, E., & Larochette, A. (2008). Investigating the quality of learning disability documentation provided by students in higher education. *Canadian Journal of School Psychology, 23*(2), 161–174. https://doi.org/10.1177/0829573507312051

Hong, B. S. S., & Himmel, J. (2009). Faculty attitudes and perceptions toward college students with disabilities. *College Quarterly, 12*(3), 6. https://files.eric.ed.gov/fulltext/EJ889557.pdf

Hong, B. S. S. (2015). Qualitative analysis of the barriers college students with disabilities experience in higher education. *Journal of College Student Development, 56*(3), 209–226. https://doi.org/10.1353/csd.2015.0032

Hurst, A. (Ed.). (2018). *Higher education and disabilities: International Approaches.* Routledge.

Ketterlin-Geller, L. R., & Johnstone, C. (2006). Accommodations and universal design: Supporting access to assessment in higher education. *Journal of Postsecondary Education and Disability, 19*(2), 163–172. https://eric.ed.gov/?id=EJ844632

Kilpatrick, S., Johns, S., Barnes, R., McLennan, D., Fischer, S., & Magnussen, K. (2015). Exploring the retention and success of students with disability in Australian higher education. *International Journal of Inclusive Education, 21*(7), 747–762. https://doi.org/10.1080/13603116.2016.1251980

Kimball, E., Vaccaro, A., & Vargas, N. (2016). Student affairs professionals supporting students with disabilities: A grounded theory model. *Journal of Student Affairs Research and Practice*, *53*(2), 175–189. https://doi.org/10.1080/19 496591.2016.1118697

Lane, H. (2002). Do deaf people have a disability? *Journal of Sign Language Studies*, *2*(4), 356–379. https://www.jstor.org/stable/26204820

Leake, D. W., & Stodden, R. A. (2014). Higher education and disability: Past and future of underrepresented populations. *Journal of Postsecondary Education and Disability*, *27*(4), 399–408. https://eric.ed.gov/?id=EJ1059990

Lederer, A. M., Hoban, M. T., Lipson, S. K., Zhou, S., & Eisenberg, D. (2021). More than inconvenienced: The unique needs of U.S. college students during the COVID-19 pandemic. *Health Education & Behavior*, *48*(1), 14–19. https://doi.org/10.1177/1090198120969372

Lombardi, A. R., & Murray, C. (2011). Measuring university faculty attitudes toward disability: Willingness to accommodate and adopt Universal Design principles. *Journal of Vocational Rehabilitation*, *34*, 43–56. https://files.eric.ed.gov/fulltext/EJ1026882.pdf

Lynn, B. (2016). *Universal Design: A student affairs perspective*. [Masters Theses, Eastern Illinois University]. https://thekeep.eiu.edu/theses/2445

Mehta, J. (2010). *Introduction to education policy course*. Harvard Graduate School of Education. https://sites.google.com/site/a100educationpolicy2010/home/udl/politics

Meyer, A., Rose, D. H., & Gordon, D. (2014). *Universal design for learning: Theory and practice*. CAST Professional Publishing.

Moriarty, M. A. (2007). Inclusive pedagogy: Teaching methodologies to reach diverse learners in science instruction. *Equity and Excellence in Education*, *40*(3), 252–265.

National Center for Education Statistics (NCES), U.S. Department of Education. (2009). Students with disabilities at postsecondary education institutions. https://nces.ed.gov/pubs2011/2011018.pdf

Pliner, S. M., & Johnson, J. R. (2004). Historical, theoretical, and foundational principles of Universal Instructional Design in higher education. *Equity & Excellence in Education*, *37*(2), 105–113. https://doi.org/10.1080/10665680490453913

Raue, K., Lewis, L., Coopersmith, J., National Center for Education Statistics, & Institute of Education Sciences. (2011). Students with disabilities at degree-granting postsecondary institutions: First look. https://nces.ed.gov/pubs2011/2011018.pdf

Schwanke, T. D., Smith, R. O., & Edyburn, D. L. (2001). A3 model diagram developed as accessibility and Universal Design instructional tool. RESNA 2001 Annual Conference Proceedings, 21, RESNA Press. https://access-ed.r2d2.uwm.edu/About_ACCESS-ed/Conceptual_Framework/

Shakespeare, T. (2012). Still a health issue. *Disability and Health Journal*, *5*(3), 129–131. https://doi.org/10.1016/j.dhjo.2012.04.002

Singleton, K. J. (2017). Integrating UDL principles and practices into the online course development process: A delphi study (Order No. 10256923). ProQuest Dissertations & Theses Global. (1934350597). http://login.proxy.lib.uiowa.edu/login?url=https://www-proquest-com.proxy.lib.uiowa.

edu/dissertations-theses/integrating-udl-principles-practices-into-online/docview/1934350597/se-2?accountid=14663

Squires, M. E., Burnell, B. A., McCarty, C., & Schnackenberg, H. (2018). Emerging adults: Perspectives of college students with disabilities. *Journal of Postsecondary Education and Disability, 31*(2), 121–134. https://eric.ed.gov/?id=EJ1192068

Sniatecki, J. L., Perry, H. B., & Snell, L. H. (2015). Faculty attitudes and knowledge regarding college students with disabilities. *Journal of Postsecondary Education and Disability, 28*(3), 259–275. https://eric.ed.gov/?id=EJ1083837

Swain, J., & French, S. (2000). Towards an affirmation model of disability. *Disability & Society, 15*(4), 569–582. https://doi.org/10.1080/09687590050058189

Tinto. V. (1993). *Leaving college: Rethinking the causes and cures of student attrition* (2nd ed.). The University of Chicago Press.

Vaccaro, A., Daly-Cano, M., & Newman, B. M. (2015). A sense of belonging among college students with disabilities: An emergent theoretical model. *Journal of College Student Development, 56*(7), 670–686. https://doi.org/10.1353/csd.2015.0072

Vaccaro, A., & Kimball, E. (2019). Navigating disability in campus housing: An ecological analysis of student affairs work. *Journal of Student Affairs Research and Practice, 56*(2), 168–180. https://doi.org/10.1080/19496591.2018.1490307

Watt, S. K. (2015). *Designing Transformative Multicultural Initiatives.* Stylus.

Weis, R., Speridakos, E. C., & Ludwig, K. (2014). Community college students with learning disabilities: Evidence of impairment, possible misclassification, and a documentation disconnect. *Journal of Learning Disabilities, 47*(6), 556–568. https://doi.org/10.1177/0022219413483175

Wentz, B., Jaeger, P. T., & Lazar, J. (2011). Retrofitting accessibility: The legal inequality of after-the-fact online access to persons with disabilities in the United States. *First Monday, (16)*11. https://doi.org/10.5210/fm.v16i11.3666

Wilson, K., Boyd, C., Chen, L., & Jamal, S. (2011). Improving student performance in a first- year geography course: Examining the importance of computer-assisted formative assessment. *Computers & Education, 57,* 1493–1500. https://www.learntechlib.org/p/50759/

World Health Organization (WHO). (2001). *International classification of functioning, disability and health.* Geneva: WHO. https://apps.who.int/iris/bitstream/handle/10665/42407/9241545429.pdf

## Bio

**Carly D. Armour** is a doctoral student in the Higher Education & Student Affairs program at the University of Iowa. She has a Social Work background and previously worked for a large research university's disability services for over a decade before returning to school to advance her education. Her research focuses on the higher education experiences of undergraduate and graduate students with disabilities and students who are d/Deaf or hard of hearing. Email: carlyarmour@gmail.com

# 9　Reshaping the Landscape

Considering COVID-19's
Uncertain Impacts on Canadian
and U.S. International Higher
Education

*Michael O'Shea, You Zhang, and Leping Mou*

**Abstract**

As the world grapples with the COVID-19 pandemic, international higher education (IHE) enters a new territory and complicates models that describe a third wave of internationalization. Against this backdrop, we apply a three-layer (country, institution, individual) analysis to understand COVID-19's impact on IHE in Canada and the United States, on particularly student mobility, and consider the future of an altered landscape. At the national level, we consider how the two countries are responding to COVID-19 regarding their policies toward international students and what long-term impact might be looming. At the institutional level, we consider the pandemic's impact on institutions' revenue, mission, internationalization strategies, and even survival. At the individual level, we examine how this pandemic impacts international students' plan of study in Canada and the United States, with their concern for the expense and experience of online learning and their consideration of other alternative destination countries.

## Keywords:

international higher education, international student mobility, COVID-19, the United States, Canada

## Introduction

The COVID-19 pandemic has affected every aspect of higher education, including international higher education (IHE). As higher education institutions (HEIs) prepare for a paradigm shift in student mobility, COVID-19 might be accelerating existing trends and pushing higher education beyond its current third wave of internationalization (Choudaha, 2018). This third wave features the emergence of new destinations for international students, amidst China's need for skilled labor, nationalism signalled by Brexit, and the anti-immigration tone and policy of former U.S. President Trump in the United

States (Choudaha, 2018). Just as COVID-19 is accelerating changes in other sectors, such as telemedicine and telework (Zakaria, 2020), the pandemic is rapidly reshaping the current landscape of IHE, even if some specific effects of COVID-19 remain uncertain.

The effects from the pandemic have been cascading and interrelated. Within days of the first cases in Canada, universities announced restrictions on travel and research abroad, especially to and from China, which saw the first outbreak of the virus in January 2020. The situation rapidly worsened in the United States, making the country the world leader in infections. International students have begun to reconsider studying in the United States and grappled with anxiety, uncertainty, and xenophobia. Government leaders in Canada and the United States sealed the borders, raising even higher obstacles to entry. Almost overnight, instruction shifted online, creating complications for students without internet access or international students who returned home to different time zones.

COVID-19 is an ongoing phenomenon but considerable COVID-19 peer-reviewed research related to COVID-19 and IHE has emerged in just the last year. A number of authors have explored the COVID-19 effects on IHE such as student mobility in different national and regional contexts (Aristovnik et al., 2020), including in Mainland China and Hong Kong (Mok et al., 2021; Peters et al., 2021) and Europe (Rumbley, 2020). Pan (2020) explores the pressures today's IHE neoliberal framework faces from COVID-19 resulting from the fallout in intentional enrollments and fees. COVID has upset a higher education financing system that has seen HEIs in Western anglophone countries aggressively court international students to compensate for declining public funding. Other authors have explored the COVID's impacts on national higher education systems around the world (Marinoni, 2020) in particular countries: in India (Jena, 2020), Latin America (Samoilovich, 2020), Nigeria (Jacob et al., 2020), Philippines (Toquero, 2020), Turkey (İnce et al., 2020), and Vietnam (Pham & Ho, 2020). A separate sizeable literature explores higher education's overnight shift to online and distance learning (Adnan & Anwar, 2020; Amemando, 2020; Crawford, 2020; Mishra et al., 2020; Paudel, 2020), and more specifically, online assessments (García-Peñalvo et al., 2020). This scholarly research is addition to the extensive ongoing journalism and growing body of grey literature on the topic (Hudzik, 2020; Martel, 2020a; 2020b).

In this chapter, we reflect on the future of student mobility to Canada and the United States by referencing government reports, university communications, news articles from reputable sources, and grey literature. We organize our discussion based on national policy, institutional response, and individual experience. Though not an empirical study, the chapter responds to current events that have taken lives, devastated livelihoods, and challenged institutions like no crisis in recent memory (Oleksiyenko et al., 2020; Zakaria, 2020). In the following sections, we reflect on the potential impact of the pandemic on IHE in Canada and the United States from national, institutional, and individual levels. The three-level approach enables us to reflect on the impact by considering different stakeholders. However, we acknowledge that the impact is far more complicated and involves interaction between different levels.

## National Level

At the national level, policies toward international students during COVID-19 are centered around student visas, Course load and their relevance to students' eligibility for work permits after graduation, and student financial relief. Canada and the United States put into place somewhat contrasting policies, which send different signals to incoming and future international students.

In Canada, the COVID-19 policy before October 20, 2020, was that international students must meet two requirements to enter Canada. First, international students must have their student visa approved before March 18, 2020, or they had to travel directly from the United States (Government of Canada [GOC], 2020). Second, they had to be travelling for a non-discretionary and non-optional purpose (GOC, 2020). In early October, the Canadian government announced that international students will be able to enter Canada if their institutions have a COVID-19 readiness plan approved by their provinces and territories (GOC, 2020).

The above policies toward international students entering Canada did not affect students' taking courses, as online courses are permitted and counted towards their degree for the application of work permits (GOC, 2020). Specifically, most institutions have opted to offer courses online due to COVID-19, meaning students have to take online courses outside of Canada. Previously, online courses taken outside of Canada were not counted toward the length of the program for their application of work permits in Canada (El-Assal & Thevenot, 2020). However, the Canadian government decided to allow students to take all courses online if their program is only eight to twelve months, and to take 50% of the courses online if their program is 12 months or longer while being outside of Canada (GOC, 2020). In addition, the lengths are counted toward their programs (GOC, 2020), allowing students to be eligible to apply for work permits.

In the United States, policies regarding students entering the country and eligibility are still strictly related to the format of their courses, particularly for new international students by January 2021. According to guidelines from U.S. Immigration and Customs Enforcement (ICE) in March and its updated version in July 2020, continuing international students were able to take online courses and return to the United States if they are outside of the United States (ICE, 2020a; 2020b). However, new students will not be able to have their student visa issued or active if they take 100% online courses (ICE, 2020b). To be able to continue their study plans, incoming students would have to travel to the United States to take at least one in-person class, putting themselves at risk of contracting COVID-19 (Quintero, 2020). For students, this policy likely exacerbated their mental health concerns and disrupted their study plans.

While policies toward international students are evolving constantly, the current policies in Canada and the United States at the start of 2021 are quite different. Canadian policies are more flexible and friendly to new incoming students. This is evidenced by allowing new students to take online courses outside of Canada and still keep the option for work permit open (GOC, 2020), depending on the length of the programs. In contrast, the United States does not allow new international students to take 100% online courses for the fall semester of 2020 (ICE, 2020b). Fortunately, continuing international students are not subject to this rule. In the case of the pandemic, new international students would have to take in-person classes, which forces students to choose between their studies and their health. As there have been changes in student mobility globally, such as new destination countries amidst intense competition for international students, U.S. policies during the COVID-19 pandemic may have implications on students' choice of destination countries.

Student relief, where it does exist, has not been made available to international students. This has taken the form of refunds, fellowships, deferred fees, direct payments, such as the Canada Emergency Student Benefit (CESB). Post-secondary students, and recent post-secondary and high school graduates could apply up to three times for CAD$1,250 in relief from May to September 2020 (Canada Revenue Agency, 2020). In the United States, relief has flown through schools via the Higher Education Emergency Relief Fund, part of the pandemic relief package. Eligible students can apply for US$1,200. Both funds, however, excluded certain student populations, including international students (Canada Revenue Agency, 2020; U.S. Department of Education, 2020). In summary, in both Canada and the U.S., international students are disadvantaged in accessing student financial relief during the pandemic, which we argue may have an adverse impact on their experience in host countries.

## Institutional Level

While the pandemic has affected all aspects of HEIs, there are unique effects on international students. While there are many effects to analyze, we focus on three themes below among the U.S. and Canadian institutions.

### *Campus Health and Travel Restrictions*

All institutions reacted quickly, following regional or national health guidance, to protect their communities' health (O'Shea & Mou, 2021). These measures would impact international students differently. Early measures included issuing travel advisories, followed by travel restrictions, and quarantine measures for returning overseas travel from China, and later northern Italy, Iran, and other hot spots of the early outbreak. Institutions ordered students studying abroad home and cancelled study and research abroad until at least the end of 2020 (Redden, 2020; Simon Fraser University, 2020; University of Saskatchewan, 2020).

As the crisis worsened, and especially after the World Health Organization declared COVID-19 a pandemic, Canadian and American HEIs moved to extend spring breaks, move classes online, send students home, close research facilities, and restrict campus access to essential personnel. By the summer of 2020, many schools, after conferring with health officials and following guidance from COVID task forces, announced phased reopening plans (O'Shea & Mou, 2021; University of Illinois at Chicago, 2020; University of Regina, 2020). These plans, however, have been complicated by a resurgence of cases—second or third waves in some cases—during the fall 2020 semester (Wilson & Kluger, 2020). This situation, when combined with restrictive policies from the federal government on international student access, make international students' access to U.S. higher education even more difficult.

International students and their unique needs are mentioned among the reopening plans and COVID-19 updates posted on university websites in Canada that enroll large numbers of international students (University of Toronto, 2021). The same is true for students at several top receiving institutions in the United States (New York University, 2020; University of Southern California, 2020; University of Illinois, 2020). Information primarily provided focuses on immigration questions and quarantine requirements.

### *Falling Enrollments*

COVID-19 travel restrictions have also led to falling international enrollments in Canada and the United States. In Canada, the number of study permits issued to international students fell by almost 25% between the spring 2019 and 2020 (Gordon, 2020). This number may rebound after Canada reopens its border to international students on October 20, 2020 at so-called "Designated Learning Institutions" (DLIs), but it is not certain. DLIs are those institutions that have a COVID-19 readiness plan in place (Thevenot, 2020). In the United States, new enrollments may fall to historic lows not seen since World War II (Fernandez, 2020). New international enrollments already fell between 2018 and 2019 in the face of a snowball of restrictive immigration policies and anti-immigrant rhetoric from the Trump administration and competition from other countries, including Canada (Trapani & Hale, 2019).

American HEIs have attempted to maintain international student enrollments even in the face of the double, interrelated threats of immigration restrictions and the pandemic. Tighter immigration policies include the executive orders from former U.S. President Trump that restricted travel from several majority Muslim countries and increased scrutiny of Chinese visas and universities' academic ties (Mou et al., 2020). Particular restrictions are related to COVID-19. For example, in the summer of 2020, with little warning, the U.S. Department of Homeland Security (DHS) announced that new study visas will not be renewed for international students taking online courses only (Fischer, 2020a). Motivation behind this restriction to F-1 visas was unclear (Whitford, 2020), but it may have been a way to pressure campuses to reopen, thereby sending a message that the pandemic was under control. Ninety percent of the U.S. HEIs said they would be switching to online or hybrid instruction for fall 2020 (Martel, 2020b).

A coalition of universities and their lawyers, backed by outraged international students and their backers, successfully filed lawsuits against DHS. As the DHS deliberated, schools, including the country's most influential and elite institutions, expressed support for their international students and promised to help them fulfill course requirements to meet visa requirements (Bacow, 2020; Klayman, 2020). In the face of such pressure, the U.S. government reversed course a week later, but the victory was only partial: a week later DHS issued guidance that said that the rule would still apply to new international students entering the United States (Fischer, 2020b; Whitford, 2020).

American higher education persists in its efforts to remain a top destination for international students. The non-profit Institute for International Education released a three-part series of reports on international education in the COVID era, including one dedicated to the topic of international Chinese student mobility (Martel, 2020a). In July 2020, 92% of institutions surveyed by the Institute of International Education (IIE) said that their foreign students would be staying on campus through Fall 2020. Over half of institutions surveyed noted international numbers are lower than "in previous years" (Martel, 2020b). International recruitment efforts continue as well among U.S. HEIs. For example, Franklin & Marshall College partnered with the University of California and the University of Illinois at Urbana-Champaign in October 2020 for a "webinar exclusively for high school counsellors, parents and students in China" (Strong, 2020).

Student mobility is not the only expression of international education, however, and COVID-19 could present an opportunity to move away from the last several decades' focus on student mobility as the yardstick of internationalization. This emphasis, Oleksiyenko et al. (2020) assert, is part of the neoliberal framework that sees higher education as a private good. Under this framework, public funding for higher education has fallen, and universities look to outside funding sources, especially international student fees to fund their operations. Hudzik (2020) urges higher education to prepare for a "paradigm shift" in how universities approach IHE (p. 2). The physical movement of students around the globe should not be an end in and of itself: internationalization should be integrated to all higher education goals. As COVID-19-related health and travel restrictions reduce student mobility, universities can still create cross-cultural learning experiences through creative uses of technology, better engagement with local communities, and deeper appreciation for cultural knowledge of international students. Doing so would also reduce perception of the latter population as only a revenue stream (Hudzik, 2020, p. 2).

### Funding and Support for International Students

As funding has been stretched and schools reel from the pandemic's fallout, international students have not always been supported. While some schools have frozen tuition, others have not, or at least not for international students. University of Toronto, though a public university, is tuition-dependent (87% of its revenue comes from tuition), and has announced an increase in international student fees, while freezing domestic tuition (Planning and Budget Office, 2020). Other Canadian and U.S. schools have announced similar international hikes, including Western University, Dalhousie, University of New Brunswick, McGill University, University of Guelph, and the University of Calgary (Erudera College News, 2020).

In a survey of 30,383 students from 62 countries, Aristovnik et al. (2020) finds that international students expressed a higher need for financial assistance for rent compared to domestic students. This makes intuitive sense: with friends and family in another country, international students may have less access to local off-campus housing if campuses close. Closure of campus and ending of on-campus jobs could also cut off their only source of income. In the United States, for example, international students are only legally authorized to work on campus for up to 20 hours and cannot work off campus in their first year. They can work with restrictions in subsequent years (U.S Immigration and Customs Enforcement, 2020). Despite this financial need of international students, little systematic financial support was available.

In the absence of government support for international students, some individual schools or even individual student groups have offered different kinds of support, including financial help (Canada Revenue Agency, 2020; U.S. Department of Education, 2020). University of Toronto students, for example, have organized a food bank to assist those impacted by food insecurity during the pandemic after the university's food bank was closed (UofT Emergency Foodbank, 2020). At Pomona College in Claremont, California, alumni and community members organized a GoFundMe to support students who lost off campus housing, among them international students (Pomona FLI Scholars, 2020).

U.S. and Canadian schools have stepped forward in various ways to attempt combat xenophobia experienced by students of Asian ethnicity, including Chinese students. Around the world, international students from China have experienced xenophobia, which have contributed to mental health problems (Zhai & Du, 2020). In addition to worrying about family back home, Chinese students experience hate crimes and derogatory headlines (Zhai & Du, 2020). For example, the University of Illinois-Chicago on April 24, 2020, sent a letter to faculty and students, "It goes without saying that we denounce these xenophobic practices and rhetoric, which are antithetical to our ethos and culture, and we will not tolerate any form of harassment against Asian and Asian American students, faculty and staff" (UIC News Staff, 2020). California State University created a website, "Racism and xenophobia in the age of COVID-19" with suggestions for faculty on fighting racism on campus (California State University, 2020). International students elsewhere, such as in the Netherlands, have also experienced mental health problems related to the anxiety and isolation that accompanied COVID-19 and campus closures (Misirlis et al., 2020).

## Individual Level

At the individual level, we reflect on how this pandemic impacts students' plans of studying abroad. In addition to major concerns about the difficulties of staying in isolation away from home, students are deliberating about the expense and experience of online learning during the pandemic, and the possibility of changing destination countries due to the pandemic.

As the world struggles to control a second wave of infections and as troubling new strains of the virus appear, a survey on international students shows that the biggest concern is staying healthy while studying in the United States (Kennedy, 2020). Bhojwani et al. (2020) identified a range of concerns among international students in the United States ranging from future employment to health insurance, from food security to visas. International students in Canada are worried about living away from home during the pandemic and lacking support both emotionally and financially (Coulton, 2020; Zhai & Du, 2020).

International students admitted to universities in the United States and Canada, still at home taking online classes, are very concerned with how long this situation will last. Due to the time difference, students taking many online synchronous classes during night time in China and India, for example, found the arrangement disruptive and could have harmful health effects (Misirlis et al., 2020; Nott, 2020). As a result, some are considering taking a gap year before returning to campus to North America—assuming the COVID-19 situation improves by then. Possible choices include taking courses from the joint-venture universities in China, such as the University of Nottingham Ningbo China. In addition, some universities from Hong Kong are trying to attract students during this pandemic. For example, universities in Hong Kong and Singapore are welcoming and offering competitive scholarships to prospective PhD students who hold an admission offer from top universities, but may not be able to commence their studies as planned due to COVID-related visa issues (Sharma, 2020). For students from China, transferring to universities in mainland China or Hong Kong could represent a safer, less stressful alternative, as these areas have managed the current pandemic relatively well and safety measures have been followed strictly.

### Expense and Experience

Tuition is another significant concern for many international students when they are taking online classes, and especially as some universities have continued with tuition increases during the pandemic (Burman, 2020). Many questioned the high tuition cost of online courses (Szperling, 2020). As an important aspect of studying overseas, knowing people and culture, living and studying with people from different backgrounds are important factors that contribute to international students' intercultural competency and capabilities for their future career and life. The online format of coursework has diminished these cultural and social experiences to a great extent. Hence, the tuition increase concerns international students, as the quality and experience of remote learning are different from pre-pandemic, in-person learning (Sarkar & Feng, 2020). In addition, summer job opportunities decreased during this pandemic and some international students who rely on summer jobs to save up and pay tuition face significant financial challenges (Charles & Øverlid, 2020).

## *Changing Destination Countries*

The choices of destination countries for international students have been impacted by the pandemic, either directly by the COVID-19 situation or indirectly by changing international relations. For example, according to a survey, with the rapid increase of COVID cases in key destination countries such as the United Kingdom, Spain, and the United States, around 20% of participants are considering a different country or not going abroad at all while 50% wanted to postpone their enrollment for at least one year (Mitchel, 2020). Moreover, as COVID-19 intensifies tensions between China and the United States, and amidst unfriendly policies of both government toward each other, international students from China may potentially considering other countries such as the United Kingdom (UK), which introduced a new visa policy allowing international students apply for two-year visa staying in the United Kingdom after graduation (Hubble & Bolton, 2020). As such, future students are likely to take into consideration the rise of xenophobia, nationalism, populism in the United States when choosing a destination country for their study (Xin, 2020). These forces make studying and living there challenging or even dangerous and pose obstacles for adapting to, living, and studying, in such an environment.

## Discussion and Conclusion

Broadly speaking, the national policies toward international students during the pandemic might affect a country's image among international students, which is important in students' decision-making (Ghazarian, 2016). In mid-July 2020 when updated restrictions from the U.S. government on international students was announced, the COVID-19 cases in the United States remained as high as over 65,000 and combined cases surpassing four million (Maxouris & Hanna, 2020). Yet, while current international students are able to take classes online, U.S. policies as of early January 2021 do not allow new international students to take the majority of their classes online while still in their home countries, which potentially forced students to choose between risking their health to travel to the United States for their study (Whitford, 2020)—or delay or even cancel their study abroad plans. By contrast, Canadian policies recognize the health crisis and allow students to still take courses outside of Canada. The contrast in policies clearly signals to international students that Canada might be much more friendly to them.

Although the United States is still the largest destination for international students, different factors suggest that other countries may be able to attract a growing number of students in the future. First, many countries are implementing policies that could attract more international students. For example, the United Kingdom has loosened work visas for international students (Hubble & Bolton, 2020). China continues to build the "Study in China" brand and set up scholarships to attract international students from developing countries (Ma & Zhao, 2018). This competition for international students aligns with Choudaha's analysis of a third wave in IHE (2018), which sees emergent top destinations for international students. What will the unfriendly policies toward international students during COVID-19 mean amidst the third wave? We argue that it potentially accelerates the changing landscape of international students mobility featuring emergent new destinations.

The differentiated national level policies and national contexts have impacts on institutional response in the United States and Canada. In Canada, where nearly all universities are public, universities followed provincial and government health guidelines and benefitted from relatively consistent and clear guidance on travel restrictions. U.S. universities suffered from inconsistent and a highly decentralized national response where individual states were asked to lead to tackle the pandemic. Immigration restrictions, already underway before the pandemic continued over summer 2020, complicate American HEIs attempts to support their international students.

In both countries, institutions sought to support and reassure international students, though often falling short, as international students' needs were sometimes considered after institutional finances and the needs of domestic students. Institutions with large international student populations made supporting international students part of their COVID-19 reopening plans. In the United States, individual institutions pushed back against national immigration restrictions and sought to support anxious international students, while not always succeeding. Therefore, at the institutional level, support for international students in the two countries are underway and largely positive, although the extent to which international students are reassured merits additional empirical research.

Looking to the future, the drop in international student enrollment in both countries will affect university systems that have become increasingly reliant on international student tuition fees (Oleksiyenko et al. 2020; Usher, 2020). In both countries, universities may need to cut expenditures, raise new revenue, and find ways to continue international education in ways that are less reliant on physical student mobility (Hudzik, 2020).

Given the complexity of the pandemic and that the level of institutional and governmental support for international students is unclear, we see anecdotal evidence that international students are considering alternatives. For example, students from large origin countries, China and India, are thinking about alternative plans of studying abroad during this pandemic. As taking full online courses may not be feasible or desirable, some students are considering alternative options, such as postponing study abroad, or transferring to other universities in a close region. Besides these immediate practical concerns of health, safety, tuition, and learning experience or outcomes, there is also a new consideration on the value of a foreign degree for the future job market amid the increasing tension exacerbated by the pandemic between countries, such as between China and the United States (Lau, 2020). All these factors working together are influencing student's and parents' choice in this challenging time. We argue that these are signs of the accelerating trend in the changing international student landscape. The changing students' choice of study abroad destinations is an important area for empirical research.

To conclude, HEIs around the world are still working hard to adapt to the new normal of pandemic that claimed millions of lives and profoundly altered nearly every institution, including higher education and international student mobility. How the new landscape of international student mobility forms depends not only on national policies, but also on progress of the pandemic itself and international cooperation to tackle the crisis, and to what extent institutions seriously address the concerns of international students.

## Acknowledgement

The authors contributed equally to this research and manuscript.

## References

Adnan, M., & Anwar, K. (2020). Online learning amid the COVID-19 pandemic: Students' perspectives. *Journal of Pedagogical Sociology and Psychology, 2*(1), 45–51.

Amemado, D. (2020). COVID-19: An unexpected and unusual driver to online education. *International Higher Education, 102,* 12–14.

Aristovnik, A., Keržič, D., Ravšelj, D., Tomaževič, N., & Umek, L. (2020). Impacts of the COVID-19 pandemic on life of higher education students: A global perspective. *Sustainability, 12*(20), 8438.

Bacow, L. (2020). COVID-19–Moving classes online, other updates [Community Message]. Harvard University.

Bhojwani, J., Joy, E., Hoxsey, A., & Case, A. (2020). Being an international student in the age of COVID-19. *Navigating Careers in the Academy: Gender, Race, and Class, 3*(2), 47–60.

Burman, D. (2020. August 27). *International students concerned about fee increases, future in Canada during coronavirus pandemic.* CityNews. https://toronto.citynews. ca/2020/08/27/intarional-student-fees-coronavirus/

California State University. (2020). Racism and xenophobia in the age of COVID-19. https://www2.calstate.edu/csu-system/news/Pages/racism-and-xenophobia-in-the-age-of-covid-19.aspx

Canada Revenue Agency. (2020, October 1). *Eligibility criteria – Closed: Canada Emergency Student Benefit (CESB).* https://www.canada.ca/en/revenue-agency/ services/benefits/emergency-student-benefit/cesb-who-apply.html

Charles, C. H., & Øverlid, V. (2020, July 3). Many international students in Canada find themselves in a precarious situation. Pandemic-driven tuition hikes will damage efforts to attract them. *Policy Opinions.* https://policyoptions.irpp. org/magazines/july-2020/tuition-hikes-exacerbating-existing-challenges-for-international-students/

Choudaha, R. (2018). A third wave of international student mobility: Global competitiveness and American higher education. *Research & Occasional Paper Series, The Center for Studies in Higher Education, UC Berkeley, CSHE, 8.*

Crawford, J., Butler-Henderson, K., Rudolph, J., Malkawi, B., Glowatz, M., Burton, R., Magni, P., & Lam, S. (2020). COVID-19: 20 countries' higher education intra-period digital pedagogy responses. *Journal of Applied Learning & Teaching, 3*(1), 1–20.

Coulton, M. (2020, November 9). How the pandemic has disrupted the lives of international students in Canada. *Maclean's.* https://www.macleans.ca/ education/how-the-pandemic-has-disrupted-the-lives-of-international-students-in-canada/

El-Assal, K., & Thevenot, S. (2020, April 9). International students now eligible for PGWP with online courses. *CIC News.* https://www.cicnews.com/2020/04/ international-students-now-eligible-for-pgwp-with-online-courses-0414082. html#gs.rleb63

Erudera College News. (2020, August 20). International students petition against tuition fee hikes at Canadian universities. *Erudera College News.* https:// collegenews.org/international-students-petition-against-tuition-fee-hikes-at-canadian-universities/

Fernandez, M. (2020, September 12). College international student enrollments plunge. *Axios.* https://www.axios.com/international-student-enrollment-trump-covid19-5caad69c-f6d4-4b79-bfb4-7b6ed038bc5b.html

Fischer, K. (2020a, July 8). As MIT and Harvard sue, colleges scramble to respond to new federal policy on international students. *Chronicle of Higher Education.* https://www.chronicle.com/article/as-mit-and-harvard-sue-colleges-scramble-to-respond-to-new-federal-policy-on-international-students

Fischer, K. (2020b, July 14). U.S. rescinds visa policy that could have forced colleges to hold some classes in person. *Chronicle of Higher Education.* https:// www.chronicle.com/article/u-s-rescinds-visa-policy-that-could-have-forced-colleges-to-hold-some-classes-in-person

García-Peñalvo, F. J., Corell, A., Abella-García, V., & Grande, M. (2020). Online assessment in higher education in the time of COVID-19. *Education in the Knowledge Society, 21*(12), 1–26.

Ghazarian, P. G. (2016). Country image and the study abroad destination choice of students from Mainland China. *Journal of International Students, 6*(3), 700–711.

Gordon, J. (2020, September 15). Staying home: Drop in foreign students bad omen for Canada's labor market. *Reuters.* https://www.reuters.com/article/ health-coronavirus-canada-universities-idUKL1N2G70C0

Government of Canada. (2020, October 28). *Coronavirus disease (COVID-19): International students.* https://www.canada.ca/en/immigration-refugees-citizenship/ services/coronavirus-covid19/students.html

Hubble, S., & Bolton, P. (2020). *Briefing paper number CBP 7976, 30 July 2020: International and EU students in higher education in the UK FAQ* [Briefing paper]/ House of Commons Library), UK Parliament.

Hudzik, J. (2020). *Post-COVID higher education internationalization.* NAFSA: Association of International Educators. https://www.nafsa.org/professional-resources/ research-and-trends/post-covid-higher-education-internationalization

Immigration Customs Enforcement. (2020a, March 9). *Broadcast message: Coronavirus disease 2019 (COVID-19) and potential procedural adaptations for F and M nonimmigrant students.* https://www.ice.gov/doclib/sevis/pdf/bcm2003-01.pdf

Immigration Customs Enforcement. (2020b, July 24). *Broadcast message: Follow-up: ICE continues March guidance for fall school term.* https://www.ice.gov/doclib/sevis/ pdf/bcmFall2020guidance.pdf

İnce, E. Y., Kabul, A., & Diler, İ. (2020). Distance education in higher education in the COVID-19 pandemic process: A case of Isparta Applied Sciences University. *Distance Education, 4*(4), 345–351.

Jacob, O. N., Abigeal, I., & Lydia, A. E. (2020). Impact of COVID-19 on the higher institutions development in Nigeria. *Electronic Research Journal of Social Sciences and Humanities, 2*(2), 126–135.

Jena, P. K. (2020). Impact of Covid-19 on higher education in India. *International Journal of Advanced Education and Research, 5*(3), 77–81.

Kennedy, K. (2020, July 1). US: health & safety a bigger worry than remote instruction – survey. *The Pie News.* https://thepienews.com/news/us-health-safety-a-bigger-worry-than-remote-instruction-for-international-students/

Klayman, J. (2020, July 7). Penn condemns ICE order requiring intl. students to take in-person classes or leave U.S. *The Daily Pennsylvanian.* https://www.thedp.com/ article/2020/07/ice-international-students-guidelines-online-only-hybrid

Lau, J. (2020, June 26). Post-pandemic, will dominant China use students as bargaining chips? *Times Higher Education.* https://www.timeshighereducation. com/news/post-pandemic-will-dominant-china-use-students-bargaining-chips

Ma, J., & Zhao, K. (2018). International student education in China: characteristics, challenges, and future trends. *Higher Education, 76*(4), 735–751.

Marinoni, G., van't Land, H., & Jensen, T. (2020). The impact of COVID-19 on global higher education. *International Higher Education, Special Issue, 102*, 7–9.

Martel, M. (2020a). *COVID-19 effects on U.S. higher education campuses academic student mobility to and from China.* Institute for International Education.

Martel, M. (2020b). *COVID-19 effects on US higher education campuses, report 3.* Institute for International Education. https://www.iie.org:443/en/Research-and-Insights/Publications/COVID-19-Effects-on-US-Higher-Education-Campuses-Report-3

Maxouris, C., & Hanna, J. (2020, July 23). US surpasses 4 million reported coronavirus cases as hospitalizations near record. *CNN.* https://www.cnn. com/2020/07/23/health/us-coronavirus-thursday/index.html

Mishra, L., Gupta, T., & Shree, A. (2020). Online teaching-learning in higher education during lockdown period of COVID-19 pandemic. *International Journal of Educational Research Open, 1*, 100012.

Misirlis, N., Zwaan, M., Sotiriou, A., & Weber, D. (2020). International students' loneliness, depression and stress levels in Covid-19 crisis: The role of social media and the host university. *Journal of Contemporary Education Theory & Research (JCETR), 4*(2), 20–25.

Mitchell, N. (2020, April 14). 40% of students changing study abroad plans, says survey. *University World News.* https://www.universityworldnews.com/post.php?story=20200414082756282

Mok, K. H., Xiong, W., Ke, G., & Cheung, J. O. W. (2021). Impact of COVID-19 pandemic on international higher education and student mobility: Student perspectives from mainland China and Hong Kong. *International Journal of Educational Research, 105,* 101718.

Mou, L., O'Shea, M., & Zhang, Y. (2020). Push and pull: International Students' motivations and decisions to do a PhD in Canada. *CHIE Perspectives.* Boston, MA, USA.

New York University. (2020). *New international students.* https://www.nyu.edu/students/getting-started-at-nyu/next-stop-nyu-fall-semester/for-new-international-students.html

Nott, W. (2020, July 28). Canada backtracks on travel ban exemption for international students. *The Pie News.* https://thepienews.com/news/canada-backtracks-on-travel-ban-exemption-intl-students/

Oleksiyenko, A., Blanco, G., Hayhoe, R., Jackson, L., Lee, J., Metcalfe, A. Sivasubramaniam, M., & Zha, Q. (2020). Comparative and international higher education in a new key? Thoughts on the post-pandemic prospects of scholarship. *Compare: A Journal of Comparative and International Education, 51*(4), 612–628.

O'Shea, M., & Mou, L. (2021, January 18). Crisis messaging: How universities are communicating the pandemic. *University Affairs.* https://www.universityaffairs.ca/opinion/in-my-opinion/crisis-messaging-how-universities-are-communicating-the-pandemic/

Pan, S. (2020). COVID-19 and the neo-liberal paradigm in higher education: Changing landscape. *Asian Education and Development Studies, 10*(2), 322–335.

Paudel, P. (2020). Online education: Benefits, challenges and strategies during and after COVID-19 in higher education. *International Journal on Studies in Education, 3*(2), 70–85.

Peters, M. A., Wang, H., Ogunniran, M. O., Huang, Y., Green, B., Chunga, J. O., Quainoo, E. A., Ren, Z., Hollings, S., Mou, C., Khomera, S. W., Zhang, M., Zhou, S., Laimeche, A., Zheng, W., Xu, R., Jackson, L., & Hayes, S. (2020). China's internationalized higher education during Covid-19: Collective student autoethnography. *Postdigital Science and Education, 2,* 968–988.

Pham, H. H., & Ho, T. T. H. (2020). Toward a 'new normal' with e-learning in Vietnamese higher education during the post COVID-19 pandemic. *Higher Education Research & Development, 39*(7), 1327–1331.

Planning and Budget Office. (2020). *Budget report 2020–21 and long range budget guidelines 2020–21 to 2024–25.* University of Toronto. https://governingcouncil.utoronto.ca/sites/default/files/agenda-items/20200318_BB_03_0.pdf

Pomona FLI Scholars. (2020, June 2). Help Pomona students impacted by COVID-19. *Gofundme.Com.* https://www.gofundme.com/f/help-house-pomona-college-students-during-covid19

Quintero, D. (2020, July 13). New ICE guidelines jeopardize international students like me. *Brookings.* https://www.brookings.edu/blog/brown-center-chalkboard/2020/07/13/new-ice-guidelines-jeopardize-international-students-like-me/

Redden, E. (2020, March 20). COVID-19 disrupts international student exchange in both directions. *Inside Higher Ed.* https://www.insidehighered.com/news/2020/03/20/covid-19-disrupts-international-student-exchange-both-directions

Rumbley, L. E. (2020, March). Coping with COVID-19: International higher education in Europe. https://www. eaie. org/our-resources/library/publication/Research-and-trends/Coping-with-COVID-19–International-higher-education-in-Europe.html

Samoilovich, D. (2020). International students' loneliness, depression and stress levels in COVID-19 crisis: The role of social media and the host university. *International Higher Education, 102,* 32–34.

Sarkar, A., & Feng, A. (2020, September 7). International students face old and new challenges amid the COVID-19 pandemic. *The Medium.* https://themedium.ca/comment/international-students-face-old-and-new-challenges-amid-the-covid-19-pandemic/

Sharma, Y. (2020, July 10). *New solution for students facing study abroad uncertainty.* University World News. https://www.universityworldnews.com/post.php?story=20200710084000947

Strong, J. (2020, October 14). *China session with UIUC, Berkeley, and F&M* [Zoom webinar]. https://illinois.zoom.us/webinar/register/WN_fga2SIbZRVS-EyZWXmLrVw

Simon Fraser University. (2020, September 16). *COVID-19 (Coronavirus) and Study Abroad—Study Abroad—Simon Fraser University.* https://www.sfu.ca/students/studyabroad/updates-on-covid-19.html

Szperling, P. (2020, July 6). Students want tuition slashed as universities and colleges go online during pandemic. *CTV News.* https://ottawa.ctvnews.ca/students-want-tuition-slashed-as-universities-and-colleges-go-online-during-pandemic-1.5013139

Thevenot, S. (2020, October 21). Canadian schools reopening to international students. *CIC News.* https://www.cicnews.com/2020/10/canadian-schools-reopening-to-international-students-1016116.html

Toquero, C. M. (2020). Challenges and opportunities for higher education amid the COVID-19 pandemic: The Philippine context. *Pedagogical Research, 5*(4), em0063.

Trapani, J., & Hale, K. (2019, September 4). Higher education in science and engineering. *National Science Foundation: Science & Engineering Indicators.* https://ncses.nsf.gov/pubs/nsb20197/

UIC News Staff. (2020, April 27). Supporting Asians and Asian Americans at UIC during COVID-19. *UIC Today.* https://today.uic.edu/supporting-asians-and-asian-americans-at-uic-during-covid-19

University of Illinois. (2020, August 17). *International students – COVID-19.* https://covid19.illinois.edu/on-campus/international-students/

University of Illinois Chicago. (2020, May 26). *UIC return to work – phase 3 recovery – information for employees and managers.* https://today.uic.edu/uic-return-to-work-phase-3-recovery-information-for-employees-and-managers

University of Regina. (2020, September 10). The University of Regina to continue with primarily remote learning for the Winter 2021 term. *University Advancement & Communications,* University of Regina. https://www.uregina.ca/external/communications/releases/current/nr-09102020.html

University of Saskatchewan. (2020, March 9). COVID19: past updates. https://covid19.usask.ca/past-updates.php#March

University of Southern California. (2020, July 8). International student FAQ – fall semester Office of International Services. https://ois.usc.edu/international-student-faq-fall-semester/

University of Toronto. (2021, June 18). *Frequently asked questions about the 2020–21 school year.* https://www.utoronto.ca/utogether2020/faqs

UofT Emergency Foodbank. (2020). A contactless foodbank for students. https://utfoodbank.tech/

U.S. Department of Education. (2020, August 13). *CARES act: Higher education emergency relief fund.* https://www2.ed.gov/about/offices/list/ope/caresact.html

U.S. Immigration and Customs Enforcement. (2020, July 28). *Employment.* https://www.ice.gov/sevis/employment

Usher, A. (2020, September 16). *The state of postsecondary education in Canada, 2020.* https://higheredstrategy.com/the-state-of-postsecondary-education-in-canada-2020/

Wilson, C., & Kluger, J. (2020, September 28). Alarming COVID-19 data shows third wave brewing for U.S. *Time.* https://time.com/5893916/covid-19-coronavirus-third-wave/

Whitford, E. (2020, July 7). Department of Homeland Security rule bans international students from online-only instruction models this fall. *Inside Higher Ed.* https://www.insidehighered.com/news/2020/07/07/department-homeland-security-rule-bans-international-students-online-only

Xin, Q. (2020, April 21). As pandemic spreads in the US, so do racism and xenophobia. *Global Times.* https://www.globaltimes.cn/content/1186329.shtml

Zakaria, F. (2020) *Ten lessons for a post-pandemic world.* W. W. Norton & Company.

Zhai, Y., & Du, X. (2020). Mental health care for international Chinese students affected by the COVID-19 outbreak. *The Lancet Psychiatry, 7*(4), e22.

## Bios

**Michael O'Shea** is a PhD Candidate in Higher Education at the University of Toronto. His doctoral research focuses on Canadian universities' historic treaty responsibility to Indigenous students on Turtle Island. Other research interests include higher education policy and equity in astronomy education. Email: michael.oshea@mail.utoronto.ca

**You Zhang** is a PhD Candidate in Higher Education at the University of Toronto. Her current research examines higher education internationalization and regionalization from a comparative perspective. Email: youzhang.zhang@mail.utoronto.ca

**Leping Mou** is a PhD Candidate in Higher Education at the University of Toronto. His doctoral research focuses on liberal arts education in the East Asian contexts. Other research interests include sociology of education and research methodology. Email: leping.mou@mail.utoronto.ca

# 10 The Vulnerability and Opportunity of Privatization in Higher Education during a Pandemic

*Ziyan Bai*

## Abstract

The COVID-19 pandemic has raised fear for an impending global economic recession that would further accelerate the privatization tendencies in public higher education in the United States. During the 2008–2009 financial crisis, university leaders pursued self-sustaining academic programs as an alternative funding model in response to the state funding austerity. Such programs have grown dramatically at the master's level. Many scholars questioned the appropriateness of these programs with the public missions of universities. This multi-site comparative case study reveals that self-sustaining master's programs do not meaningfully contribute to student diversity, despite the highlight of diversity in home institutions' mission statements. Recommendations for public universities to be more attentive to diversity and inclusion according to most universities' missions are made at the end of the chapter.

## Keywords:

comparative case study, diversity, and inclusion, master's education, privatization, public higher education, state funding

## Introduction

Higher education scholars have emphasized the educational values of a diverse graduate student body for all students (Hurtado et al., 1999; Milem, 2003; Page, 2007; Smith, 2015). To meaningfully contribute to the university diversity and inclusion missions, Milem et al. (2005) recommended achieving student compositional diversity first, since it can play a key symbolic role in indicating diversity as a priority for the institution and its leaders. However, they also cautioned institutions to seek to develop beyond just this one dimension of diversity. Although in some cases, mission statements are not always operationally substantive (Morphew & Hartley, 2006), all programs should adhere substantively to the same mission statements of their respective public institutions.

Prior to the COVID-19 global pandemic, recent history suggested that along with the decline in state appropriations during and after the economic downturns in 2001–2002 and 2008–2009 and the increase in revenue-generating behaviors of public higher education institutions that resulted, a funding model for some master's programs in public research universities has appeared and expanded at a fast pace: self-sustaining master's programs SSMPs (Hagigi, 2014; Kinne-Clawson, 2017). These are master's programs that reside in public universities but do not rely on direct state appropriations, rather, generating virtually all their revenue from student tuition. Hagigi (2014), the only research on SSMPs thus far, found that none of the informants from two public health SSMPs in two universities within the same state mentioned the importance of student diversity. Furthermore, revenue-generating behaviors of public universities that resulted in rising tuition without adequate aid tend to hurt the access of students from low-socioeconomic status to these institutions (Bok, 2003; Ehrenberg, 2002).

The COVID-19 pandemic has raised fear for an impending global economic recession that would further accelerate the privatization of public higher education in the United States. This pandemic has already affected students in the US higher education when many institutions that traditionally provide in-person instruction abruptly moved to a virtual space with little preparation or structured guidance regarding how to do so in the spring of 2020 (Marinoni & van't Land, 2020). Along with the emergency responses from universities, students from non-dominant ethnic groups and internationally also faced discrimination, such as a rise in anti-Asian sentiment and hate crimes in the wake of the pandemic (Chen et al., 2020). These problems made revenue-generating programs, including SSMPs, more vulnerable when trying to attract students from underrepresented minority backgrounds and internationally.

SSMPs have been expanding, further accelerated the privatization of public higher education. Public higher education institutions are encouraged to uphold diversity and inclusion in their mission statements. However, whether SSMPs adhere to the diversity and inclusion missions is unknown, especially considering how the COVID-19 pandemic has intensified racial economic inequality. Therefore, this research aims to answer the following three research questions: (1) Is the expansion of self-sustaining master's programs undermining the mission of diversity and inclusion in public research universities? If so, how and why? (2) What lessons can self-sustaining master's programs offer public universities that want to make up for revenue loss during the COVID-19? (3) How can such programs create a more inclusive academic environment?

## Literature Review

This research is informed by the literature on the privatization of higher education and diversity in US higher education. In most higher education contexts, privatization is defined as "the retreat of public dollars from public universities and a corresponding increased reliance on private money and diverse revenue streams, increased competition for resources, and freedom from excessive public regulations" (Eckel et al., 2005). Since the 1980s, the emergence and subsequent expansion of SSMPs in public universities followed a similar timeline to the movement of privatization. Publicly available institutional policy documents from university and program webpages (for example, the University of Virginia, the University of Maryland, and the University of California), indicate that SSMPs can be in any discipline with a professional focus and with any modality of instruction delivery, and are allowed to set tuition rates based on a competitive market rate. In general, when facing declines in state appropriations, public research universities resort to raising tuition as one of the primary mechanisms to increase revenue. Raising tuition at institutions relying on external sources of full-paying students could lead to problematic disparities in the socio-economic profiles of in-state versus out-of-state students and international students (Ehrenberg, 2006; Toutkoushian, 2009). Concurring with Ehrenberg's (2006) and Toutkoushian's (2009) arguments, the American Academy of Arts and Sciences (2016) cautioned institutions that a financial model, with sharply rising tuition and more dependence on this revenue, had put the public character of these institutions at risk. Further, students coming from low socio-economic backgrounds could suffer more financially from attending public research universities, where tuition is generally higher than other types of public higher education institutions (Toutkoushian, 2009), and even worse they could be deterred from enrolling in these institutions (Heller, 1999; Paulsen & St. John, 2002; Perna et al., 2005).

In the US higher education system, the racial and ethnic diversity of student enrollment has been increasing (Espinosa et al., 2019). Educational scholars like Turner et al. (1996) have argued that to ensure the educational outcomes of an increasingly diverse student population, higher education institutions should seize the opportunity that diversity brings, reexamine their missions, values, and conventional practices, and take actions accordingly (Turner et al., 1996). More recently, the Association of American Colleges and Universities (AAC&U, 2015) called for institutional commitment to equity and inclusive excellence, emphasizing the importance of expanding access to quality education, which can ultimately make the opportunity to enroll in higher education real for all people. However, the reality, as the report revealed, was that "at all levels of US education, there are entrenched practices that reinforce inequalities—and that lead to vastly different outcomes for low-income students and for students of color" (AAC&U, 2015, p. 3) than for students from higher social-economic status groups and other racial groups. Thus, the focus of this research is to unravel the implications of SSMPs on the diversity and inclusion mission of public universities, especially in light of the COVID-19 public health pandemic that intensified racial economic inequality.

## Research Method

Considering the lack of unified terminology of SSMPs across institutions and no distinction between SSMPs and state-funded programs in the federal databases, the study is designed as a qualitative multi-site comparative case study using a purposeful sampling strategy (Merriam, 2009; Patton, 2002, Yin, 2014). The case study methodology is appropriate for answering the research questions because it is designed for researchers who aim to explore the "how" and "why" of a contemporary social phenomenon that the researcher has little or no control over (Yin, 2014).

## Data Sources

The sample includes six graduate programs in three flagship public research universities in three states (see Table 10.1). To protect the confidentiality of the institutions and especially the individual informants within each institution, the comparison table presents detailed information about each institution without naming them. Table 10.1 provides an overview of key characteristics among the three sample institutions, including location, control, state higher education governance, Carnegie classification (2018), total enrollment (Fall 2018), graduate enrollment (Fall 2018), master's degrees conferred (2017–2018), the first year an SSMP was started on record, the total number of SSMPs by September 2017, and state appropriations as a percentage of institutional revenue in 2017. These three states represent different state higher education governing structures that vary in their impact on institutional governance and

*Table 10.1* Sample State and Institutional Profiles

| Institutions | University A | University B | University C |
|---|---|---|---|
| Location | West Coast | Midwest | South |
| Control | Public | Public | Public |
| State and/or University system higher education governance | State higher education coordinating board | No single statewide higher education coordinating or governing board; system-wide governing board (Board of Regents of University B System) | State higher education coordinating board; system-wide governing board (Board of Regents of University C System) |
| Carnegie basic classification (2018) | Doctoral university: very high research activity | Doctoral university: very high research activity | Doctoral university: very high research activity |
| Total enrollment (Fall 2018) | > 47,000 | > 44,000 | > 51,000 |
| Graduate enrollment (Fall 2018) | > 12,000 | > 8,000 | > 11,000 |
| Master's degrees conferred (2017–2018) | > 3,900 | > 2,200 | > 3,000 |
| Year first SSMP established | 1983 | 1999 | 1995 |
| Total number of SSMPs (September 2017) | 111 | 48 | 26 |
| State appropriations (Percentage of total revenue in 2017) | 9% | 10% | 14% |

management (Lacy, 2011; McGuinness, 2011). The universities in the sample, one in each state, are similar in size, have more than ten full-time SSMPs, and have their first SSMP established earlier than 2001.

Within each institution, SSMPs were sampled based on the following criteria (see Table 10.2 for sample program profiles): (a) full-time program for

*Table 10.2* Sample Program Profiles

|  | *University A* | | |
| --- | --- | --- | --- |
| *Programs* | *Information management* | *Mechanical engineering* | *Statistics* |
| Year of establishment | 2001 | 2012 (Conversion from state-funded program) | 2012 (Conversion from state-funded program) |
| Credit requirement | 65 | 42 | 49 |
| Tuition 2018–2019 | $52,585 | $22,470 (In-state); $41,370 (Out-of-state) | $26,950 (In-state); $45,325 (Out-of-state) |
| Enrollment 2017–2018 | 96 | 114 | 32 |
| Acceptance 2017–2018 | 32% | 81% | 17% |
| International students | Eligible to apply | Eligible to apply | Eligible to apply |
| Administrative staff 2018–2019 | 1 full-time staff academic advisor; 3 staff administrators shared by 3 SSMPs | 1 full-time staff academic advisor | 1 full-time staff academic advisor |

|  | *University B* | *University C* | |
| --- | --- | --- | --- |
| *Programs* | *Data Science* | *Software engineering* | *Economics* |
| Year of establishment | 2013 | 1998 | 2013 |
| Credit requirement | 30 | 10 courses | 30 |
| Tuition (total) 2018–2019 | $48,000 (non-VISP); $24,000 (VISP) | $34,000 | 10-month: $29,250 (In-state); $45,325 (Out-of-state) |
| Enrollment 2017–2018 | 65 | 17 | 56 |
| Acceptance 2017–2018 | 68% | 63% | 64% |
| International students | Eligible to apply | Ineligible to apply | Eligible to apply |
| Administrative staff 2018–2019 | 1 full-time staff student services/ career advisor | 1 full-time administrative staff; 2 staff administrators shared by 4 SSMPs | 1 full-time staff administrator hired after the program started |

students, (b) in-residence program, and (c) programs that have graduated more than one cohort of students. The reason for choosing only full-time programs was that international students could only be enrolled full-time due to visa requirements, and they are an important part of US graduate education and my research interest. The choice for in-residence programs is based on the fact that funding models, structure, and student populations are different from those of online programs. Online programs do not require international students to obtain visas since they are not physically on campus long enough to trigger the visa requirement. The reason for choosing programs that have

*Table 10.3* Interview Participants by State, University, Program, and Role

| State A | | | |
|---|---|---|---|
| **University A** | | | |
| University Extension Unit administrators | 2 | | |
| The Graduate School administrators | 3 | | |
| College dean, associate deans | 4 | | |
| | Information Management | Mechanical Engineering | Statistics |
| Dept. chair, faculty, staff | 2 | 2 | 2 |
| Subtotal by university | 15 | | |
| | | | |
| **State B** | | | |
| **University B** | | | |
| University Extension Unit administrator | 1 | | |
| The Graduate School administrators | 2 | | |
| | Data Science | | |
| Dept. chair, faculty, staff | 3 | | |
| Subtotal by university | 6 | | |
| | | | |
| **State C** | | | |
| University system high-level administrator | 1 | | |
| **University C** | | | |
| The Graduate School administrators | 2 | | |
| College dean, associate deans | 2 | | |
| | Software Engineering | Economics | |
| Dept. chair, faculty, staff | 4 | 2 | |
| Subtotal by university | 11 | | |
| | | | |
| Totals by State | | | |
| All of University A | 15 | | |
| All of University B | 6 | | |
| All of University C | 11 | | |
| **Total Participants** | 32 | | |

graduated more than one cohort of students is that usually the number of graduates in the first year of a new program differs from later years, and having alumni of the program helps with the understanding of student placement. At the graduate level, disciplinary differences profoundly affect culture, program design, and program outcomes (Berelson, 1960; Golde & Walker, 2006). In most cases, SSMPs in similar disciplines were sampled across institutions; at the same time, within each institution, a maximized variation across programs was adopted to obtain a spectrum of disciplinary differences.

This study utilized multiple data sources, including 40 semi-structured interview data collected from June 2017 to June 2019 with university system leaders, university central administrators, faculty and departmental staff (see Table 10.3), secondary administrative data acquired from public websites or requested through university administrators, and online and archived policy documents and reports. Multiple sources of evidence were used for the purpose of triangulation to achieve "convergence of evidence" (Yin, 2014, p. 121).

## Findings

This research found that diversity, with respect to US minority students, is neither the mission nor the priority of SSMPs, despite the fact that all three sample universities included and elaborated on "diversity" in their mission and vision statements. This finding corroborated Hagigi's (2014) observation with evidence from student demographics and informants' accounts of reinvestment of the generated revenue from SSMPs. This study also found that students who enrolled in SSMPs were either capable of paying the tuition including relying on loans or receiving a subsidy from their employer. Interviewees (faculty and deans) generally referred to SSMPs as "revenue-generating programs." Increased resource allocation for diversity-related efforts may reflect universities' commitment to diversity, access, and affordability for all students (Taylor et al., 2016), yet the choice of investment of revenue generated by SSMPs, as determined by colleges or schools, does not reflect the value of diversity. None of the SSMPs in the sample invested the revenue into diversity-related efforts, such as recruitment and admission of students, inclusive student experience, and funding and financial support for students in need.

*Admission.* One of the design principles of SSMPs at the sample institutions is to attract either a new student population or a student population that has not been served traditionally. These student populations are supposed to be a new source of students in the market that has not been tapped into by higher education institutions regionally or nationally. Table 10.4 shows the breakdown of accessible information on student demographics for the entry class in the 2017–2018 academic year, with much lower-than-average underrepresented minority (URM) student enrollment in sample SSMPs compared to the university average in all master's programs. The URM column is a subset of students in the US column, and "-" means unavailable information due to the small number of URM students in sample SSMPs at the University C might be identifiable. When asked during the interviews, no informants from

*Table 10.4* Select Student Demographic Information in the Sample SSMPs: 2017–2018

| University | SSMP | Total | International | U.S. | URM (%) | University URM (%) |
|---|---|---|---|---|---|---|
| A | Statistics | 23 | 20 | 3 | 0% | 12.9% |
| | Information Management | 96 | 58 | 38 | 6% | |
| | Mechanical Engineering | 128 | 72 | 56 | 3% | |
| B | Data Science | 46 | 46 | 0 | 0% | 8.6% |
| C | Economics | 61 | 28 | 33 | - | 17% |
| | Software Engineering | 60 | 7 (work visa) | 53 | - | |

any SSMP voiced concerns about not enrolling diverse domestic students into their programs. Comments regarding student admission and enrollment fall into two major categories: either to enroll a minimum number of students to meet the financial target or to enroll as many students as possible.

*Student experience.* Given the historical underrepresentation of particular student populations in higher education institutions, even in the 21st century, it is more pivotal than ever to recruit the most diverse students into higher education. SSMPs are established under the premise of preparing students for the future workforce and equipping students with more employable skills or, in some cases, with academic skills to pursue advanced graduate education such as a doctoral degree. Having a diverse student composition is the first step in creating a space where diverse perspectives are appreciated. Research in graduate education has proved the value of having a diverse team working on problem-solving or project development (Harvey & Allard, 2014; Page, 2007). Based on the review of documents and interviews, faculty and administrators in sample SSMPs have not considered diversifying students, URM students in the United States, in their programs as a priority. As a result, students did not benefit from being part of a learning environment with diverse perspectives. Besides, the low staff-to-student ratio in SSMP student service is particularly problematic when sufficient institutional and departmental support has been identified as a key to the master's student success (Conrad et al., 1993).

*Funding and financial support.* For conventional stand-alone master's programs, such as a Master of Business Administration (MBA) or master's of law, professional schools tend not to fund their students but provide merit-based scholarships for a few select students (Glazer-Raymo, 2005). The assumption that terminal master's degrees lead to certain well-paying professions is the foundation of many SSMPs, and students may pay their tuition or take out loans in the hope of earning a rewarding post-graduation salary. However, most first-generation graduate students in the United States come from low-income families and consider funding an essential factor in the pursuit of higher education (Holley & Gardner, 2012; Terenzini et al., 1996);

as such, having no financial support creates a financial barrier for students from underrepresented communities. The prevalent messages on the websites of SSMPs include the ineligibility of students for state-subsidized funding opportunities, such as teaching or research assistantships. The available financial support for students with insufficient funding includes all types of student loans, from federal to private sources. Nevertheless, international master's students are ineligible for any federal student loans. While some colleges or schools offer a minimal number of merit-based scholarships, to which students from all graduate programs, both state-funded and self-sustaining, are eligible to apply, no SSMPs in the sample offered non-merit-based scholarships.

To summarize, although public research universities claim to uphold diversity and inclusion at the center of their missions, SSMPs within these universities are operating without attending to these missions. The lack of diversity-informed practice makes one suspect that diversity and inclusion is simply institutional rhetoric not reflected in actual policies and practices. The findings of this study suggest that the expansion of SSMPs did undermine the mission of diversity and inclusion in the sample public research universities.

## Discussion and Conclusions

Based on the analysis of this organizational study, the following recommendations are geared toward the state, institution, and program levels. Besides responding to the research questions, the many lessons learned from this research could potentially guide higher education leaders to design more equitable professionally oriented master's programs in public research universities, particularly during the COVID-19 pandemic.

First, public higher education leaders should endeavor to secure state funding for innovative master's programs, for example, master's programs in data science, computational chemistry, or innovation management, and should be more cautious when creating any academic programs that require tying revenue to enrollment. This strict relationship between revenue and enrollment damages academic quality (Bok, 2003), especially when coupled with a high acceptance rate and rapid enrollment expansion without attentive recruiting diverse students. Such innovative master's programs could train qualified candidates, including students from low-income backgrounds who are rarely served when programs must break even from tuition alone, for particular careers that would benefit the state and simultaneously diversify its workforce. During the COVID-19 pandemic, the staffing shortage in the public health fields (CDC, 2021) raised the question of how our education system can prepare sufficient next-generation health care workers in face of crises. SSMPs could be a viable option to train more public health professionals and to diversify the workforce if they recruit students from low socio-economic backgrounds and provide adequate financial support.

Second, Colleges that operate SSMPs should also actively seek external funding opportunities, such as from private industry, to provide financial packages for students from low-income backgrounds, which would make admission a more equitable process. For example, one SSMP beyond the sample at University A receives funding from a large technology company in the form of student scholarships. The caution is that this type of external funding should not interfere with any decisions relating to the academic quality of the program. Although funding resources are more limited during COVID-19, new funding opportunities also emerged in response to the crisis in the health-related and medical fields (see U.S. Department of Health and Human Services, 2021).

Third, the institutional reporting process should ensure data transparency by disaggregating data about academic programs with different funding mechanisms. Currently, the enrollment and graduation data published by the federal government (e.g., the Department of Education) does not distinguish between state-funded programs and self-sustaining programs, which is a serious limitation. Additionally, state mandatory reporting requirements vary by state, depending on the role of the state higher education governing agency. As a result, the proportion of state-funded degrees out of the total number of degrees produced by public universities is debatable due to the ambiguity of counting degrees produced by self-sustaining programs toward the total number. For example, if attempting to measure the impact of COVID-19 on the privatization of higher education by calculating student enrollment or the number of graduates at the regional or national level, SSMPs should be counted separately from state-funded programs.

Finally, to assure academic program quality and student experience, academic program review for SSMPs should be separated from other state-funded programs in the same department or college and be implemented at the same frequency as the schedule of financial reviews, to assure that SSMPs are not primarily financially healthy secondarily academically sound. In particular, the alignment of SSMPs to the institutional diversity missions should be added as part of the academic review process. For example, when counting the number or calculating the proportion of underrepresented students in any department or college, students in SSMPs should not be grouped with state-funded master's and doctoral students. Further, the COVID-19 public health crisis affected both domestic and international students in the United States when many institutions that traditionally provide in-person instruction abruptly moved to a virtual space with little preparation or structured guidance regarding how to do so in the Spring of 2020 (Marinoni & van't Land, 2020). International students coming to the United States in ordinary times need to navigate visa processes, adjust to new cultural norms, and adapt to a new academic system that is often very different from that in their home country (Gold, 2016). Many of the SSMPs in the sample enrolled a decent number of international students, thus, faculty and academic staff in SSMPs are encouraged to stay connected with international students and provide tailored instructional support for their needs (Wilson, 2020).

## Implications

In light of the COVID-19 pandemic, universities are facing unprecedented challenges, including moving instruction online, funding uncertainties from the state and federal governments, and unpredictability in international student mobility (Altbach & de Wit, 2020). Although SSMPs can be a viable revenue-generation opportunity for public research universities during state funding austerity, they can also expose public institutions to the potential vulnerability of compromising their diversity and inclusion missions. Thus, when considering offer SSMPs, higher education leaders need to strive for more equitable practice in aspects of admission, student experience, and funding opportunities, especially in preparation for post-pandemic recovery.

## References

Altbach, P. G., & de Wit, H. (2020). Postpandemic outlook for higher education is bleakest for the poorest. *International Higher Education, 102*, 3–4. The Boston College Center for International Higher Education.

American Academy of Arts and Sciences. (2016). Public research universities: Recommitting to Lincoln's Vision—An educational compact for the 21st century. https://www.amacad.org/publication/public-research-universities-recommitting-lincolns-vision-educational-compact-21st

Association of American Colleges and Universities (AAC&U). (2015). Committing to equity and inclusive excellence: A campus guide for self-study and planning. https://www.aacu.org/sites/default/files/CommittingtoEquityInclusiveExcellence.pdf

Berelson, B. (1960). *Graduate education in the United States*. McGraw-Hill.

Bok, D. (2003). *Universities in the marketplace: The commercialization of higher education*. Princeton University Press.

Centers for Disease Control and Prevention [CDC]. (2021, March 20). *Strategies to mitigate healthcare personnel staffing shortages*. Centers for Disease Control and Prevention. https://www.cdc.gov/coronavirus/2019-ncov/hcp/mitigating-staff-shortages.html

Chen, H A., Trinh, J., & Yang, G. P. (2020). Anti-Asian sentiment in the United States - COVID-19 and history. *American Journal of Surgery, 220*(3), 556–557. doi:10.1016/j.amjsurg.2020.05.020.

Conrad, C. F., Haworth, J. G., & Miller, S. B. (1993). *A silent success: Master's education in the United States*. Johns Hopkins University Press.

Eckel, P. D., Couturier, L., & Luu, D. T. (2005). Peering around the bend: The leadership challenges of privatization, accountability, and market-based state policy. Paper 4 in the Changing Relationship between States and Their Institutions Series. Washington, DC: American Council of Education.

Ehrenberg, R. G. (2002). *Tuition rising: Why college costs so much*. Harvard University Press.

Ehrenberg, R. G. (2006). The perfect storm and the privatization of public higher education. *Change, 38*(1), 46–53.

Espinosa, L. L., Turk, J. M., Taylor, M., & Chessman, H. M. (2019). *Race and ethnicity in higher education: A status report*. American Council on Education.

Glazer-Raymo, J. (2005). Professionalizing graduate education: The master's degree in the marketplace. *ASHE Higher Education Report, 31*(4), 1–137.

Gold, S. J. (2016). International students in the United States. *Society, 53*(5), 523–530.

Golde, C. M., & Walker, G. E. (2006). *Envisioning the future of doctoral education: Preparing stewards of the discipline.* Jossey-Bass.

Hagigi, F. A. (2014). *The hybrid public research university: A comparative case study of two self-sustaining degree programs in public health.* (Publication No. 3614087) [Doctoral dissertation, University of California, Los Angeles] ProQuest Dissertations Publishing.

Harvey, C., & Allard, M. J. (2014). *Understanding and managing diversity: Readings, cases, and exercises* (6th ed.). Pearson.

Heller, D. E. (1999). The effects of tuition and state financial aid on public college enrollment. *The Review of Higher Education, 23*(1), 65–89.

Holley, K. A., & Gardner, S. (2012). Navigating the pipeline: How socio-cultural influences impact first-generation doctoral students. *Journal of Diversity in Higher Education, 5*(2), 112–121.

Hurtado, S., Milem, J., Clayton-Pedersen, A., & Allen, W. (1999). *Enacting diverse learning environments.* ASHE-ERIC.

Kinne-Clawson, A. M. (2017). *Service and reputation: An examination of the growth in graduate education at public master's universities.* (Publication No. 10261741) [Doctoral dissertation, University of Washington]. ProQuest Dissertations Publishing.

Lacy, Jr., T. A. (2011). Measuring state postsecondary governance: Developing a new continuum of centralization. University of Georgia Thesis and Dissertation. https://getd.libs.uga.edu/pdfs/lacy_thomas_a_201105_phd.pdf

Marinoni, G., & van't Land, H. (2020). The impact of COVID-19 on global higher education. *International Higher Education, 102*, 7–9.

McGuinness, A. C. (2011). The states and higher education. In P. G. Altbach, P. J. Gumport, & R. O. Berdahl (Eds.), *American higher education in the twenty-first century: Social, political, and economic changes* (3rd ed.) (pp. 139–169). The Johns Hopkins University Press.

Merriam, S. B. (2009). *Qualitative research: A guide to design and implementation.* Jossey-Bass.

Milem, J. F. (2003). The educational benefits of diversity: Evidence from multiple sectors. In M. J. Chang, D. Witt, J. Jones, & K. Hakuta (Eds.), *Compelling interest: Examining the evidence on racial dynamics in colleges and universities* (pp. 126–169). Stanford University Press.

Milem, J. F., Chang, M. J., & Antonio, A. L. (2005). *Making diversity work on campus, a research-based perspective.* Association of American Colleges and Universities. https://www.aacu.org/sites/default/files/files/mei/MakingDiversityWork.pdf

Morphew, C. C., & Hartley M. (2006). Mission statement: A thematic analysis of rhetoric across institutional type. *The Journal of Higher Education, 77*(3), 456–471.

Page, S. E. (2007). *The difference: How the power of diversity creates better groups, firms, schools, and societies.* Princeton University Press.

Patton, M. Q. (2002). *Qualitative research and evaluation methods* (3rd ed.). Sage Publications.

Paulsen, M. B., & John, E. P. S. (2002). Social class and college costs: Examining the financial nexus between college choice and persistence. *The Journal of Higher Education, 73*(2), 189–236.

Perna, L. W., Steele, P., Woda, S., & Hibbert, T. (2005). State public policies and the racial/ethnic stratification of college access and choice in the state of Maryland. *The Review of Higher Education, 28*(2), 245–272.

Taylor, E. E., Milem, J. F., & Coleman, A. L. (2016). Bridging the research to practice gap: Achieving mission-driven diversity and inclusion goals. https://www.aacu.org/sites/default/files/BridgingResearchPracticeGap.pdf

Smith, D. G. (2015). *Diversity's promise for higher education: Making it work* (2nd ed.). Johns Hopkins University Press.

Terenzini, P. T., Springer, L., Yaeger, P. M., Pascarella, E. T., & Nora, A. (1996). First- generation college students: Characteristics, experiences, and cognitive development. *Research in Higher Education, 37*(1), 1–22.

Toutkoushian, R. (2009). An economist's perspective on the privatization of public higher education. In C. C. Morphew & P. D. Eckel (Eds.), *Privatizing the public university: Perspectives from across the academy* (pp. 60–87). Johns Hopkins University Press.

Turner, C., Garcia, M., Nora, A., & Rendon, L. I. (Eds.). (1996). *Racial & ethnic diversity in higher education*. ASHE Reader Series. Simon & Schuster Custom Publishing.

U.S. Department of Health and Human Services. (2021, April 29). *NIH to invest $29 million to address COVID-19 disparities*. National Institutes of Health. https://www.nih.gov/news-events/news-releases/nih-invest-29-million-address-covid-19-disparities.

Wilson, D. M. (2020). *The role of teaching assistants and faculty in student engagement*. American Society for Engineering Education Annual Conference.

Yin, R. K. (2014). *Case study research: Design and methods*. Sage Publications.

## Bio

**Ziyan Bai** holds a Ph.D. in Educational Leadership and Policy Studies— Higher Education from the University of Washington. As a mix-method researcher and higher education practitioner, her research focuses on examining the impact of education policies and practices on diversity, equity, and inclusion. Email: baiziyan@uw.edu.

# Part III

# COVID-19, Wellbeing, and Humanity in Higher Education

International Perspectives and Experiences

# 11 COVID-19 and Health Disparities

## Opportunities for Public Health Curriculum Enhancement

*Anuli Njoku*

### Abstract

COVID-19, the pandemic of highly contagious respiratory disease, presents a global public health emergency. The COVID-19 pandemic has increased awareness of the role of public health and its professionals in responding to the pandemic. Racial and ethnic minority groups in the United States are more likely to contract and die from COVID-19 versus Whites, highlighting health disparities. Higher education schools and programs in public health can help prepare students to address this global pandemic through expanded curriculum on social determinants of health disparities in COVID-19 outcomes, teachings on implicit bias and anti-racism, interprofessional education, and practice-based learning. Moreover, eliminating health disparities is a leading public health priority in the United States and can help attain the World Health Organization goal of achieving health equity. This chapter highlights the need for public health curriculum that outlines strategies to address racial and ethnic disparities in COVID-19 to prepare and motivate a future healthcare workforce.

### Keywords

COVID-19, health curriculum, health disparities, health equity, public health, social determinants of health, anti-racism

### Introduction

The world has been gripped by "coronavirus disease 2019" (COVID-19), a pandemic of lower respiratory tract disease resulting in severe illness and potential death from pneumonia-like symptoms (Ameh et al., 2020; Sohrabi et al., 2020; Young et al., 2020; Zhu et al., 2020). The COVID-19 pandemic presents an international public health emergency. The Centers for Disease Control and Prevention (CDC) has issued guidelines to prevent the spread of COVID-19, including washing your hands often, maintaining social distancing, avoiding close contact with people who are sick, wearing a mask in public settings and when around others who don't live in one's household, avoiding crowds and poorly ventilated spaces, and getting a COVID-19 vaccine when it is available. The CDC also advises people to seek medical care if they are sick with COVID-19 (CDC, 2021a). Persons at higher risk for COVID-19 include adults of any age with certain underlying medical conditions such as cancer, heart conditions, HIV infection, chronic kidney disease, liver disease, chronic lung diseases, dementia or other neurological conditions, weakened immune system, Down syndrome, overweight and obesity, smoking, diabetes mellitus, pregnancy, solid organ or blood stem cell transplant, sickle cell disease or thalassemia, stroke or cerebrovascular disease, and substance use disorders (CDC, 2021b). In addition, US data indicates that racial and ethnic minority groups are bearing a disproportionate burden of COVID-19-associated outcomes (CDC, 2021c).

Data from the CDC shows that:

- Compared to non-Hispanic Whites, cases are 1.7 times higher among American Indian or Alaska Native, Non-Hispanic persons (AI/ANs), 1.3 times higher among Hispanic/Latino persons, 1.1 times higher among Black/African Americans, and 0.7 times higher among Asians.
- Compared to non-Hispanic Whites, hospitalizations are 3.7 times higher among AI/ANs, 3.1 times higher among Hispanic/Latino persons, 2.9 times higher among Black/African Americans, and 1.0 times higher among Asians.
- Compared to non-Hispanic Whites, deaths are 2.4 times higher among AI/ANs, 2.3 times higher among Hispanic/Latino persons, 1.9 times higher among Black/African Americans, and 1.0 times higher among Asians (CDC, 2021c).

While propensity to underlying health conditions such as hypertension, diabetes, high blood pressure and asthma play a role, systemic barriers such as systematic racism with the healthcare system, likelihood of being uninsured, reduced access to affordable medical testing, diagnosis, and management; work-related exposures; food insecurity; and housing insecurity and also likely contribute to racial and ethnic health disparities in COVID-19 (Egede & Walker, 2020; Hooper et al., 2020). Thus, the known risk factors for COVID-19 complications need to be examined within the context of adverse social determinants of health that put minority communities at increased risk for disease and mortality. The key categories of social determinants of health that contribute to racial and ethnic disparities in COVID-19 include neighborhood and physical environment, health and healthcare, occupation and job conditions, income and wealth, and education (CDC, 2021d). Discrimination, including racism and associated chronic stress, influences each of these key critical topic areas (CDC, 2021d; Egede & Walker, 2020). This pandemic has shed a new light on racial and ethnic disparities in health and creates an opportunity to enhance public health curriculum to address these inequities.

## Literature Review

Health disparities are defined as differences in health outcomes among segments of the population that are linked to socioeconomic disadvantage and related to factors such as race or ethnicity, socioeconomic status, gender, geographic location, or other factors related to discrimination or exclusion (U.S. Department of Health and Human Services [USDHHS], 2008). COVID-19 highlights disparities in health outcomes due to race and ethnicity. As discussed, CDC data shows that the percentage of Hispanic or Latino, non-Hispanic Black, and non-Hispanic American Indian or Alaska Native people who have died from COVID-19 is higher than the percentage of these racial and ethnic groups among the total US population (CDC, 2020a).

Eliminating health disparities can enhance the health and well-being of all groups and achieve health equity, defined as "the absence of avoidable or remediable differences among groups of people, whether those groups are defined socially, economically, demographically, or geographically" (World Health Organization [WHO], 2018a, para. 1). The WHO describes the social determinants of health as "the conditions in which people are born, grow, live, work and age" (WHO, 2018b). These conditions include biology, genetics, individual behavior, socioeconomic status, physical and social environment, racism, discrimination, health services, literacy levels and legislative policies (WHO, 2018c). Social determinants of health are primarily responsible for health inequities, or avoidable and unfair differences in health status between countries and between different groups of people within the same country (WHO, 2013, 2018b). Reducing health inequities is imperative because health is a fundamental human right, and failure to overcome inequities results in health disparities (WHO, 2018a). Health inequities are gaining increasing national and international attention due to few countries being able to systematically reduce them (WHO, 2013).

### *Conceptual Framework*

The WHO conceptual framework for action on the social determinants of health (Solar & Irwin, 2010) analyzes the impact of social determinants on specific health conditions, identifies possible entry-points and causal points of mediating factors, and explores potential interventions to improve health equity by addressing social determinants of health (Figure 11.1). Social, economic, and political mechanisms contribute to a set of socioeconomic positions in which populations are stratified according to race/ethnicity, gender, income, education, occupation, and other factors. These socioeconomic positions shape intermediary determinants of health (e.g., material circumstances such as housing and neighborhood quality and physical work environment, behavioral and biological factors such as nutrition and physical activity, and psychosocial factors such as stressful living circumstances and relationships). The health system itself is a social determinant of health and becomes relevant

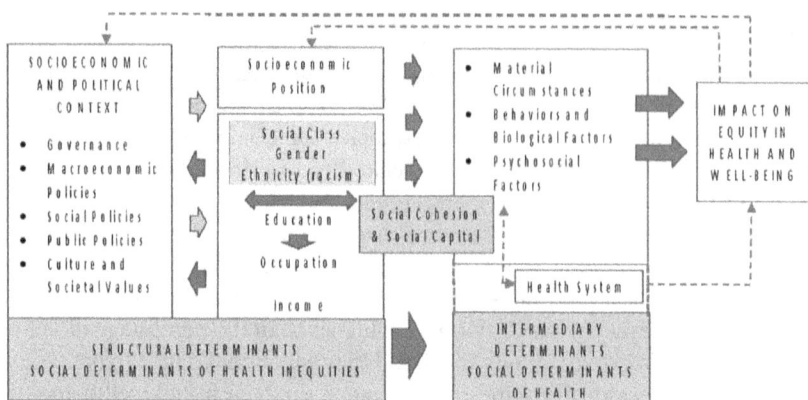

*Figure 11.1* WHO conceptual framework for social determinants of health.

through the issue of access. These various factors interact to play a central role in the social determinants of health and health inequities, with an ultimate impact on health equity and well-being (WHO, 2010).

Therefore, the recognized risk factors for COVID-19 complications need to be examined within the context of the social determinants of health that put minority communities at increased risk for disease and mortality. For example, COVID-19 illuminates medical mistreatment and mistrust in the African American community. Members of racial and ethnic minority groups tend to receive lower quality of care than Whites, which can contribute to poorer COVID-19 outcomes (Laurencin & Walker, 2020). There have been several high-profile cases of denied access to COVID-19 testing among African Americans (Basler, 2020; Fox 2 Detroit, 2020a, 2020b; Mitropoulos & Moseley, 2020). Research has shown that despite being at increased risk of exposure to the virus and requiring a higher level of care at the time they tested positive for COVID-19, people of color, particularly African Americans, do not have markedly higher testing rates and face increased barriers to care (Lieberman-Cribbin et al., 2020; Rubin-Miller et al., 2020).

Furthermore, access to COVID-19 testing may depend on where you live. One study found that in four cities in Texas, testing centers were disproportionately located in White communities compared to communities with predominantly Black persons (McMinn et al., 2020). In other instances, officials have been slow to make testing facilities available and accessible to people living in exclusively Black neighborhoods (Farmer, 2020; Peak, 2020). These factors contribute to greater demand, longer wait times for testing, and increase in travel time to testing sites (Artiga et al., 2020; Vann et al., 2020). Therefore, racial, and ethnic minority groups are particularly susceptible to COVID-19 exposure due to the social determinant of access to care.

The disparate racial impact of COVID-19 also manifests through African American workers facing more economic and health insecurity from

COVID-19 than White workers. Patterns of racism and discrimination mean that African Americans have been more likely to be exposed to the virus through work, and less likely to have access to high-quality healthcare and the resources such as health insurance to maintain their health. Racial discrimination in the labor market means that African Americans are more likely to be paid less, overrepresented in jobs that cannot be done from home, terminated, unemployed longer, and to have their unemployment claims denied, compared to their White peers (Liu, 2020). Effects of the pandemic on African American workers include devastating job losses, spiking unemployment rates, and increased likelihood to be in front-line jobs as essential workers (Gould & Wilson, 2020).

Hispanic/Latino communities are especially vulnerable to COVID-19 due to various factors including differential exposure, susceptibility, and access to healthcare (Calo et al., 2020; Quinn & Kumar, 2014). Living conditions may increase exposure to COVID-19 among Hispanic families. A quarter of Hispanic people live in multigenerational families (compared to 15% of non-Hispanic Whites), which may hinder efforts to socially distance or self-isolate when sick, if household space is limited (CDC, 2020b; Cohn & Passel, 2018). Also, the lack of reliable information in Spanish has hampered efforts to fight the spread of COVID-19 in Hispanic communities (Velasquez et al., 2020). This is especially true among those with language barriers, making them more likely to be unaware of best practices. Moreover, Hispanic people are the largest population group without health insurance coverage in the United States, leaving those with probable symptoms or with a positive COVID-19 test with limited access to necessary healthcare (Calo et al., 2020).

Other considerations include that African American and Hispanic/Latino workers are less likely to be able to work from home during the COVID-19 crisis, putting their health at risk (Gould & Shierholz, 2020). For instance, many Hispanic people work in frontline jobs in food delivery, grocery stores, cleaning and sanitation services, and waste management, putting them at constant exposure to and risk of becoming infected with COVID-19 (Bucknor, 2016). Many women of color are also essential workers on the frontlines of the COVID-19 pandemic, which may lead to higher risks of contracting COVID-19 (Frye, 2020). Policies are needed to improve access to COVID-19 testing, diagnosis, and medical treatment, particularly among uninsured individuals and people of color. Recently enacted federal legislation has required all public agencies and some private firms to provide paid sick leave during this public health crisis. This law excludes employees at businesses with over 500 employees, therefore not reaching all uninsured workers (Tolbert, 2020). Other barriers to accessing care include not having a usual source of care, prohibitive medical costs for uninsured individuals, and lack of a national, comprehensive hospital charity care policy. Therefore, racial, and ethnic minorities are especially vulnerable to COVID-19 exposure. These COVID-19 racial and ethnic disparities necessitate the expansion and continuation of higher education public health curriculum to improve health equity.

## Health Disparities Curriculum

COVID-19 presents an opportunity to shine a spotlight on public health, highlight racial and ethnic health disparities, and enhance public health curriculum. Being amidst a global pandemic emphasizes the crucial role of public health in responding to the COVID-19 outbreak. Public health can be defined as the science and art of preventing disease, promoting health, and improving the health of people in their communities. This work is accomplished by promoting healthy lifestyles, preventing injury, and stopping, detecting, investigating, and responding to infectious diseases. Public health also involves limiting healthcare disparities and promoting healthcare quality, equity, and accessibility (CDC Foundation, 2020). Public health is interdisciplinary due to its examination of the biological, social, psychological, and other factors that affect health. Students can concentrate in a variety of study paths that are relevant to COVID-19 response including biostatistics, health education, environmental health, epidemiology, public health policy, and preparedness response and recovery (Association of Schools and Public Health, 2020).

Since eliminating health disparities is a leading public health priority in the United States (USDHHS, n.d.), there is an opportunity to highlight the susceptibility of communities of color to COVID-19 due to discrimination, refused access to health services, and other factors. While many undergraduate and graduate health professions programs are incorporating health disparities content into their curricula to promote greater understanding among students (Batada, 2018; Dimaano & Spigner, 2016; Elias et al., 2017; Gutierrez & Wolff, 2017; Njoku, 2019; Njoku & Baker, 2019), curriculum can be expanded to teach about the social determinants of health that contribute to racial and ethnic disparities in COVID-19 outcomes. Furthermore, the accreditation criteria for schools and programs of public health in the United States stipulates that all Master of Public Health (MPH) graduates demonstrate competency in Public Health and Health Care Systems by discussing "the means by which structural bias, social inequities and racism undermine health and create challenges to achieving health equity at organizational, community and societal levels" (Council on Education for Public Health [CEPH], 2016, p. 17). This competency is not specified for the undergraduate curriculum, though there is encouragement for cross-cutting concepts and experiences such as "cultural contexts in which individuals work (CEPH, 2016, p. 28). While there is a growing number of Public Health programs in the United States (CEPH, 2020a), a review of overall MPH curriculum design trends revealed that about 11% of curricula contained a single concentration program in Health Equity or Priority Populations (CEPH, 2020b). This suggests an opportunity to incorporate such content into public health curriculum.

Due to the coronavirus pandemic, public health and disaster preparedness are likely to become a greater focus of many medical schools' curriculum. However, health disparities have been a critical issue before and during this pandemic. Medical schools should integrate social determinants of health and health disparities into the curriculum to provide students with an understanding of cultural competence, help them identify and address racial bias in medicine, and elucidate how health disparities can adversely affect both patient and healthcare system outcomes (Lucey & Johnston, 2020). Health disparities can result in excess medical care costs, lost productivity, and premature deaths. Addressing health disparities and the social determinants that contribute to them in medical education and training can help reduce healthcare system costs and improve care for everyone (Vickers, 2020). Therefore, it is warranted to develop anti-racism public health and medical school curricular approaches (Hagopian et al., 2018; Hardeman et al., 2018).

There are various advantages of offering health disparities courses in an undergraduate curriculum. A health disparities course could encourage collaboration among departments to develop interdisciplinary courses. With the surge of the COVID-19 pandemic, schools and programs in public health have an opportunity to expand interprofessional education and practice and service-based learning to train students for meaningful, long-term careers in public health (Brisolara & Smith, 2020). CEPH accreditation requirements of cross-cutting concepts and experiences such as teamwork and leadership and systems thinking lend themselves nicely to skills needed within health departments (Bogaert et al., 2019; CEPH, 2016).

To respond to COVID-19 disparities, schools and program should incorporate community-based participatory research and academic service learning to promote student engagement in the community, provide reflection opportunities on contextual factors affecting health, apply course concepts to real-world settings, and enhance cultural competence among students (Metcalf & Sexton, 2014; McElfish et al., 2015; Sabo et al., 2015). Curriculum development should also consider interprofessional, collaborative efforts with other health professions disciplines (e.g. Nursing, Pharmacy, Dental Hygiene, Respiratory Therapy, Allied Health professions) as well as non-health disciplines (e.g. Education, Social Work, Psychology, Science, Technology, Engineering, and Mathematics) to share resources and develop health disparities-related course content and collective projects, to assemble a wider set of future stakeholders to commit to eliminating health disparities (Benabentos et al., 2014).

## Approach

In addressing COVID-19 effect on minority communities and suggested response, proposed curriculum can prioritize minority health needs in and out of the classroom, emphasize academic-community partnerships to enrich student training and development, and develop academic-practice linkages to enhance community-based practice and research conducted by students.

Proposed curriculum components can:

- Apply a human rights framework and incorporate concepts of social determinants of health, health equity, and social justice to highlight racial and ethnic disparities in COVID-19 disease and mortality

- Encourage students to understand COVID-19 health disparities within the context of social determinants of health rather than race-based biological differences
- Train students to assess needs, develop solutions, and advance health equity in underserved and minority populations by concentrating on experiences and training in community settings
- Plan virtual learning to reinforce class material and connect students to local community partners doing COVID-19 prevention and treatment
- Teach students to conduct literature reviews on the COVID-19 outbreak
- Provide geographic information system (GIS) training, develop population health through organizational collaboration, and prepare students for a career in public health
- Summarize national and state-level programs that promote health and well-being among minority populations and assess their response to COVID-19 disease and mortality within these communities
- Describe work of key federal government agencies to support research, share findings, and develop healthy living guidelines
- Recognize key surveillance surveys and activities to monitor the health of the US population
- Train health and social workers of communities to provide enhanced screening and contact tracing of suspected cases
- Develop online health disparities courses to increase the reach of such curricula

Moreover, strategies are needed to support faculty in developing curriculum to further student awareness of racial and ethnic disparities in COVID-19 outcomes. Faculty development programs can be instrumental in inspiring and supporting faculty efforts to employ intentional instructional approaches to promote student learning about health disparities, particularly as it relates to COVID-19 disease outcomes. Successful development of faculty can be described as an ongoing, intentional, and meticulous process (Guskey, 2000). Opportunities to enhance faculty teaching and student learning can encourage faculty to stimulate critical thinking, active learning, problem-solving, and collaboration among students (Weimer, 2013).

## Discussion and Implications

The existence of racism as a root cause of COVID-19 health disparities among racial and ethnic minority groups in the United States necessitates the enhancement of public health curriculum to prepare and sustain a public health workforce to improve health equity. Due to the salient racial and ethnic disparities in COVID-19 disease outcomes, future directions and recommendations include the need for continued institutional commitment to provide and sustain health disparities curriculum for students, including those in the health professions. Such curriculum may help to engage, prepare, and motivate a future healthcare workforce that is committed to addressing health disparities, particularly as it relates to racial and ethnic disparities in COVID-19 disease outcomes.

Disparities in healthcare outcomes is one of the pressing current public health concerns. Promoting awareness of factors contributing to healthcare disparities can also allow students to contextualize current societal issues that affect health and promote engagement, preparation, and motivation of a future healthcare workforce (Benabentos et al., 2014). Promoting awareness of factors contributing to healthcare disparities can also allow students to contextualize current societal issues that affect health. Developing culturally competent learners and increasing their awareness of health disparities may help to alleviate this issue by encouraging students to consider addressing these issues in the educational, research or practice pursuits (Vela et al., 2010).

Additionally, faculty should continue to seek professional development to enhance their teaching. Faculty should incorporate learner-centered teaching to enrich student learning and embrace the teacher-scholar model where their teaching fosters continued scholarship (Trigwell et al., 2000; Weimer, 2013). Professional development has been stated as essential to the role of the teacher-scholar in that it has important implications for lifelong learning; the academic is considered an adult learner and such training can also influence faculty's growth as effective educators (Adams, 2009; Nicholls, 2014).

Ultimately, evaluation of these curricular efforts will be essential to determining and ensuring effectiveness of proposed strategies to address COVID-19 health disparities. Efforts toward infusing awareness of health disparities and social determinants of health in course development and delivery will help improve public health program goals of helping future health professionals to address needs of underserved populations. As COVID-19 has increased awareness of the role of public health and its professionals in responding to the pandemic, effective responses will ultimately help advance Public Health practice.

## Conclusions

The emergence of COVID-19 presents an opportunity to examine racial disparities in health outcomes. The experiences from this pandemic may yet offer a unique opportunity to implement an academic curriculum that promotes students' interest in public health and disease management in communities of color. Public health curriculum that highlights the social determinants of health disparities in the COVID-19 pandemic can provide students with the relevant tools needed to assess and tackle this global crisis. Higher education schools and programs in public health can help equip students to address this global pandemic through enhanced curriculum on social determinants of health disparities in COVID-19 outcomes, effect of racial bias on health outcomes, the need for anti-racism in public health, interprofessional education, and practice-based learning.

These efforts will produce future public health professionals who are better prepared to address health disparities in their surrounding community as well as broader health disparities at the national and global levels (Njoku and Wakeel, 2019). Now more than ever before, education, science, and advocacy matter.

## Summary

In summary, the COVID-19 pandemic presents a public health emergency of global concern. The role of public health is critical in responding to the COVID-19 outbreak. The predisposition of racial and ethnic minority groups in the United States to the disproportionate burden of COVID-19 illuminates the discourse of health inequalities within the framework of racial and ethnic health disparities. Eliminating health disparities is a leading public health priority in the United States and can help attain the World Health Organization goal of achieving health equity. Known risk factors for COVID-19 complications need to be examined within the context of social determinants that increase risk to COVID-19 among racial and ethnic minorities. The COVID-19 pandemic creates an opportunity to enhance Public Health curriculum to emphasize a robust approach to understanding racial health disparities and promote a greater understanding of the social determinants of health that contribute to COVID-19 racial and ethnic disparities, with an ultimate goal of providing students with the necessary tools for disease prevention and management in communities of color. The COVID-19 pandemic encourages development of medical school curriculum on social determinants of health and implicit bias to equip students to address racial and ethnic disparities in health. Curriculum development should also consider interprofessional, collaborative efforts with other health professions disciplines to encourage a multidisciplinary approach to addressing health disparities. Moreover, faculty should seek ongoing professional development to enhance their teaching and incorporate learner-centered teaching to enrich student learning.

## References

Adams, P. (2009). The role of scholarship of teaching in faculty development: Exploring an inquiry-based model. *International Journal for the Scholarship of Teaching and Learning, 3*(1), 6.

Ameh, G. G., Njoku, A., Inungu, J., & Younis, M. (2020). Rural America and Coronavirus epidemic: Challenges and solutions. *European Journal of Environment and Public Health, 4*(2), em0040. https://doi.org/10.29333/ejeph/8200

Artiga, S., Corallo, B., & Pham, O. (2020, August 17). Racial disparities in COVID-19: Key findings from available data and analysis. Retrieved from https://www.kff.org/report-section/racial-disparities-in-covid-19-key-findings-from-available-data-and-analysis-issue-brief/

Association of Schools and Programs of Public Health. (n.d.). Areas of study. Retrieved from https://www.aspph.org/study/all-areas-of-study/

Basler, C. (2020, April 21). Son's death highlights testing barriers for Black residents. Retrieved from https://www.wshu.org/post/sons-death-highlights-testing-barriers-black-residents

Batada, A. (2018). Utilizing contemplative practices with undergraduate students in a community-engaged course on health disparities. *Pedagogy in Health Promotion, 4*(1), 71–76.

Benabentos, R., Ray, P., & Kumar, D. (2014). Addressing health disparities in the undergraduate curriculum: An approach to develop a knowledgeable biomedical workforce. *CBE—Life Sciences Education, 13*(4), 636–640.

Brisolara, K. F., & Smith, D. G. (2020). Preparing students for a more public health–Aware market in response to COVID-19. *Preventing Chronic Disease, 17.* DOI: http://dx.doi.org/10.5888/pcd17.200251external

Bogaert, K., Castrucci, B. C., Gould, E., Rider, N., Whang, C., & Corcoran, E. (2019). Research full report: Top training needs of the governmental public health workforce. *Journal of Public Health Management and Practice,* 25(2 Suppl), S134.

Bucknor, C. (2016). Hispanic workers in the United States (No. 2016–19). Center for Economic and Policy Research (CEPR).

CDC Foundation. (2020). What is public health? Retrieved from https://www.cdcfoundation.org/what-public-health

Calo, W. A., Murray, A., Francis, E., Bermudez, M., & Kraschnewski, J. (2020). Reaching the Hispanic community about COVID-19 through existing chronic disease prevention programs. *Preventing Chronic Disease, 17.* DOI: http://dx.doi.org/10.5888/pcd17.200165

Centers for Disease Control and Prevention. (2020a, December 15). COVID-19 racial and ethnic health disparities. Retrieved from https://www.cdc.gov/coronavirus/2019-ncov/community/health-equity/racial-ethnic-disparities/disparities-deaths.html#ref3

Centers for Disease Control and Prevention. (2020b, July 24). Health equity considerations and racial and ethnic minority groups. Retrieved from https://www.cdc.gov/coronavirus/2019-ncov/community/health-equity/race-ethnicity.html?CDC_AA_refVal=https%3A%2F%2Fwww.cdc.gov%2Fcoronavirus%2F2019-ncov%2Fneed-extra-precautions%2Fracial-ethnic-minorities.html

Centers for Disease Control and Prevention. (2021a, March 8). How to protect yourself and others. Retrieved from https://www.cdc.gov/coronavirus/2019-ncov/prevent-getting-sick/prevention.html

Centers for Disease Control and Prevention. (2021b, March 29). People with certain medical conditions. Retrieved from https://www.cdc.gov/coronavirus/2019-ncov/need-extra-precautions/groups-at-higher-risk.html

Centers for Disease Control and Prevention. (2021c, March 12). COVID-19 hospitalization and death by race/ethnicity. Retrieved from https://www.cdc.gov/coronavirus/2019-ncov/covid-data/investigations-discovery/hospitalization-death-by-race-ethnicity.html

Centers for Disease Control and Prevention. (2021d, December 10). COVID-19 racial and ethnic health disparities. Retrieved from https://www.cdc.gov/coronavirus/2019-ncov/community/health-equity/racial-ethnic-disparities/index.html

Cohn, D. V., & Passel, J. S. (2018). *Record 64 million Americans live in multigenerational households.* Washington, DC: Pew Research Center.

Council on Education for Public Health. (2016, October). Accreditation criteria: Schools of public health & public health programs. Retrieved from https://media.ceph.org/documents/2016.Criteria.pdf

Council on Education for Public Health. (2020a). CEPH trends 2020. Retrieved from https://ceph.org/trends2020/

Council on Education for Public Health. (2020b). CEPH trends 2020. MPH curriculum. Retrieved from https://media.ceph.org/documents/MPH_Curriculum_Design.pdf

Dimaano, C., & Spigner, C. (2017). Teaching from The Immortal Life of Henrietta Lacks: Student perspectives on health disparities and medical ethics. *Health Education Journal, 76*(3), 259–270.

Egede, L. E., & Walker, R. J. (2020). Structural racism, social risk factors, and Covid-19—A dangerous convergence for Black Americans. *New England Journal of Medicine, 383*(12), e77.

Elias, T. I., Williams, K. R., Hershey, T. B., Documet, P. I., Barinas-Mitchell, E., & Gary-Webb, T. (2017). The health equity certificate program: A targeted approach to reducing health disparities and increasing the competence of health professional students. *Pedagogy in Health Promotion, 3*(3), 187–194.

Farmer, B. (2020). The coronavirus doesn't discriminate, but U.S. health care showing familiar biases. (2020, April 7). Retrieved from https://www.npr.org/sections/health-shots/2020/04/02/825730141/the-coronavirus-doesnt-discriminate-but-u-s-health-care-showing-familiar-biases

Fox 2 Detroit. (2020a, April 23). Beaumont worker turned away 4 times with COVID-19 symptoms before dying. Retrieved from https://www.fox2detroit.com/news/beaumont-worker-turned-away-4-times-with-covid-19-symptoms-before-dying

Fox 2 Detroit. (2020b, April 22). Man says dad was turned away by 3 hospitals while sick with COVID-19, then died at home. Retrieved from https://www.fox2detroit.com/news/man-says-dad-was-turned-away-by-3-hospitals-while-sick-with-covid-19-then-died-at-home

Frye, J. (2020, April 23). On the frontlines at work and at home: The disproportionate economic effects of the Coronavirus pandemic on women of color. Retrieved from https://www.americanprogress.org/issues/women/reports/2020/04/23/483846/frontlines-work-home/

Gould, E., & Shierholz, H. (2020, March 19). Not everybody can work from home: Black and Hispanic workers are much less likely to be able to telework. Retrieved from https://www.epi.org/blog/black-and-hispanic-workers-are-much-less-likely-to-be-able-to-work-from-home/

Gould, E., & Wilson, V. (2020, June 1). Black workers face two of the most lethal preexisting conditions for coronavirus—racism and economic inequality. Retrieved from https://www.epi.org/publication/black-workers-covid/

Guskey, T. (2000). *Evaluating professional development.* Thousand Oaks, CA: Corwin Press.

Gutierrez, C. S., & Wolff, B. (2017). Using photovoice with undergraduate interprofessional health sciences students to facilitate understanding of and dialogue about health disparities within communities. *Pedagogy in Health Promotion, 3*(1), 42–49.

Hagopian, A., West, K. M., Ornelas, I. J., Hart, A. N., Hagedorn, J., & Spigner, C. (2018). Adopting an anti-racism public health curriculum competency: The University of Washington Experience. *Public Health Reports, 133*(4), 507–513.

Hardeman, R. R., Burgess, D., Murphy, K., Satin, D. J., Nielsen, J., Potter, T. M.,… & Cunningham, B. A. (2018). Developing a medical school curriculum on racism: Multidisciplinary, multiracial conversations informed by Public Health Critical Race Praxis (PHCRP). *Ethnicity & Disease, 28* (Suppl 1), 271.

Hooper, M. W., Nápoles, A. M., & Pérez-Stable, E. J. (2020). COVID-19 and racial/ethnic disparities. *JAMA.* doi:10.1001/jama.2020.8598

Laurencin, C. T., & Walker, J. M. (2020). A Pandemic on a pandemic: Racism and COVID-19 in Blacks. *Cell Systems, 11*(1), 9–10. https://doi.org/10.1016/j.cels.2020.07.002

Lieberman-Cribbin, W., Tuminello, S., Flores, R. M., & Taioli, E. (2020). Disparities in COVID-19 testing and positivity in New York City. *American journal of Preventive Medicine, 59*(3), 326–332.

Liu, J. (2020, September 1). Just 13% of Black people out of work are getting unemployment benefits during the pandemic. Retrieved from https://www.cnbc.com/2020/09/01/just-13percent-of-black-people-out-of-work-get-pandemic-unemployment-benefits.html

Lucey, C. R., & Johnston, S. C. (2020). The transformational effects of COVID-19 on medical education. *Jama, 324*(11), 1033–1034.

McMinn, S., Carlsen, A., Jaspers, B., Talbot, R., & Adeline, S. (2020, May 27). In large Texas cities, access to Coronavirus testing may depend on where you live. Retrieved from https://www.npr.org/sections/health-shots/2020/05/27/862215848/across-texas-black-and-hispanic-neighborhoods-have-fewer-coronavirus-testing-sit

Metcalfe, S. E., & Sexton, E. H. (2014). An academic-community partnership to address the flu vaccination rates of the homeless. *Public Health Nursing, 31*(2), 175–82. doi: 10.1111/phn.12088

McElfish, P. A., Kohler, P., Smith, C., Warmack, S., Buron, B., Hudson, J.,… & Rubon-Chutaro, J. (2015). Community-driven research agenda to reduce health disparities. *Clinical and Translational Science, 8* (6):690–695. doi: 10.1111/cts.12350. Epub 2015 Nov 17.

Mitropoulos, A., & Moseley, M. (2020, April 28). Beloved Brooklyn teacher, 30, dies of coronavirus after she was twice denied a COVID-19 test. Retrieved from https://abcnews.go.com/Health/beloved-brooklyn-teacher-30-dies-coronavirus-denied-covid/story?id=70376445

Nicholls, G. (2014). *Professional development in higher education: New dimensions and directions.* Routledge.

Njoku, A. (2019). Effect of online courses on US college students' knowledge about health disparities. *Health Education Journal, 78*(5), 510–523.

Njoku, A., & Baker, U. (2019). Teaching about cultural competence and health disparities in an online graduate public health course. *Journal of Health Disparities Research and Practice, 12*(2), 14–39. https://digitalscholarship.unlv.edu/jhdrp/vol12/iss2/2/

Njoku, A., & Wakeel, F. (2019). Infusing health disparities awareness into public health curricula at a rural Midwestern university. *Pedagogy in Health Promotion, 5*(2), 139–146.

Peak, C. (2020, July 15). Failing to protect Black lives: How Washington, D.C., mishandled its response to the coronavirus. Retrieved from https://www.apmreports.org/story/2020/07/15/washington-dc-response-to-coronavirus

Quinn, S. C., & Kumar, S. (2014). Health inequalities and infectious disease epidemics: A challenge for global health security. *Biosecurity and Bioterrorism: Biodefense Strategy, Practice, and Science, 12*(5), 263–273.

Rubin-Miller, L., Alban, C., & Artiga, S. (2020, September 16). COVID-19 racial disparities in testing, infection, hospitalization, and death: Analysis of Epic patient data. Retrieved from https://www.kff.org/report-section/covid-19-racial-disparities-in-testing-infection-hospitalization-and-death-analysis-of-epic-patient-data-issue-brief/

Sabo, S., De Zapien, J., Teufel-Shone, N., Rosales, C., Bergsma, L., & Taren, D. (2015). Service learning: A vehicle for building health equity and eliminating health disparities. *American Journal of Public Health, 105*(S1), S38–S43.

Sohrabi, C., Alsafi, Z., O'Neill, N., Khan, M., Kerwan, A., Al-Jabir, A., Iosifidis, C., & Agha, R. (2020). World Health Organization declares global Emergency: A review of the 2019 Novel Coronavirus (COVID-19). *International Journal of Surgery (London, England), 76*, 71–76. https://doi.org/10.1016/j.ijsu.2020.02.034

Solar, O., & Irwin, A. (2010). *A conceptual framework for action on the social determinants of health.* WHO Document Production Services.

Tolbert, J. (2020). What issues will uninsured people face with testing and treatment for COVID-19? The Henry J. Kaiser Family Foundation. Available at: https://www.kff.org/uninsured/fact-sheet/what-issues-will-uninsured-people-face-with-testing-and-treatment-for-covid-19/ (Accessed: 30 August, 2021).

Trigwell, K., Martin, E., Benjamin, J., & Prosser, M. (2000). Scholarship of teaching: A model. *Higher Education Research & Development, 19*(2), 155–168.

U.S. Department of Health and Human Services. (2008). The Secretary's Advisory Committee on National Health Promotion and Disease Prevention Objectives for 2020. Phase I report: Recommendations for the framework and format of Healthy People 2020 [Internet]. Section IV: Advisory Committee findings and recommendations. Retrieved from http://www.healthypeople.gov/sites/default/files/PhaseI_0.pdf

U.S. Department of Health and Human Services (USDHHS) (n.d.) Healthy people 2020. Available at: https://www.healthypeople.gov/ (accessed 30 August 2021).

Vann, M., Kim, S. K., & Bronner, L. (2020). COVID-19 test access disparities in some south Florida communities fall along racial, socioeconomic lines: ANALYSIS. Retrieved from https://abcnews.go.com/Politics/covid-19-test-access-disparities-south-florida-communities/story?id=71884733

Vela, M. B., Kim, K. E., Tang, H., & Chin, M. H. (2010). Improving underrepresented minority medical student recruitment with health disparities curriculum. *Journal of General Internal Medicine, 25*, S82–S85. doi: 10.1007/s11606-010-1270-8

Velasquez, D., Uppal, N., & Perez, N. (2020). *Equitable access to health information for non-English speakers amidst the novel coronavirus pandemic.* Health affairs blog.

Vickers, S. (2020, April 30). Medical students need to learn about health disparities to combat future pandemics. Retrieved from https://www.aamc.org/news-insights/medical-students-need-learn-about-health-disparities-combat-future-pandemics

Weimer, M. (2013). *Learner-centered teaching: Five key changes to practice* (2nd ed.). San Francisco, CA: Jossey-Bass.

World Health Organization. (2013). Closing the health equity gap: Policy options and opportunities for action. Retrieved from https://apps. who.int/iris/bitstream/handle/10665/78335/9789241505178_eng. pdf;jsessionid=85C111FD861E02760C27FC65BD24BDCF?sequence=1

World Health Organization (WHO). (2018a). *Equity*. Retrieved from http://www.who.int/healthsystems/topics/equity/en/

World Health Organization (WHO). (2018b). *Social determinants of health*. Retrieved from http://www.who.int/social_determinants/sdh_definition/en/

World Health Organization (WHO). (2018c). *Healthy people*. Retrieved from https://www.who.int/westernpacific/health-topics/equity

Young, B. E., Ong, S., Kalimuddin, S., Low, J. G., Tan, S. Y., Loh, J., Ng, O. T., Marimuthu, K., Ang, L. W., Mak, T. M., Lau, S. K., Anderson, D. E., Chan, K. S., Tan, T. Y., Ng, T. Y., Cui, L., Said, Z., Kurupatham, L., Chen, M. I., Chan, M., … Singapore 2019 Novel Coronavirus Outbreak Research Team (2020). Epidemiologic features and clinical course of patients infected with SARS-CoV-2 in Singapore. *JAMA*, *323*(15), 1488–1494. Advance Online Publication. https://doi.org/10.1001/jama.2020.3204

Zhu, N., Zhang, D., Wang, W., Li, X., Yang, B., Song, J., Zhao, X., Huang, B., Shi, W., Lu, R., Niu, P., Zhan, F., Ma, X., Wang, D., Xu, W., Wu, G., Gao, G. F., Tan, W., & China Novel Coronavirus Investigating and Research Team (2020). A novel Coronavirus from patients with pneumonia in China, 2019. *The New England Journal of Medicine*, *382*(8), 727–733. https://doi.org/10.1056/NEJMoa2001017

## Bio

**Anuli Njoku, DrPH, MPH,** is an Associate Professor of Health Equity/Health Promotion in the Department of Public Health at Southern Connecticut State University. Her research and teaching specialties include cultural competency in higher education, health disparities, health promotion and education, health equity, environmental health, rural health, and the scholarship of teaching and learning. Email: njokua3@southernct.edu

# 12 Internationalizing Trauma-Informed Perspectives to Address Student Trauma in Post-Pandemic Higher Education

*Joshua M. Anzaldúa*

## Abstract

The COVID-19 pandemic has been a time saturated with economic, health, and natural crises, resulting in immeasurable human suffering. Civil-political movements have erupted in the United States that exposed the world to a disheartening view of western injustice, violence, and death as human rights violations increased, seemingly unabated. US students also witnessed a world riddled with global crises. The impact of such potentially traumatic exposures on the future of college students' mental health and academic wellness clearly points to a need for college and university systems to reimagine more trauma-informed organizational structures. A trauma-informed human rights perspective could make significant contributions to post-secondary education systems to maximize mental health and academic benefits for present and future college students—a generation of student pandemic survivors predicted to experience pandemic-era psychosocial repercussions impacting their education for years to come.

## Keywords

COVID-19, educational leadership, higher education, human rights, student mental health, trauma, trauma-informed

## Introduction

The worldwide outbreak of COVID-19 brought tremendous distress to the global community. Medical research knew little about COVID-19, a new strain of Coronavirus, before the WHO (World Health Organization, 2020a) declared it a global pandemic in March 2020. Countries across the world were forced to take strategic actions to prevent the spread of the dangerous virus which, when transmitted through close human contact, can cause lethal respiratory complications. For instance, country leaders and governing bodies worldwide issued stay-at-home orders, encouraged individuals to wear protective masks, promoted physical distancing in public spaces, and implemented other regulations to help slow the rise in COVID-19 infections (Adhanom Ghebreyesus, 2020; Griffin, 2020; Gruber et al., 2020; Horesh & Brown, 2020). Other measures to combat the virus involved economic shutdowns and school system closures.

In the United States, the COVID-19 public health crisis had a tremendous impact on local and state economies as the nation experienced mass economic shutdowns. Countless frontline and essential workers in healthcare, law enforcement, food supply and delivery, public transportation, and other public service fields were deemed vital in maintaining the health, order, and well-being of the general public. In many cases, these workers were also placed at highest risk for bringing contagion to their personal living spaces; they often experienced feelings of overwhelming concern and fear for their safety (Greene, 2020). Millions of other workers filed for unemployment after being furloughed or let go from their day jobs. The Pew Research Center recorded a three times higher unemployment rate in the first three months of the COVID-19 pandemic than during the two years of the 2008 Great Recession (Kochhar, 2020). Not only did the growing threat of an invisible enemy contribute to an exploding unemployment rate and burgeoning economic stressors for everyday citizens, it also impacted systems of education.

As COVID-19 outbreaks began to spread uncontrollably throughout the world, national governments called for system-wide school closures at all educational levels (Van Lancker & Parolin, 2020). Within the first months of the COVID-19 pandemic, more than 1.5 billion students in 190 countries were not able to attend school in person (Bhagat & Kim, 2020; UNICEF, 2020). In the United States, these closures caused tremendous stress on students, teachers, and all other stakeholders as they tried to adjust to unfamiliar ways of delivering education through virtual means. Some educational barriers were insurmountable for many young and adult students; researchers found existing inequalities such as access to technology, reliable internet, childcare, and food insecurity to be amongst the most prevalent factors that disrupted student learning, growth, and development during the COVID-19 pandemic (The Education Trust, 2020; García & Weiss, 2020; Gundersen et al., 2020). Consequently, many students and families from lower socioeconomic and other marginalized backgrounds were disproportionately impacted as many who relied on gainful employment, human service programs, and campus support systems prior to the pandemic became further disenfranchised as school systems and the country weathered a storm of unfamiliar health and social conditions (Van Lancker & Parolin, 2020). As a result of the dramatic shift from in-person instruction to distance learning, higher education systems saw decreases in student attendance (INSA, 2020) and shifts in attitudes toward college enrollment as students and families prioritized other pressing hardships which challenged their very survival (Burke, 2020; Whitmire, 2020). Clearly, the COVID-19 pandemic took a tremendous toll across every human service system in the United States and across the global map, including higher education systems. However, before discussing the connection between the deleterious impacts of the COVID-19 pandemic on student mental health and conceptualizing the role of higher education in a COVID-19-afflicted global society, it is important to take a closer look at other potentially traumatic events taking place simultaneously throughout the world which could potentially have lasting effects on student mental health.

## World Exposure to Civil Uprisings and Traumatizing Events

Amidst the increasingly concerning public health threat of the Coronavirus (COVID-19) in the United States, civilians took to the streets in outrage over the country's legacy of civil and racial injustices. Supporters of civil rights activist groups like the Black Lives Matter movement mobilized to commemorate and protest the untimely deaths of innocent Black victims whose names were added to the list of countless others who died while in police custody. The country drew global attention and scrutiny as mass protests and civil uprisings erupted in every state and countless cities across the nation. Global news outlets reported a nation estranged as people across the world witnessed the United States' ongoing civil rights and race battles. In fact, 2020 was a year of intercontinental civil unrest as some groups in other countries around the world protested in solidarity with US social justice movements and other domestic injustices taking place (Pleyers, 2020).

People of the United States were not only forced to endure the compounding threats of economic distress and civil unrest during a global health crisis but also the nation's inadequate means of minimizing the number of COVID-19 outbreaks (Lipton et al., 2020; Wise & Chappell, 2020). Johns Hopkins University's Center for Systems Science and Engineering (JHUCSSE) reported on August 8, 2020 the United States was leading the world with the highest numbers of COVID-19 infections (4,986,345) and untimely deaths (162,244). By October 16, 2020, in just nine short weeks, the US COVID-19 infections almost doubled (8,027,412) whereas the number of COVID-19 deaths increased by over 34% (218,266). As the country pushed through the wintery months, the country had reached a staggering 16,079,922, reported infections, a 100.3% increase, and 297,886 deaths from COVID-19 by December 2020 (JHUCSSE, 2020/2021).

The country's mismanaged efforts to control the COVID-19 outbreaks not only lead to an uncontrollable rise in the number of infections and deaths for the general US population, but also contributed to unsettling disproportionalities in the number of COVID-19 infections and deaths amongst communities of color and other vulnerable populations (Chappell, 2020; Miller, 2020; Rodriguez-Diaz et al., 2020; Thebault & Fowers, 2020; Thebault et al., 2020). By mid-October, Coronavirus (COVID-19) was the cause of death for over 43,953 Latina/o/x Americans, 43,844 Black Americans, 8,182 Asian Americans, and 1,886 Indigenous Americans (APM Research Lab, 2020). By the end of October 2020, the racial minority collective experienced a disproportionately high number of reported deaths in the United States. They also endured the harsher effects of a global health and economic crisis while also being further exposed to episodic events showcasing a nation's continued legacy of systemic racial injustice (Kola, 2020).

Evidently, what took place in the United States created prolonged hardships and potentially traumatic conditions for the domestic community; however, the transnational community also bore witness to *other* traumatic worldly events. In developing countries such as Afghanistan, Venezuela, Somalia, and Yemen, ongoing issues with poverty, famine, medicine shortages, disease, natural disasters, civil wars, or other economic or sociopolitical turmoil made containing COVID-19 outbreaks, infections, and deaths even more complex (International Rescue Committee, 2020). In a May 2020 155-country survey, over 50% of the countries reported—including countries with more-developed economies—had tremendous difficulties in treating those living with non-communicable diseases/illnesses (i.e., hypertension, diabetes, cancer, cardiovascular diseases) and providing rehabilitative services as a growing number of hospital beds became occupied with COVID-19 patients (WHO, 2020a). By the first week of August 2020 to October 16, 2020, JHUCSSE (2020/2021) reported a staggering increase from 19,481,330 total COVID-19 cases globally to 39,131,360, a 100.4% increase in just over nine weeks. By mid-October, the world reached a COVID-19 death toll of over one million people (1,101,083). Although large-scale COVID-19 vaccination efforts began slowing the spread of COVID-19 within the first quarter of 2021 in the United States and across the world, by June 2021 the national total of COVID-19 infections and deaths had already reached 33,137,285 and 590,167, respectively. COVID-19 cases had also reached an astonishing global total of 167,045,252 and humanity continued to mourn the deaths of 3,467,796 COVID-19 victims worldwide. Despite exceeding 1,677,742,273 administered COVID-19 vaccinations by June 2021 (JHUCSSE, 2020/2021), the illness continues to threated and claim lives in countries, regions, and sovereignties across the world.

Additionally, the world collectively witnessed the unspeakable horrors of other instances of violence and destruction taking place amidst a pandemic. In August 2020, an enormous explosion in Lebanon's capital of Beirut made world news as it claimed the lives of over 135 people, injured over 5,000, and left more than 300,000 people homeless (Giordano, 2020). Societies around the world were exposed to graphic media footage of injured civilians, death, and destruction caused by the explosion. In the United States, an onslaught of natural disasters devastated communities such as historically large conflagrations in western states causing mass displacement of tens of thousands of civilians (Alonso & Sanchez, 2020), a growing frequency of torrential rains, flooding, and hyperactive hurricane season which wreaked havoc in southern states (Dolce, 2020a), record-breaking occurrences of earthquakes and seismic activity among fault line states (Childs, 2020), and an extremely rare 140-miles-per-hour derecho in the Midwest which destroyed over $7.5 billion in land and property and much of its agricultural (i.e., soybean and corn) industry (Dolce, 2020b). It is clear that the United States and the world were forced to cope with an unfamiliar range of human distress, tragedy, and pain caused by economic, civil-political, cultural, educational, biological, humane, and more dangerous forces of nature, all of which warrant the question of how such unique forms of collective psychological suffering will impact systems of higher education and student overall well-being. Such inquiry must involve a closer look at mental health in the age of Coronavirus (COVID-19).

The subsequent sections of this chapter purposefully situate pandemic-era topics at the intersection of mental health and higher education in the United States as the primary focus. This focus is necessary as during the time of this writing, the United States not only surpassed every global country in the number of COVID-19 infections and deaths; it has also endured its third wave of Coronavirus cases (Hellman, 2020; Leatherby, 2020). It is urgent to note, narrowing this chapter's contextual focus this way is *not* an attempt to delay or diminish any sense of urgency for global higher education systems to examine the depth and implications of pandemic-era domestic traumatization taking place in countries across the world. However, this specific focus may provide timely insight that paints a more vivid portrait of a future relationship between mental health, student wellness, and higher education after COVID-19's eradication.

### Mental Health Suffering

Living in a world plagued by a dangerous virus, individuals in societies across the world struggled with adapting to what the World Health Organization (2020b) refers to as *the new normal*, a time when humans were expected to normalize stressful social and health conditions while taking preventative measures to minimize COVID-19 exposure. Mental health experts assert such intense collective experiences with distress may contribute to higher levels of human psychological disturbances over time (Cassata, 2020; Perel, 2020; Wright, 2020). Mental health experts highlight the following pandemic-era stress factors as ones that may have long-term mental health implications globally: (a) maintaining a sense of normalcy when a lingering disease threatens lives; (b) personal or secondary experience of virus-induced illness and loss of life; (c) overwhelming distress caused by uncertain health and economic outcomes (i.e., unknown timeline of pandemic duration, unknown cure, job security and financial stress; and (d) other *threat multipliers* such as natural disasters and civil unrest (Luest et al., 2020). Those weathering the pandemic became increasingly likely to experience intrusive emotions, problems with sleep or concentration, being constantly on guard, difficult emotions, feeling numb, avoidance behaviors, negative thoughts, or changes in eating patterns (Center for Disease Control and Prevention, 2020; Gillihan, 2020). Based on well-documented, empirically based psychological research regarding natural disasters and human-caused tragedies (Miller, 2006, 2017; Neria et al., 2011), mental health experts foresaw long-term traumatic complications with individual and collective mental health beyond a time when COVID-19 is eradicated (Zhai & Du, 2020). The significance of this prediction means that the state of mental health will not look the same in the foreseeable future as it was before the global pandemic. The chapter challenges the reader to reimagine the role global higher education will play vis-à-vis lingering traumas of a generation of student COVID-19 era survivors.

## Prevalence and Impact of Student Trauma in Higher Education

Prior to the COVID-19 pandemic, trauma researchers estimated 66%–85% of college-age students in the United States had experienced one to several traumatic events in their lifetime including but not limited to family violence, childhood neglect, painful interpersonal relationships, sexual assault, and other physiological/psychological forms of maltreatment (Carello & Butler, 2015; Costa, 2020; Frazier et al., 2009; Smyth et al., 2008). Students with traumatic histories and those from vulnerable or disadvantaged backgrounds (e.g., racial/ethnic minorities, gender/sexual minorities, low-income, immigrants and refugees, students with physical/intellectual disabilities) have higher risks of experiencing trauma-related stress factors such as posttraumatic stress, destructive social behaviors, poorer physical health, substance abuse, revictimization, depression, and various other traumatic risk variables during their postsecondary education (Anders et al., 2012; Carello & Butler, 2014; Cless & Nelson Goff, 2017). Students with unaddressed or ongoing posttraumatic stress are at highest risk to encounter academic risk factors such as lower grade point averages, poorer classroom performance and attendance, and dropping out of college (Bachrach & Read, 2012; DeBerard et al., 2004; Miller, 2020).

Systems of higher education can expect dramatic shifts in percentages of students living with trauma histories as an entire generation of students will have survived one of the world's most deadly global health crises and other traumatic worldly events taking place simultaneously across the world. Most students will have been exposed to traumatic experiences personally or vicariously during the COVID-19 era such as Coronavirus-related pain or death; widespread civic distress such as financial and food insecurities; intensified education and health disparities; heightened domestic, political, and personal violence; horrific tragedies like the Beirut explosion; or through devastating natural disasters. Given that post-secondary students with traumatic histories are at higher risk for experiencing academic challenges, the traumatic impacts of the COVID-19 pandemic, and evidence predicting higher rates of human trauma (Gruber et al., 2020), global higher education must redirect attention to the severity, prevalence, and implications of a traumatizing era in human history when addressing student post-pandemic mental health challenges postsecondary education.

## Trauma-Informed Frameworks and Higher Education

Clinical researchers have made groundbreaking contributions to the study of human psychological trauma since its origins in psychoanalysis (Carello & Butler, 2014; Freud, 1989). Most advancements in psychological trauma studies have been oriented to improve the ways clinical disciplines and professions (i.e., counseling, social work, psychology, psychiatry, neuroscience, and others) engage in trauma research, evaluation, intervention, and treatment. Although inquiries of the study of trauma have covered vast trauma-related content areas (e.g., the etiology of trauma, the biopsychosocial sequelae of trauma across the lifespan, trauma symptomatology, psychopharmacological intervention) which have primarily examined human responses to traumatic circumstances, the study of trauma has pushed beyond such a medicalized scope to include inquiry regarding the psychosocial repercussions of broader oppressive social conditions (APA, 2013; Herman, 1997). Such progressive paradigm shifts have resulted in new *trauma-informed* (TI) perspectives which examine the links between human trauma psychopathology, broader macro trauma exposure (i.e., oppressive socioenvironmental milieu, ideological, structural conditions), and a push for various human service organizations (e.g., mental health facilities, community centers, colleges and universities) to develop TI organizational cultures.

Being Trauma-informed or TI means understanding the dynamic ways in which violence, victimization, and various human trauma exposures affect individuals, families, and communities (Bent-Goodley, 2019; Butler et al., 2011). Harris and Fallot (2001) developed five basic principles (i.e., safety, trustworthiness, choice, collaboration, empowerment) which have set the foundation of what it means to be TI. Further, TI principles make up what is known as *trauma-informed care* (TIC). TIC approaches help organizations minimize individual-level trauma reemergence through policy and practice, while maximizing opportunities for individuals to heal and recover from past traumatic experiences (Fallot & Harris, 2009), and works as a way to minimize the potential of people who have already experienced past trauma from developing posttraumatic stress disorder or PTSD (Brown, 2018). For the sake of clarity, Carello et al. (2019) highlight two distinctions between TIC and what is known as *trauma-specific services* (TSS). TSS are specific to treating individual trauma cases in clinical settings. For example, a university student survivor of a natural disaster seeking mental health services may receive TSS services (e.g., Trauma-Focused Cognitive Behavioral Therapy and other forms of psychotherapy) from their university's mental health intervention program to help strengthen self-regulation and coping strategies. A second distinction between TSS and is that the latter considers the pervasive nature of human trauma and helps transform organizational structures and human service delivery in ways that respect and appropriately respond to the effects of trauma at all levels (Bloom, 2010; Harris & Fallot, 2001). In the same vein of the previous example, the student's teacher could engage in TIC in the classroom by becoming familiar with the potential impacts posttraumatic stress has on student behavior (e.g., class avoidance, declining grades) and restructure the course in ways that prioritizes student safety and success (e.g., alternative assignments, flexible deadlines, mental health days).

Carello and colleagues (2019) also note that human service systems could offer trauma-specific services without being trauma-informed or be trauma-informed without offering trauma-specific services. Therefore, it should be understood that TI organizational systems recognize the prevalence of trauma, its impact on human lives, and incorporate those understandings in policy, procedure, and practice (Collin-Vézina et al., 2020; Yatchmenoff et al., 2017). Although TIC was originally developed for clinical organizational systems, in the past 20 years the intellectual community outside the clinical sciences has begun to examine traumatic experiences as outcomes of oppressive social systems and structures and broadened TIC models that reach other non-health related human service systems—including systems of higher education.

Carello and Butler (2014) highlight the prevalence of trauma amongst college students and the potential for learning environments to become ground zero for traumatization, retraumatization, or vicarious/secondary traumatization. In response, Carello and Butler (2015) developed a *trauma-informed educational practice* (TIEP) teaching model which integrate TIC elements in pedagogical practices which aim to reduce student traumatization and promote student resilience and emotional safety. Other trauma and education scholars have also contributed recent and relevant work to the growing efforts of creating more trauma-informed education cultures in both higher education and K12 education contexts (see *Equity-Centered Trauma-Informed Education* [Venet, 2021]; *Building a trauma-informed restorative school: Skills and approaches for improving culture and behavior* [Brummer & Thorsborne, 2021]; Trauma-*Informed Classroom Care Model* [Cless & Nelson Goff, 2017]; *ISTSS Best Practice Parameters* [International Society for Trauma and Traumatic Stress, 2016]; *Trauma-Informed Practices for Postsecondary Education* guide [Davidson, 2017]; *Safeguarding Mindfulness in Schools and Higher Education: A Holistic and Inclusive Approach* [Burrows, 2017]; Nikischer's [2018] trauma-informed recommendations for writing and teaching about violence; *Trauma-Informed Teaching & Learning in Times of Crisis* [Carello, 2020]; and *A Model for Trauma-Informed Education and Administration* [Harper & Neubauer, 2020]).

These TI educational models and approaches have tremendous potential to help minimize student (re)traumatization in K12 and higher education settings. However, conversations regarding the traumatic implications of the COVID-19 era on college student education must expand to include other broader, progressive conceptualizations of human trauma such as human rights violations created by existing oppressive social conditions such as institutionalized racism, gender-based violence, generational poverty, inequitable access to education and healthcare services, food insecurities, inadequate housing and unsafe living conditions, warfare, bigotry—all of which were exacerbated by the COVID-19 pandemic.

## Human Rights and Trauma Perspectives in Post-Pandemic Education

As educational systems work to create methods to minimize the traumatization of COVID-affected students, it is critical that they welcome a trauma-informed perspective toward understanding often-overlooked transgressions afflicting generations of students navigating worldly social systems. Broadly, such historical and contemporary encroachments on human rights have far-reaching, systemic, and potentially traumatic effects on global peoples' physical and mental wellness particularly for the world's most vulnerable and historically marginalized populations.

The Universal Declaration of Human Rights was developed in 1948 by a collective of global national leaders who believe humans are born with certain inherent, indivisible, fundamental rights and protected freedoms regardless of place of residence, race, ethnic or national origin, religion, language, gender and sexual orientation, color, or any other social status (United Nations, n.d.). The evolution of human rights discourse has roots spanning various global philosophical and theological foundations, several socialist and collectivist movements (e.g., universal suffrage movements, international labor movement, Civil Rights movement, Feminist Movement), and other historically significant eras of human history (e.g., Enlightenment, Anti-colonial, French Revolution) (Butler & Critelli, 2019). International human rights discourse has been instrumental in the fight to end global human degradation, economic/social/health inequalities, discrimination, torture, and in the protection and preservation of the planet humans occupy (Moyn, 2010). Considering the aforementioned traumatic events/exposures taking place simultaneously in the United States and throughout the world during the COVID-19 pandemic (e.g., death, violence, destruction, racial/social injustice)—it is crucial to conceptualize ways both trauma-informed and human rights perspectives can help strengthen awareness of and forecast the implications of COVID-19 pandemic student traumatic exposures. This kind of complex critical inquiry is unique to the study of higher education; however, such transdisciplinary perspectives may yield a new vantage point for how higher education institutions view historical, pandemic-era, and contemporary student trauma and help inform systems-level approaches toward addressing and minimizing student (re)traumatization.

Butler and Critelli (2019) amalgamate human rights and trauma-informed lenses to conceptualize a *Trauma-Informed Human Rights* (TIHR) framework which expands the scope of human traumatic stress beyond a medicalized model. TIHR integrates the trauma-informed perspective, human rights principles, and historical/sociopolitical dimensions to contextualize human trauma as products of broader institutionalized social problems (de Jong, 2002). More succinctly, TIHR is a holistic framework encompassing the full spectrum of *traumatic exposures* (TE) and *human rights violations* (HRV). Butler and Critelli (2019) recognize that "TEs and HRVs often occur together and in some cases are simply different descriptions emphasizing different aspects of the same experience" (p. 40). Further, they argue potentially traumatic experiences may look and feel different across individuals, groups and social contexts, may often overlap, and range from: (a) natural disasters (i.e., tsunamis, earthquakes, hurricanes); (b) mental and physical factors (i.e., disease/illness, neuropsychological ailments; physiological injury); (c) incidental events (i.e., motor vehicle accidents, exposure to death, violence, destruction); (d) human behavior (i.e., sexual victimization, child abuse and/or neglect, warfare, terroristic acts); (e) institutional forces (e.g., systemic racism and xenophobia, transnational colonialism, slavery, genocide, institutional negligence and betrayal). Given the aforementioned evidence shared earlier in this chapter, the range of TEs and HRVs may very well include the potentially traumatic repercussions of global health pandemics. Thus, an integrative, multidimensional, multidisciplinary perspective such as TIHR is one possible, trauma-informed approach to frame what mass complex trauma—such as trauma manifested during the COVID-19 pandemic—looks like in tertiary education. Moreover, the TIHR framework's theoretical foundation may help push the study of higher education toward achieving a more nuanced understanding of individual, groups, communities, societies, and generations of complex human suffering and trauma emerging where Butler and Critelli (2019) describe the *nexus* of traumatic exposures and human rights violations.

## TIHR Perspective in University and Higher Education Practice

In a new trauma-laden post-pandemic educational landscape, global tertiary education systems will need to develop trauma-informed criteria that better accommodate emergent student mental health challenges. A TIHR framework can help shift colleges and universities toward a more trauma-informed education system which addresses the full range of student trauma spanning across all TE and HR violations. To be clear, the goal of a TIHR approach is not for school agents or education systems to play a therapist role, rather, it is to help higher education systems deliver an education that understands the implications of trauma on students' ability to learn and grow. Utilizing the TIHR framework to help develop more trauma-informed educational structures and cultures could unveil a promising pathway toward improving learning and increase successful outcomes for a higher proportion of students predicted to live with trauma histories in a post-pandemic society. This next several statements help unpack the *chronic food insecurity* (CFI) social phenomenon, its relationship to the COVID-19 pandemic, and formulate a conceptual example of how tertiary education could envision what a TIHR perspective could look like in post-pandemic university and higher education practice.

Beyond CFI's association with *Adverse Childhood Experiences* or ACEs (i.e., childhood exposure to adverse forms of abuse, neglect, violence, or toxic stress) in trauma research (Chilton, 2015), the negative consequences of CFI have also posed as complex barriers facing students on their pursuit of financial and academic success in adulthood (Broton et al., 2018). Food insecurity is also one of many potentially traumatic adverse risk factors contributing to anxiety, stress, depression, drug addiction, and overall occupational and educational wellness (Chilton et al., 2015; Raskind et al., 2019). Although CFI has impacted the lives of generations of students and families, the impacts of the COVID-19 pandemic exacerbated and made CFI a more pervasive issue for millions of students and families in the United States (Gundersen et al., 2020). Given the increased severity and prevalence of food-insecure students and families in the wake of a devastating pandemic, tertiary education systems might consider innovative, systems-level TIHR-informed policies, procedures, processes, and practices which: (a) reframe CFI as a systemic, potentially traumatic, human rights violation deep-rooted in a legacy of unjust social conditions; (b) disarm institutional structures and forces contributing to student and family CFI in university and higher education settings; (c) reduce the number of students and families enduring CFI; (d) function in ways that do not subject students and families to CFI (re)traumatization; and (e) strengthens student and family overall safety, empowerment, agency, dignity, and mutual trustworthiness long after the COVID-19 pandemic.

A TIHR perspective in higher education practice might begin with university systems' recognition of sociohistorical contexts regarding state-sanctioned food (in)accessibility across generations of diverse student populations, particularly those from the most marginalized backgrounds. Further, higher education systems may also benefit from understanding the adverse impacts of food insecurity on student biopsychosocial and educational well-being, and begin centering the sociohistorical, sociocultural, socioeconomic, dietetic, affective, among other defining characteristics of what food (in)security and (in)accessibility means for a generation of student pandemic survivors and an increasingly more diverse future college student population. Practical approaches toward this distant future may involve consideration of existing trauma-informed CFI research which recommends the development and implementation of systems-level, non-stigmatizing, developmentally appropriate, trauma-informed screening protocol may help identify students and families currently enduring and/ or at risk of enduring CFI among other maladaptive health behaviors and outcomes in the future (Raskind et al., 2019). In other work, Chilton and colleagues (2015) recommend the potential of integrating nutrition and other public assistance programs (e.g., food/cash allotments, access to affordable childcare, behavioral health support, prior exposure to potentially traumatic experiences) that holistically address a spectrum of risk factors which may contribute to student and family CFI.

Although the example provided of what TIHR in higher education practice could look like from a conceptual understanding, empirical research regarding TIHR's broader applicability, efficacy, and implications in university and higher education contexts is vastly underexplored given that the TIHR's framework was recently conceptualized (see Butler & Critelli, 2019). Nonetheless, this chapter highlights TIHR's tremendous potential to ground trauma-informed and human rights discourse and theoretical traditions to transform existing higher education cultures that holistically and systematically addresses and minimizes student (re)traumatization while simultaneously promoting student success. As the pandemic persists during the final writing stage of this chapter, there is significant promise for the future of trauma-informed work in education as trauma-informed education researchers continue to develop COVID-19 sensitive, trauma-informed approaches and practices that human and education service systems can enact as the United States and the world continue to endure prolonged uncertainty, ambiguous loss, anticipatory grief, lasting psychological stress, and other mental wellness challenges (see Carello, 2020; Collin-Vézina et al., 2020; Harper & Neubauer, 2020; Luest et al., 2020; Perel, 2020; Wright, 2020). These COVID-19 sensitive trauma-informed approaches and the TIHR framework have potential to complement one another when designing a trauma-informed higher education system aimed at minimizing acute trauma and human rights-related trauma risk factors in post-pandemic tertiary education. Such integration could potentially yield new iterations of TI perspectives relevant to post-pandemic higher education systems, help reimagine and normalize pre-COVID-19 TI teaching/service models (see Burrows, 2017; Carello & Butler, 2014; Cless & Nelson Goff, 2017; Davidson, 2017; ISTSS, 2016; Nikischer, 2018) and help inform TIHR organization-specific policy, procedures, and practices. Moving forward, this chapter advocates for domestic and global tertiary education to reimagine and internationalize ways COVID-19 sensitive trauma-informed education models and the conceptual TIHR framework considers the spectrum of pervasive traumatic exposures and human rights violations and the historical, contemporary, systemic, and transcendent relationships to student (re)traumatization and vicarious traumatization.

## Conclusion

This chapter does not proclaim a universal trauma-informed approach to remedy all student trauma-related barriers in higher education. Rather, this chapter asserts that operationalizing TIHR perspective(s) may more adequately address an anticipated mental health curve for students and the greater society. It is imperative for higher education systems to consider trauma-informed approaches when facing lingering mental health challenges which are likely to impact academic success of a generation of student pandemic survivors. It is difficult to gauge what the state of mental health will look like for students beyond the COVID-19 era, however, despite such uncertainty, a few things are certain. First, the adverse implications of the COVID-19 pandemic on systems of education will be a topic studied by many across all academic disciplines and professions far beyond the time when the

Coronavirus (COVID-19) is eradicated. Second, the years 2020 and 2021 will be marked in global history as the year that sparked reform and transformation of national economies, politics, healthcare, and human and social relations and what will shift the day-to-day lives of generations of global citizens to come, including tertiary education systems. Lastly, as the world moves forward, so must higher education systems that, too, will be recovering from the remanence of COVID-19 era setbacks. Therefore, it is in the best interest of higher education systems to play a stronger, holistic, truly transformative role in addressing a new social era riddled with unforeseen traumatic exposures, human rights violations, biopsychosocial and other emerging critical issues and challenges—all of which will play a role in how higher education systems enroll, serve, and graduate present-day and future student pandemic survivors.

## References

Adhanom Ghebreyesus, T. (2020). Addressing mental health needs: An integral part of COVID -19 response. *World Psychiatry, 19*(2), 129 –130. http://dx.doi.org/10.1002/wps.20768

Alonso, M., & Sanchez, R. (2020, October 17). California's record-breaking wildfires consume nearly 1 million acres in a month. Retrieved October 23, 2020, from https://www.cnn.com/2020/10/17/us/california-wildfires-saturday/index.html

American Psychiatric Association [APA]. (2013). *Diagnostic and statistical manual of mental disorders* (5th ed.). American Psychiatric Publishing.

Anders, S., Frazier, P., & Shallcross, S. (2012). Prevalence and effects of life event exposure among undergraduate and community college students. *Journal of Counseling Psychology, 59*(3), 449–457. https://doi.org/10.1037/a0027753

APM Research Lab. (2020, October 15). COVID-19 deaths analyzed by race and ethnicity. Retrieved October 16, 2020, from https://www.apmresearchlab.org/covid/deaths-by-race

Bachrach, R., & Read, J. (2012). The role of posttraumatic stress and problem alcohol involvement in university academic performance. *Journal of Clinical Psychology, 68*(7), 843–859.

Bent-Goodley, T. (2019). The necessity of trauma-informed practice in contemporary social work. *Social Work, 64*(1), 5–8. https://doi.org/10.1093/sw/swy056

Bhagat, S., & Kim, D. J. (2020). Higher education amidst COVID-19: Challenges and silver lining. *Information Systems Management,* 1–6. https://doi.org/10.1080/10580530.2020.1824040

Bloom, S. L. (2010). Organizational stress as a barrier to trauma-informed service delivery. In M. Becker & B. A. Levin (Eds.), *Public Health Perspective of Women's Mental Health* (pp. 295–311). Springer.

Broton, K., Weaver, K., & Mai, M. (2018). Hunger in higher education: Experiences and correlates of food insecurity among Wisconsin undergraduates from low-income families. *Social Sciences, 7*(10), 179. https://doi.org/10.3390/socsci7100179

Brown, V. (2018). *Through a trauma lens: Transforming health and behavioral health systems* [eBook edition]. Routledge. https://doi.org/10.4324/9781315626109

Brummer, J., & Thorsborne, M. (2021). *Building a trauma-informed restorative school: Skills and approaches for improving culture and behavior.* Jessica Kingsley Publishers.

Burke, L. (2020, May 14). *Cal State pursuing online fall.* Inside Higher Ed. https://www.insidehighered.com/news/2020/05/14/cal-state-pursuing-online-fall?utm_source=Inside+Higher+Ed

Burrows, L. (2017). *Safeguarding mindfulness in schools and higher education: A holistic and inclusive approach.* Routledge.

Butler, L., & Critelli, F. (2019). Traumatic experience, human rights violations, and their intersection. In L. Butler, F. Critelli, & J. Carello (Eds.), *Trauma and human rights: Integrating approaches to address human suffering* (pp. 11–53). Palgrave Macmillan.

Butler, L. D., Critelli, F. M., & Rinfrette, E. S. (2011). Trauma-informed care and mental health. *Directions in Psychiatry, 31,* 197–210.

Carello, J. (2020, April 6). *Trauma-informed teaching & learning in times of crisis* [Video]. YouTube. https://www.youtube.com/watch?v=AuRxxPK9Hyc&feature=youtu.be

Carello, J., & Butler, L. (2014). Potentially perilous pedagogies: Teaching trauma is not the same as trauma-informed teaching. *Journal of Trauma & Dissociation, 15*(2), 153–168. https://doi.org/10.1080/15299732.2014.867571

Carello, J., & Butler, L. (2015). Practicing what we teach: Trauma-informed educational practice. *Journal of Teaching in Social Work, 35*(3), 262–278. https://doi.org/10.1080/08841233.2015.1030059

Carello, J., Butler, L., & Critelli, F. (2019). Introduction to trauma and human rights: Context and content. In L. Butler, F. Critelli, & J. Carello (Eds.), *Trauma and human rights: Integrating approaches to address human suffering* (pp. 1–10). Palgrave Macmillan.

Cassata, C. (2020, May 19). *The pandemic will cause PTSD for some. What we can do about it.* HealthLine. https://www.healthline.com/health-news/the-pandemic-will-cause-ptsd-for-some-heres-what-we-can-do-about-it

Chappell, B. (2020, April 9). *Fauci says U.S. coronavirus deaths may be 'more like 60,000'; antibody tests on way.* NPR. https://www.npr.org/2020/04/09/830664814/fauci-says-u-s-coronavirus-deaths-may-be-more-like-60-000-antibody-tests-on-way

Childs, J. W. (2020, May 12). *Utah's Wasatch Fault lines are bigger than previously thought, new research says.* The Weather Channel. https://weather.com/news/news/2020-05-12-utah-wasatch-fault-lines-bigger-than-previously-thought

Chilton, M., Knowles, M., Rabinowich, J., & Arnold, K. (2015). The relationship between childhood adversity and food insecurity: 'It's like a bird nesting in your head'. *Public Health Nutrition, 18*(14), 2643–2653. https://doi.org/10.1017/S1368980014003036

Centers for Disease Control and Prevention [CDC]. (2020, July 1). Mental health and coping during COVID-19. Center for Disease Control and Prevention. https://www.cdc.gov/coronavirus/2019-ncov/daily-life-coping/managing-stress-anxiety.html

Cless, J., & Nelson Goff, B. (2017). Teaching trauma: A model for introducing traumatic materials in the classroom. *Advances in Social Work, 18*(1), 25–38. https://doi.org/10.18060/21177

Collin-Vézina, D., Brend, D., & Beeman, I. (2020). When it counts the most: Trauma-informed care and the COVID-19 global pandemic. *Developmental Child Welfare.* https://doi.org/10.1177/2516103220942530

Costa, K. (2020). *Cameras be damned.* LinkedIn. https://www.linkedin.com/pulse/cameras-damned-karen-costa/?fbclid=IwAR1PN8XYVH6HPI5aMHry0Ku8K312ZlhFg_6pG6U-rB1nUrnSNR_SVVixN5c

Davidson, S. (2017). *Trauma-informed practices for postsecondary education: A guide* (Rep.). Education Northwest. https://www.acesconnection.com/g/san-diego-state-university-aces-connection/fileSendAction/fcType/5/fcOid/473769386034974384/fodoid/473769386034974383/Trauma-informed%20Practices%20for%20Post%20Secondary%20Education_A%20Guide_28%20pages_Education%20Northwest.pdf

DeBerard, M., Spielmans, G., & Julka, D. (2004). Predictors of academic achievement and retention among college freshmen: A longitudinal study. *College Student Journal, 38*(1), 66–80.

de Jong, J. (2002). *Trauma, war, and violence: Public mental health in socio-cultural context.* Springer Press.

Dolce, C. (2020a, September 21). *All the records the 2020 hurricane season has broken so far.* The Weather Channel. https://weather.com/storms/hurricane/news/2020-09-21-atlantic-hurricane-season-2020-records

Dolce, C. (2020b, October 19). *August Midwest derecho was costliest to hit the U.S. in 4 decades, NOAA says.* The Weather Channel. https://weather.com/news/weather/news/2020-10-19-midwest-derecho-august-2020-billion-dollar-disaster

The Education Trust. (2020). *COVID-19: Impact on education equity resources & responses.* The Education Trust. https://edtrust.org/covid-19-impact-on-education-equity-resources-responding/?pagenum=3

Fallot, R. D., & Harris, M. (2009). *Creating cultures of trauma-informed care (CCTIC): A self -assessment and planning protocol.* Community Connections. https://www.theannainstitute.org/CCTICSELFASSPP.pdf

Frazier, P., Anders, S., Perera, S., Tomich, P., Tennen, H., Park, C., & Tashiro, T. (2009). Traumatic events among undergraduate students: Prevalence and associated symptoms. *Journal of Counseling Psychology, 56*(3), 450–460. https://doi.org/10.1037/a0016412

Freud, S. (1989). The aetiology of hysteria. In P. Gay (Ed.), *The Freud reader* (pp. 97–110). Norton. (Original work published 1896).

García, E., & Weiss, E. (2020, September 10). COVID-19 and student performance, equity, and U.S. education policy: Lessons from pre-pandemic research to inform relief, recovery, and rebuilding. Economic Policy Institute. https://www.epi.org/publication/the-consequences-of-the-covid-19-pandemic-for-education-performance-and-equity-in-the-united-states-what-can-we-learn-from-pre-pandemic-research-to-inform-relief-recovery-and-rebuilding/

Gillihan, S. (2020, April 07). The COVID-19 crisis may trigger emotions from past trauma. *WebMD.* https://blogs.webmd.com/mental-health/20200407/the-covid19-crisis-may-trigger-emotions-from-past-trauma

Giordano, C. (2020, August 6). *Beirut explosion: At least 135 killed and 300,000 homeless overnight after Lebanon port blast.* MSN. https://www.msn.com/en-ae/news/world/beirut-explosion-at-least-135-killed-and-300-000-homeless-overnight-after-lebanon-port-blast/ar-BB17C8LG?ocid=ob-fb-enae-21

Greene, J. (2020). Treating the collective trauma of COVID-19; Therapy company sees widespread PTSD cases from frontline workers to fearful children. *Crain's Detroit Business, 36*(19), 7.

Griffin, G. (2020). Defining trauma and a trauma-informed COVID-19 response. *Psychological Trauma, 12*(S1), S279–S280. https://doi.org/10.1037/tra0000828

Gruber, J., Prinstein, M., Clark, L., Rottenberg, J., Abramowitz, J., Albano, A., Aldao, A., Borelli, J., Chung, T., Davila, J., Forbes, E., Gee, D., Hall, G., Hallion, L., Hinshaw, S., Hofmann, S., Hollon, S., Joormann, J., Kazdin, A., … Weinstock, L. (2020). Mental health and clinical psychological science in the time of COVID-19: Challenges, opportunities, and a call to action. *The American Psychologist.* https://doi.org/10.1037/amp0000707

Gundersen, C., Hake, M., Dewey, A., & Engelhard, E. (2020). Food insecurity during COVID-19. *Applied Economic Perspectives and Policy.* https://doi.org/10.1002/aepp.13100

Harper, G. W., & Neubauer, L. C. (2020). Teaching during a pandemic: A model for trauma-informed education and administration. *Pedagogy in Health Promotion.* https://doi.org/10.1177/2373379920965596

Harris, M., & Fallot, R. D. (Eds.) (2001). *Using trauma theory to design service systems.* Jossey-Bass.

Hellmann, J. (2020, October 17). *COVID-19 surge prompts warnings that anticipated 'third wave' is now here.* The Hill. https://thehill.com/policy/healthcare/521414-as-coronavirus-cases-surge-in-the-us-experts-warn-the-third-wave-has

Herman, J. (1997). *Trauma and recovery: The aftermath of violence—from domestic abuse to political terror.* Basic Books.

Horesh, D., & Brown, A. D. (2020). Traumatic stress in the age of COVID-19: A call to close critical gaps and adapt to new realities. *Psychological Trauma: Theory, Research, Practice, and Policy, 12*, 331–335. http://dx.doi.org/10.1037/tra0000592

International Network for School Attendance [INSA]. (2020, April 7). *The impact of COVID-19 on school attendance problems: Our response.* INSA. https://www.insa.network/images/pdf/2020-04-07_INSA_RESPONSE_COVID-19.pdf

International Rescue Committee. (2020, January 07). *The top 10 crises the world should be watching in 2020.* International Rescue Committee. https://www.rescue.org/article/top-10-crises-world-should-be-watching-2020

International Society for Trauma and Traumatic Stress [ISTSS]. (2016). *ISTSS best practice parameters.* ISTSS. https://istss.org/ISTSS_Main/media/Documents/ISTSS_Best_Practice_Parameters1.pdf

Johns Hopkins University [JHU]. (2020/2021). *COVID-19 dashboard by the Center for Systems Science and Engineering (CSSE) at Johns Hopkins University (JHU).* JHU. https://gisanddata.maps.arcgis.com/apps/opsdashboard/index.html

Kochhar, R. (2020, July 27). Unemployment rose higher in three months of COVID-19 than it did in two years of the Great Recession. *Pew Research Center.* https://www.pewresearch.org/fact-tank/2020/06/11/unemployment-rose-higher-in-three-months-of-covid-19-than-it-did-in-two-years-of-the-great-recession/

Kola, A. (2020, April 14). How collective is the trauma of COVID-19? The pandemic is traumatic for all, but the burden of suffering may be unequal. *Psychology Today.* https://www.psychologytoday.com/us/blog/hyphenated/202004/how-collective-is-the-trauma-covid-19

Leatherby, L. (2020, October 15). U.S. virus cases climb toward a third peak. *New York Times.* https://www.nytimes.com/interactive/2020/10/15/us/coronavirus-cases-us-surge.html

Lipton, E., Sanger, D. E., Haberman, M., Shear, M. D., Mazzetti, M. Barnes, J. E., (2020, April 11). He could have seen what was coming: Behind Trump's failure on the virus. *New York Times.* https://nytimes.com/2020/04/11/us/politics/coronavirus-trump-response.html

Luest, H., Di Biase, C., & Roberto, M. (2020). *Trauma-informed COVID-19 considerations in virtual human services* (pp. 1–9, Issue brief). Manhattan Strategy Group [MSG]. http://www.manhattanstrategy.com/download/Trauma_Informed_COVID-19_Considerations_in_Virtual_Human_Services.pdf

Miller, E. D. (2006). Can Americans ever feel safe in a post-9/11 and Hurricane Katrina world? In J. Forest (Ed.), *Homeland security: Protecting America's targets* (Vol. 2, pp. 350–364). Praegar.

Miller, E. (2017). Making sense of the brutality of the Holocaust: Critical themes and new perspectives. *The Journal of Psychology, 151*(1), 88–106. https://doi.org/10.1080/00223980.2016.1217191

Miller, E. (2020). The COVID-19 pandemic crisis: The loss and trauma event of our time. *Journal of Loss & Trauma, 25*(6–7), 560–572. https://doi.org/10.1080/15325024.2020.1759217

Moyn, S. (2010). *The last utopia: Human rights in history.* Harvard University Press.

Neria, Y., DiGrande, L., & Adams, B. (2011). Posttraumatic stress disorder following the September 11, 2001, terrorist attacks: A review of the literature among highly exposed populations. *The American Psychologist, 66*(6), 429–446. https://doi.org/10.1037/a0024791

Nikischer, A. (2018). Vicarious trauma inside the academe: Understanding the impact of teaching, researching and writing violence. *Higher Education, 77*(5), 905–916. https://doi.org/10.1007/s10734-018-0308-4

Perel, E. (2020). *What is this feeling? Anticipatory grief and other new pandemic-related emotions.* Esther Perel. https://estherperel.com/blog/anticipatory-grief?utm_campaign=August+2020+Newsletter+%28U3QQLM%29&utm_medium=email&utm_source=April+Workshop&_ke=eyJrbF9lbWFpbCI6ICJydXN0aS5xdWFybGVzQGdtYWlsLmNvbSIsICJrbF9jb21wYW55X2lkIjogIk41dWJEUyJ9

Pleyers, G. (2020). The Pandemic is a battlefield. Social movements in the COVID-19 lockdown. *Journal of Civil Society,* 1–18. https://doi.org/10.1080/17448689.2020.1794398

Raskind, I., Haardörfer, R., & Berg, C. (2019). Food insecurity, psychosocial health and academic performance among college and university students in Georgia, USA. *Public Health Nutrition, 22*(3), 476–485. https://doi.org/10.1017/S1368980018003439

Rodriguez-Diaz, C., Guilamo-Ramos, V., Mena, L., Hall, E., Honermann, B., Crowley, J., Baral, S., Prado, G., Marzan-Rodriguez, M., Beyrer, C., Sullivan, P., & Millett, G. (2020). Risk for COVID-19 infection and death among Latinos in the United States: Examining heterogeneity in transmission dynamics. *Annals of Epidemiology.* https://doi.org/10.1016/j.annepidem.2020.07.007

Smyth, J., Hockemeyer, J., Heron, K., Wonderlich, S., & Pennebaker, J. (2008). Prevalence, type, disclosure, and severity of adverse life events in college students. *Journal of American College Health, 57*(1), 69–76. https://doi.org/10.3200/jach.57.1.69-76

Thebault, R., & Fowers, A. (2020, July 31). Pandemic's weight falls on Hispanics and Native Americans, as deaths pass 150,000. *The Washington Post.* https://www. washingtonpost.com/health/2020/07/31/covid-us-death-toll-150k/?arc404=true

Thebault, R., Tran, A., & Williams, V. (2020, April 07). The coronavirus is infecting and killing black Americans at an alarmingly high rate. *The Washington Post.* https:// www.washingtonpost.com/nation/2020/04/07/coronavirus-is-infecting-killing-black-americans-an-alarmingly-high-rate-post-analysis-shows/?arc404=true

United Nations [UN]. (n.d.). *The foundation of international human rights law.* United Nations. https://www.un.org/en/sections/universal-declaration/foundation-international-human-rights-law/index.html

United Nations Children's Fund [UNICEF]. (2020). *Children at increased risk of harm online during global COVID-19 pandemic.* UNICEF. https://www.unicef. org/ press-releases/children-increased-risk-harm-onlineduring-global-covid-19-pandemic

Van Lancker, W., & Parolin, Z. (2020). COVID-19, school closures, and child poverty: A social crisis in the making. *The Lancet Public Health, 5*(5), e243–e244.

Venet, A. S. (2021). *Equity-centered trauma-informed education.* W.W. Norton & Company.

Whitmire, R. (2020, May 17). Due to COVID-19, thousands of low-income students are deferring and dropping college plans. *The Hill.* https://thehill. com/opinion/education/498231-due-to-covid-19-thousands-of-low-income-students-are-deferring-and-dropping

Wise, A., & Chappell, B. (2020, July 29). More than 150,000 people have died from Coronavirus in the U.S. *NPR.* https://www.npr.org/sections/coronavirus-live-updates/2020/07/29/896491060/more-than-150-000-people-have-died-from-coronavirus-in-the-u-s

World Health Organization [WHO]. (2020a). *Coronavirus disease (COVID-19) - events as they happen.* WHO. https://www.who.int/emergencies/diseases/novel-coronavirus-2019/events-as-they-happen

World Health Organization. (2020b). *COVID-19 transmission and protective measures.* WHO. https://www.who.int/westernpacific/emergencies/covid-19/information/covid-19-new-normal

Wright, A. (2020, April 23). When your past is present: Trauma triggered by COVID-19. https://www.anniewright.com/when-your-past-is-present-trauma-triggered-by-covid-19/

Yatchmenoff, D. K., Sundborg, S. A., & Davis, M. A. (2017). Implementing trauma-informed care: Recommendations on the process. *Special Issue: Trauma-Informed Practice, 18,* 167–185. https://doi.org/10. 18060/21311

Zhai, Y., & Du, X. (2020). Addressing collegiate mental health amid COVID-19 pandemic. *Psychiatry Research, 288,* 113003–. https://doi.org/10.1016/j. psychres.2020.113003

## Bio

**Joshua M. Anzaldúa** is a fourth-year doctoral student in the Department of Educational Leadership and Policy Studies at the University of Texas at San Antonio. His research agenda aims to help transform ways educational systems respond to distinct academic and non-academic needs of society's most underserved and vulnerable student populations. Email: mgw139@ my.utsa.edu

# 13 Global Collaboration for Global Solution in Academia

## Opportunities and Challenges

*Ekaterina Minaeva and Giorgio Marinoni*

### Abstract

The COVID-19 pandemic has created health, economic, and social crises globally and the rapid spread of the virus has hit the higher education sector hard with disrupting traditional academic programs and campus life. As Higher Education Institutions (HEIs) grapple with these unprecedented challenges, they must realize that they can play a major role in finding and implementing solutions given their expertise in different fields and scientific capacity. International collaboration between governments, non-governmental organizations, business and other societal actors can be one of those strategies to consider. As such, this chapter investigates opportunities and challenges for global collaborations between HEIs and various stakeholders. We argue whether the COVID-19 situation will serve as an impetus for triggering innovative and sustainable global collaborations as a global solution.

## Keywords:

global cooperation, sustainability, internationalization of higher education, COVID-19

## Higher Education in the COVID-19 Crisis

In the COVID-19 crisis, higher education can be one of the key pillars for mitigating the negative impact of this pandemic, and its consequences on society, and provide solutions. Due to the global nature of the pandemic, it is only through global collaboration that higher education can be part of the answer, as global challenges can only be met by global solutions. Therefore, the first step in order to understand the role of higher education in finding solutions to the challenges posed by the pandemic is to identify which are the consequences of the pandemic on global cooperation in higher education. Has the pandemic stimulated more cooperation among HEIs and between HEIs and other stakeholders at global level, or has it acted as an inhibitor for global collaboration?

The COVID-19 crisis stimulated a profound internal transformation of the higher education sector in relation to all its three missions: teaching, research, and community engagement. Scholars emphasize that "tertiary education around the globe has been affected in a way not seen since World War II" (Basset, 2020, p. 6). Although the pandemic has affected higher education in all its aspects and brought educators to reconsider the overall functioning of HEIs in order to adapt to the new conditions created by the crisis, the most notable transformation has happened in teaching. The delivery mode of higher education is what has changed the most. The massive move to online teaching provides an opportunity to apply this mode of delivery more widely in the future; the academic profession, the role and competencies needed by professors are changing as well and there will be a growing need of pedagogical training (Rapanta et al., 2020).

In addition to changes in the delivery mode, the significant changes that have occurred in the job market due to the pandemic happened at a global level with repercussions at a local level. Experts emphasize the necessity to reconsider curriculum and put more attention on the skills for the post-pandemic economy, such as digital literacy, data analytics, critical and innovative thinking, digital and coding skills, communication intelligence, and flexibility (McKinsey, 2020).

Internationalization in all its aspects, but especially student mobility and the education export industry associated with it, have transformed significantly, because of the slowdown (or even a complete stop) of all types of mobility, the change in global student flows, the emergence of new products for "education export" (such as hybrid learning and virtual exchange), and the change in admission procedures, etc.

In this chapter, we pursued two goals: (i) to provide a snapshot and comparison of the current situation at HEIs in all regions of the world in teaching, research, and community engagement, and (ii) to understand the effect of the COVID-19 pandemic on global collaboration of HEIs and to discuss how global collaboration can help mitigate the consequences of the COVID-19 pandemic for the higher education sector and for the society.

## Research Method

In order to grasp the scope and state-of-the-art teaching, research, and community engagement of higher education institutions globally during the pandemic, we used pre-existing data collected by the International Association of Universities (IAU) in March/April 2020. The survey was built around four blocks of 25 close-ended questions and 2 open-ended: institutional profile, teaching and learning, research, and social (community) engagement sections. We sent the online questionnaire to all HEIs with contacts present in the IAU database (WHED). WHED lists about 20, 000 HEIs around the world, which is basically the whole population of recognized HEIs in the world. For this survey, it was difficult to calculate a return rate as there was no precise way to know many HEIs received the survey or filled it out. The survey was disseminated through other channels as well, such as websites, social media, and mailing lists of IAU and partners organizations. For this chapter, we used 424 usable responses from different HEIs in 109 countries and two Special Administrative Regions of China (Hong Kong and Macao). The profile of respondents is broad with Faculty members (20%), Heads of institutions (17%), and Heads of international offices (16%) being the most common respondents.

While the original IAU report covers the data, the aim of this chapter is to explore the challenges and opportunities and state-of-the-art of global collaboration based not only on statistical data but also to explore the implications and domains of global collaboration in a more detailed way.

The data collected by IAU has several limitations. First, the data provides global and regional perspectives but the number of replies is too low to allow any national analysis. Moreover, institutions within regions and countries can have very different capacity for mitigating the pandemic risks and consequences, The additional research on the responses to COVID-19 in different types of HEIs (e.g. research-intensive universities or teaching institutions, comprehensive universities or specialized institutions, public or private institutions, institutions based in rural areas or in metropolitan areas, etc.) can contribute to a more comprehensive picture. Second, some regions of the world were underrepresented in the survey (namely, Americas, Asia & Pacific).

In addition to data collected by IAU, we performed an extensive literature review and used data from reports and research papers in order to provide a more comprehensive perspective on current challenges and good practices of global collaboration and to validate the findings of the survey. It is worth mentioning that while there is some data gathered in reports and opinion pieces from researchers and expert organizations, the number of scientific articles on the impact of COVID-19 on global collaboration in higher education is still relatively low.

It is therefore important to keep in mind the intrinsic limitations of this study, which does not pretend to be a comprehensive and detailed analysis supported by data of the current situation of global collaboration in higher education, nor of the effects of the COVID-19 pandemic on it. On the contrary, more research on these topics is definitely needed in the future and this article could be seen as a first attempt to understand it and how COVID-19 could be the trigger for more and better global HE collaboration for global solutions.

Global collaboration in higher education has the potential to solve several major issues. First, in teaching and learning, by educating globally competent citizens, who have an understanding of the global challenges and possess the necessary skills and sensitivity to address them in different national and cultural contexts. Second, collaboration in research and the joint research capacity is a promising instrument for boosting research productivity, avoiding multiplication of efforts and waste of resources, which can lead to faster and more efficient solutions both to the health crisis and to the wider effects of the pandemic on the economy and society. Third, by sharing experiences and good practices of societal engagement globally, HEIs can help in solving local problems by translating and adapting societal solutions already developed in other parts of the world. However, global collaboration does not happen spontaneously and a strategic approach is needed for collaboration in all the three pillars of teaching and learning, as well as research and social engagement. We discuss more in detail global collaboration in these three pillars in the following sections. For each section, we provide a data analysis and a set of possible solutions.

## Results and Implications

### *An Unequal Landscape*

The way the COVID-19 pandemic has affected higher education around the world and the responses of the higher education community varies considerably throughout the world.

Some higher education systems, mostly in developed countries, possessed the capacity to address the challenges posed by the pandemic even in times of financial shortage and overall turbulence. Nevertheless, multiple reports indicate significant gaps in research and teaching capacity, in availability of methodological and organizational support, and in developed managerial practices and crisis mitigation expertise across the globe (International Association of Universities, 2020; Rumbley, 2020; World Bank, 2020a). In addition, different countries and regions of the world have different financial capacity for coping with the crisis, and one of the biggest dangers of the pandemic is that it can further deepen the already existing gap between developed and developing countries, causing further economic lag and instability in particular regions and countries.

This can be seen, for instance, in the results of the IAU global survey on the impact of COVID-19 on higher education (International Association of Universities, 2020), for the question concerning the effects of the pandemic on international partnerships. In Africa, 73% of HEIs reported that the effect of COVID-19 was negative, and that it weakened existing partnerships. This percentage is much higher than in all other regions (47% in Europe, 44% in Asia & Pacific, and 41% in the Americas). On the other hand, Asia & Pacific is the region with the highest percentage of HEIs reporting the creation of new opportunities (44%), a higher percentage than in all other regions and especially when compared to Africa (14%). Also in Europe (34%), and the Americas (32%) the percentage of HEIs reporting the creation of new opportunities is substantial. Unfortunately, the IAU survey data do not allow national analysis and an investigation of a possible relation between these results to the national economic indicators such as GDP, but they already point out the existence of inequality among various regions of the world.

## Teaching and Learning

The effects of the pandemic on teaching and learning at HEIs globally is very inhomogeneous due to high differentiation in the higher education field "with public and private institutions with vastly differing resources and serving different needs'" (Altbach & de Wit, 2020). In addition to high diversification by the type of institutions, HEIs operate in very different national and regional contexts which also results in their different ability to cope with the crisis. However, there are several common challenges in teaching and learning that are seen across the globe.

First and foremost, education experts express concerns about the growing inequality in quality of teaching and access to higher education (World Bank, 2020a). The issue of global inequality in education was one of the biggest challenges even before the pandemic, however, the COVID-19 crisis deepened the gap between different regions of the world and different HEIs. Some institutions had the capacity to switch to teaching online within a few weeks, and others had to stop teaching altogether or provided a very limited set of solutions for distance learning. The IAU COVID-19 report shows that Europe, Americas and—to a lesser extent—Asia and Pacific, tend to be more successful in moving their teaching online than African countries (Table 13.1).

This might be related to different reasons, but most probably the socio-economic background of many countries in Africa plays a major role, especially regarding access to technology which allows online teaching and learning.

Inequality is not only present among regions, but also within each region. For example, in South-East Asia, different countries coped with online teaching resulting in a different degree of success: while Singapore, Brunei, and Malaysia had relatively high internet access rates, other countries (for example, Myanmar and Vietnam) had less than 40% of internet accessibility (Jalli, 2020) which causes difficulties for the university students and leaves the financially vulnerable groups most affected.

*Table 13.1* Impact on Teaching and Learning by Region, International Association of Universities, 2020

|  | Not affected (%) | Classroom teaching replaced by distance teaching and learning (%) | Teaching suspended but the institutions is developing solutions (%) | Teaching cancelled (%) |
|---|---|---|---|---|
| Africa | 3 | 29 | 43 | 24 |
| Americas | 3 | 72 | 22 | 3 |
| Asia & Pacific | 1 | 60 | 36 | 3 |
| Europe | ≈0 | 85 | 12 | 3 |

These results show that the move to online teaching and learning, although overall performed quite rapidly and somehow successfully, is still more an emergency solution with many challenges, rather than a long-term transformation. Inequality in access is the most visible and probably the easiest to measure, but the issue of quality of teaching and learning is equally relevant. Preparation of teachers and students for online teaching and learning is paramount, training for teachers and support for students are needed. As it is the case for access, also quality of online teaching and learning is unequally distributed, with poorly resourced higher education institutions and isolated students from low socio-economic backgrounds being the groups most at risk of a low-quality online education experience, even if access is guaranteed.

*Solutions for Keeping an International Perspective in Teaching*

The COVID-19 pandemic and the travel restrictions caused by it strongly affected all types of academic mobility, both for students and staff with no signs of a quick recovery on the horizon. The relative lack of international students in the classroom and the absence of visiting professors had a negative effect on providing an international perspective in teaching. However, at the same time, this lack stimulated other forms of internationalization at home.

According to the IAU survey cited above, virtual mobility and/or collaborative online learning has lately increased in 60% of the higher education institutions that responded to the survey. Asia & Pacific is the region with the highest percentage, three quarters of HEIs in the region have done so. Even in the other regions, this percentage is higher than (Europe and the Americas) or close to (Africa) 50% of the institutions.

Moreover, in the open questions, respondents mentioned that the enhancement of the digital infrastructure and the shift to more blended and online learning would increase the opportunities for international exposure of both students and academics.

Both virtual mobility and collaborative online learning are useful tools to offer intercultural perspectives to a larger number of students, they can help not only to keep an international perspective on teaching, but also to increase the number of students exposed to international opportunities, making the process of internationalization more inclusive.

In addition to the internationalization agenda, teaching collaboration between different institutions can provide a necessary transfer of expertise, helping institutions to fill in the gaps in their curriculum and methodology and ensuring a more sustainable global education system altogether.

### Research

The effectiveness of global collaboration in research was widely discussed in the literature long before the pandemic. Scholars emphasize that collaborative research results in wider expertise due to the wider availability of data

(Georghiou, 1998), it has a more significant research impact (Adams, 2013), and it addresses and involves a wider audience (Lee & Haupt, 2020; Sun et al., 2013). In addition, "international research collaborations offset domestic skill shortages, even in the most advanced economies, including the USA and UK" (Adams, 2013; Lee & Haupt, 2020), and it proves to be the most effective in the applied fields of research.

During the pandemic crisis, not all institutions were able to sustain their own research capacity at the pre-COVID-19 level. According to the IAU survey (International Association of Universities, 2020), 80% of HEIs reported that research had been affected by the COVID-19 pandemic at their institutions. The most common impact of COVID-19, not surprisingly, has been the cancelling of international travel (at 83% of HEIs) and the cancellation or postponement of scientific conferences (81% of HEIs). However, most importantly, scientific projects appeared to be at risk of not being completed at a bit more than half of HEIs (52%) and at 21% of HEIs scientific research has even completely stopped. From the regional perspective, Africa is the region that has suffered the most when it comes to research activities—they are reported to have been stopped at 43% of HEIs. The same has happened at 31% of HEIs in Asia & Pacific, but only at 12% of HEIs in the Americas and even less in Europe (9%). This regional divide follows the already existing divide in research capacity among regions, underlying the fact that the pandemic aggravates existing inequalities.

There are several areas for which collaboration at global level would be enviable: medical and pharmaceutical research, including on COVID-19, research on post-pandemic socio-economic issues, and sharing data and resources.

*Medical and Pharmaceutical Research, Including on COVID-19*

A pandemic such as COVID-19 affects humanity as a whole, viruses do not discriminate on the basis of nationality and do not care about borders. It is the global health which is in danger when a pandemic appears and no one can feel safe if her/his neighbors are affected. Only if the disease is overcome at a global level will each single individual feel safe.

Therefore, it would seem logical that in times of a pandemic researchers all around the world join forces in search of the most effective way of defeating the disease, being that of a cure or a vaccine. However, short-term, limited, and narrow-thinking, putting self-interest before the common good can lead to completely different decisions which jeopardize international collaboration.

For these reasons, the research related particularly to medical and epidemiological inquiries caused a lot of tension between countries. As Lee and Haupt (2020) emphasized, "geopolitical tensions are rising, particularly around the source of the coronavirus and information sharing," which, together with considerations for national security, is to a large extent explained by the expectations of prestige and financial revenue from the vaccine for COVID-19.

There is a considerable risk of competition between countries and pharmaceutical companies in the race to develop the vaccine and to secure exclusive rights over it. Earlier this year (2020), a claim (later retracted) from the head of a big pharmaceutical company in France that the US government had "the right to the largest pre-order [of COVID-19 vaccines] because it [had] invested in taking the risk" made the headlines in the news (BBC, 2020).

If competition between governments and pharmaceutical companies can somehow be understood, at an institutional level, especially in medical and pharmaceutical research, despite all the pressure that HEIs might be subjected to, cooperation and not competition should be the way forward.

As a Stanford University statement reads: "Important lessons on disease management can be learned from around the world as each nation brings its expertise and experience to bear on addressing this crisis."

> In some countries, testing and case-tracking have been extensive. In others, previous experiences with other highly contagious diseases such as Ebola and SARS have informed their pandemic preparedness and response.... Collaboration with both well-established and emerging international scientific partners alike is critical (A Statement from the Academy project on Challenges for International Scientific Partnerships, 2020).

Fortunately, different COVID-19 related scientific publications in 2020 showed that "despite the tense geopolitical climate, countries increased their proportion of international collaboration and open-access publications during the pandemic" (Lee & Haupt, 2020). However, according to the same study, as can be expected, not all countries are engaged globally, therefore the risk of growing inequality in research is particularly relevant.

Many HEIs were directly involved in epidemiologic research. According to the IAU global report on COVID-19 (International Association of Universities, 2020), 35% of HEIs participating in the survey indicated that they were involved in COVID-19 research and their researchers contributed to public policy for their own countries. In addition to that 65% of HEIs had members of their senior management being consulted by public or government officials in the context of public policies relating to COVID 19. Overall, almost three quarters of HEIs were contributing to public policies either through their institutional leadership or through their researchers. This is a very interesting result pointing out the importance of higher education for society.

In fact, HEIs carry out an important societal mission, by providing support for students and staff in times of crisis, by providing support to their local communities, for instance through medical or nursing schools, by conducting community engagement activities, and, last but not least, by producing and disseminating scientific knowledge, which increases literacy on pandemic-related issues and crisis mitigation practices.

*Sharing Data and Research Expertise*

In addition to collaboration in medical research activities, there are a number of other initiatives launched by HEIs, research centers, and supra-national agencies aimed at sharing up-to-date research data and knowledge. Among organizations which provide comparative data and analytical expertise, we can cite UNESCO, World Bank, etc.

HEIs are showing examples of collaboration also through their associations, for instance the European University Association is active in the European Open Science Cloud (EOSC), a major effort to connect research data services, such as storage, analysis and transfer, across Europe, started by the European Commission to "enhance the possibilities for researchers to find, share and reuse publications, data, and software leading to new insights and innovations, higher research productivity and improved reproducibility in science" (European University Association, 2020).

In addition, the COVID-19 pandemic has contributed to increasing Open Access to scientific publications, as a matter of fact, among the 111 countries combined 3401 COVID-19 articles, three-fourths are open access (Lee & Haupt, 2020).

*Research on Post-Pandemic Issues*

While the immediate responses to the short-term challenges of the COVID-19 crisis, especially health-related, were the first priority for many governments, the experts emphasize the importance of the long-term effects that can significantly transform education, industry, and public policy across the world. Deeply rooted implications for social and economic sectors, production, business, politics, global trade, and many other areas will be seen long after the pandemic is over. According to the World Bank (2020b), "deep recessions associated with the pandemic will likely exacerbate the multi-decade slowdown in economic growth and productivity, the primary drivers of higher living standards and poverty reduction."

Responding to these challenges will require policies and practices based on analytics, data, and research. Comparative and collaborative research on possible consequences and risk mitigation mechanisms will allow the development of more elaborated responses as well as enhance joint efforts on the elimination of long-term challenges of the pandemic crisis. Therefore, economists and social scientists have a major role to play to investigate the long-term impacts of the pandemic and to provide research results, which will help policy makers to come up with appropriate decisions to mitigate these effects.

In addition, collaboration in research can be very helpful for educators. A good example of global collaboration for research on teaching and learning is the COVID-19 Social Science Lab at the University of Ljubljana funded by the Slovenian Research Agency and developed in collaboration with 11 international partners. During the pandemic, the research hub performed comparative research on student learning experiences in 62 countries (Aristovnik et al. 2020), highlighted the government responses and provided data; this can serve as a valuable reference point for policymakers and university professionals from different countries.

## *Community/Societal Engagement*

The COVID-19 pandemic has come with risks and opportunities also for the third mission of HEIs, the one of support and engagement with local communities and society in general. According to the IAU Global Survey, the pandemic had a mixed effect on community engagement, especially at regional level, where an unequal impact can easily be identified, with COVID-19 having mainly increased community engagement in the Americas and in Europe, while it has mainly decreased in Asia & Pacific. In Africa, there are almost two equal groups of HEIs, those for which their community engagement increased during this COVID-19 period and those for which COVID-19 decreased their community engagement.

Among the most common social activities, the participants of the survey named an increase in community actions (52%), science communication initiatives (49%), medical care and support (40%), and student volunteering for people that were affected by the pandemic (28%).

While institutions took part in social engagement mostly at the local level, global collaboration in this domain can also be a great help, especially for the regions that were affected the most by the pandemic. Providing support for medical training is, perhaps, one of the most crucial activities.

Some universities have already taken a proactive stand on these challenges. For example, "Imperial College has established a virtual space for surgeons in the front line of the COVID-19 crisis to work together" (Buitendijk et al., 2020, p. 2). However, these efforts can take a more systemic nature and involve more institutions across the globe, as well as hospitals and medical professional communities.

Another type of social engagement—support of the underprivileged groups—is a very locally based activity. However, sharing practices in service and volunteering can help institutions to develop their own volunteering and community programs, find partners, and raise awareness on both local and global social issues. One example of this kind of collaboration is the European Observatory of Service learning in Higher Education (EOSLHE), created in 2019, with the aim of enhancing and disseminating the knowledge of service-learning in higher education in Europe, as an educational approach that enhances students' civic engagement, brings them closer to different social realities while allowing them to work in a real environment (EOSLHE, 2020).

Finally, a very important issue during the turbulent times of the crisis—pandemic literacy—can benefit significantly from the global collaboration among HEIs. Even before the pandemic, the scholars emphasized that the lack of health literacy is one of the main obstacles to health (National Academies of Sciences, Engineering, and Medicine, 2017). This issue was particularly relevant during the crisis due to what the World Health Organization called "an infodemic" —a large amount of information on COVID-19 and its treatment which is in many cases unverified and even hazardous (Zarocostas, 2020). One of the most helpful COVID-19 trackers was the one initiated at Johns Hopkins University (Coronavirus Resource Center, 2020); it is a successful example of timely and clear scientific data collection and provision and recommendations for the wider public provided by a higher education institution. International partnerships aiming at supporting health literacy and providing verified information across the globe produce transparent comparative data on pandemic-related issues, help avoid unreliable and speculative data, and eventually help the spreading of knowledge by making it available to a wider audience. This will allow people to make safe and rational decisions in their daily life, recognize the level of hazard, and decrease the panic and social anxiety which is reported to be one of the most serious psychological implications of the pandemic (Ayers et al., 2020).

## Conclusion

The data from the IAU Global Survey and other sources confirm that HEIs in different regions of the world coped with the challenges of the pandemic crisis at a different pace. Some of them managed to find sustainable solutions, others were lagging behind and were held back by the lack of resources and risk mitigation capacity.

There are many ways to address the challenges of the pandemic through global collaboration initiatives, and many of these initiatives can be addressed by higher education institutions as hubs of knowledge, expertise, and social awareness. Some practices of global collaboration for crisis mitigation are already shaping up in different parts of the world. However, in order to develop global cooperation in higher education as a systemic phenomenon rather than as a collection of localized more sporadic initiatives, it is crucial to have both the political will and dedicated leadership with a global mindset.

The pandemic is not the first crisis in the history of mankind. Looking back at the challenges of the previous decades and centuries, we can certainly learn from these lessons and see that global issues do have long-lasting effects, they impact every region of the world, and sustainable development even at local level is impossible if the global crisis is not solved with a joint effort at a global level. Higher education has a major role to play in providing solutions to the crisis and holds the great responsibility of doing it, and many universities already have a capacity to do so.

## References

Adams, J. (2013). The fourth age of research. *Nature, 497*, 557–560.

Altbach, P. G., & de Wit, H. (2020). Post pandemic outlook for HE is bleakest for the poorest. *University World News*. https://www.universityworldnews.com/post. php?story=20200402152914362

Aristovnik, A., Keržič, D., Ravšelj, D., Tomaževič, N., & Umek, L. (2020). Impacts of the COVID-19 pandemic on life of higher education students: A global perspective. https://doi.org/10.20944/preprints202008.0246.v2.

Ayers J. W., Leas, E. C., Johnson, D. C. et al. (2020). Internet searches for acute anxiety during the early stages of the COVID-19 pandemic. *JAMA Intern Med.* Published online.

Basset, R. (2020). Sustaining the values of tertiary education during the COVID-19 crisis. *International Higher Education, 101*, 5–7.

BBC. (2020). https://www.bbc.com/news/world-europe-52659510

Buitendijk, S., Ward, H., Shimshon, J., Sam, A. H., Sharma, D., & Harris, M. (2020). COVID-19: An opportunity to rethink global cooperation in higher education and research. *BMJ Glob Health, 5*(7), http://dx.doi.org/10.1136/bmjgh-2020-002790.

Coronavirus Resource Center. (2020). Johns Hopkins University. https://coronavirus.jhu.edu [27.08.2020]

European Observatory of Service learning in Higher Education. (2020). https://www.eoslhe.eu/ [30.08.2020]

European University Association. (2020). https://eua.eu/events/141-eua-webinar-universities-and-the-european-open-science-cloud.html [31.07.2020]

International Association of Universities. (2020). *The impact of COVID-19 on Higher Education around the world.* Paris: International Association of Universities.

Jalli, M. (March 17, 2020). Lack of internet access in Southeast Asia poses challenges for students to study online amid COVID-19 pandemic. *The Conversation.* https://theconversation.com/lack-of-internet-access-in-southeast-asia-poses-challenges-for-students-to-study-online-amid-covid-19-pandemic-133787

Georghiou, L. (1998). Global cooperation in research. *Research Policy, 27*(6), 611–626.

Lee, J., & Haupt, J. (2020). Scientific globalism during a global crisis: Research collaboration and open access publications on COVID-19. *Higher Education, 81*(5), 949–966.

McKinsey (2020, February). Beyond hiring: How companies are reskilling to address talent gaps. https://www.mckinsey.com/business-functions/organization/our-insights/beyond-hiring-how-companies-are-reskilling-to-address-talent-gaps [27.08.2020]

National Academies of Sciences, Engineering, and Medicine. (2017). *Science literacy: Concepts, contexts, and consequences.* Washington, DC: The National Academies Press.

Rapanta, C., Botturi, L., Goodyear, P. et al. (2020). Online university teaching during and after the Covid-19 Crisis: Refocusing teacher presence and learning activity. *Postdigital Science and Education*, https://doi.org/10.1007/s42438-020-00155-y

Rumbley, L. (2020). *Coping with COVID-19: International higher education in Europe.* Amsterdam: European Association for International Education. https://www.eaie.org/our-resources/library/publication/Research-and-trends/Coping-with-COVID-19--International-higher-education-in-Europe.html [21.05.2021]

A Statement from the Academy project on Challenges for International Scientific Partnerships. (2020). American Academy of Arts and Sciences. https://www.amacad.org/international-science-COVID-19

Sun, X., Kaur, J., Milojevic, S., Flammini, A., & Menczer, F. (2013). Social dynamics of science. *Scientific Reports, 3*, 1–6.

World Bank. (2020a). *The COVID-19 pandemic: Shocks to education and policy responses.* Washington, DC: World Bank.

World Bank. (2020b). https://www.worldbank.org/en/news/press-release/ 2020/06/02/countries-can-take-steps-now-to-speed-recovery-from-covid-19 [27.08.2020]

World Health Organisation Europe. (2020). Retrieved 7/31/2020, from https:// www.euro.who.int/en/health-topics/health-emergencies/coronavirus- covid-19/technical-guidance/mental-health-and-covid-19 [30.08.2020]

Zarocostas, J. (2020). How to fight an infodemic. *The Lancet, 395*(10225), 676.

## Bios

**Ekaterina Minaeva** is an analyst at the Institute of Education, Higher School of Economics, Russia. Her research interests include international student experiences, international education policy, and digital internationalization. She is a coordinator of the Observatory of Higher Education Transformations, which aims to analyze the research trends in higher education worldwide and includes the education leading research centers from around the globe. Before her current position, Ekaterina worked at the International Association of Universities and still keeps collaboration with IAU on selected projects. Email: eminaeva@hse.ru

**Giorgio Marinoni** is Manager of Higher Education and Internationalization at the International Association of Universities (IAU). He oversees Internationa- lization as one of the four strategic priorities of the Association. Previously, Giorgio Marinoni worked for UNICA, the Network of Universities from the Capitals of Europe, in the field of internationalization and higher education policy and reform at the European level and beyond. He has been an active member of the Erasmus Student Network (ESN) at local, national, and international level, and served the ESN as its President in 2007–2008. Email: g.marinoni@iau-aiu.net

# 14 Humanizing the Academic Advising Experience with Technology

## An Integrative Review

*Charles Liu and Ravichandran Ammigan*

### Abstract

The use of information and communication technologies, such as Zoom, Canvas, Blackboard, and Microsoft Teams, have dramatically revolutionized student learning and academic advising at the time of the COVID-19 global pandemic. This chapter builds on previous research to explore how humanizing academic advising with technology impacts student interaction, technological engagement, and the online community in a higher education context. We examine how current and future technological advancement can be leveraged to reach and support students and argue that the academic advising process needs to put human beings at the center of the student experience. This integrative review provides a snapshot into the higher education landscape that may garner future conceptualization of advising practices, implementations, and policies.

### Keywords:

academic advising, COVID-19, humanizing, information and communication technologies

### Introduction

In March 2020, the COVID-19 global pandemic brought in-person learning and class instruction to a stop, and many universities had to resort to emergency e-learning protocols by moving courses and academic support services to the virtual environment (Murphy, 2020, p. 492). Almost 91% of students worldwide shifted to online education last year (Abumalloh et al., 2021) as institutions scrambled to enhance their technological infrastructure to continue supporting students and limit disruptions to their academic trajectories (Fried & McDaniel, 2020). As such, the role of academic advisors has been expanded to "first responders" to help alleviate students' stress, anxiety, and urgent situations in the post-era of COVID-19 pandemic

(Flaherty, 2020, p. 6). Now, more than ever, academic advisors are expected to be equipped with equanimity and quality while balancing their added responsibilities.

The historical and philosophical foundation of academic advising involves shaping students' worldview in a post-secondary educational environment (Frost, 2000). As faculty members find themselves more responsibilities in teaching, research, and service, the role of advising emerged as a key feature of the college experience (Hayes, 1841). More recently, Larson et al. (2018) revealed that academic advising cannot simply be defined as a term but rather as a verb "to empower students and campus and community members to successfully navigate academic interactions related to higher education" (p. 86). At its best, academic advising is "a supportive and interactive relationship between students and advisors" (Nutt, 2000, p. 220). It guides students in curriculum review (e.g., degree audit), provides general support to students' academic or personal matters, and refers them to university resources for further consultation.

Prior to the COVID-19 health crisis, there was ongoing technological advancement that supported student learning (Chang & Gomes, 2017; Gray et al., 2010; Leask, 2004). Namely, information and communication technologies (ICTs) have been found to be beneficial in enhancing the quality of learning. Leask (2004) posits that "ICTs can be used effectively to assist students in developing international perspectives, interacting with people from other cultures, and engaging actively in intercultural learning" (p. 350). However, it may be a challenging process for students to adapt to a new digital environment on campus (Gray et al., 2010). The ICT experience for international students, for instance, may be unique in the sense that the sources of online information they relied on while in their home country may be very different from what they have to grapple with on their new campus (Chang & Gomes, 2017). Language barriers and cultural differences may also impact how some students adapt to their online learning environment (Beckstein, 2020; Liu et al., 2010; Peters et al., 2020) and, by analogy, to the academic advising and support services that are offered in a virtual setting. It is therefore vital that online solutions are offered in alignment with adequate and intentional, technical, and administrative support so that students can fully benefit from the learning process (Leask, 2004).

The increase in technological integration in US higher education has inevitably changed in the practices, implementation, and organization of student support services (Amador & Amador, 2014; McDonald, 2008; Schwebel et al., 2012). While these advancements have traditionally been focused on tracking students' academic progress (Gutiérrez et al., 2020; Loucif et al., 2020; Pasquini & Eaton, 2019), in-person advising has been found to be generally more effective than online-advising (Kalamkarian & Karp, 2017; Pasquini & Steele, 2016; Steele, 2016). With the knowledge that students who have commonly needed the most help have been those who have not sought assistance (Museus & Ravello, 2010), this chapter builds on previous research to further investigate and analyze whether academic advising through current and future technological integration can be leveraged to reach and help these students (Feghali et al., 2011; Glass et al., 2021; LaPadula, 2003). It particularly explores, through an integrative literature review, how humanizing academic advising with technology impacts student interaction, technological engagement, and online community, and makes an overarching claim that academic advising needs to focus on putting human beings in the center of the student experience (i.e., technology-to-human-to-human-to-technology), and not solely focus on technological advancement (Castañeda & Selwyn, 2018; Selwyn, 2016).

## Method

Through synthesis and critical evaluation, we reviewed, critiqued, and synthesized existing literature and research from 2005 to 2020 on the topic of academic advising and the use of technology within the higher education context. This process is also referred to as meta-synthesis, which typically includes highly structured search strategies with inclusion and exclusion criteria such as data type, data range, and topic focus (Catalano, 2013). Integrative and systematic reviews, from both quantitative and qualitative research, have been widely used in the field of higher education to evaluate and synthesize literature, methodologies, and relevant findings (Bearman et al., 2012; Iatrellis et al., 2017; Storrie et al., 2010).

### *Inclusion and Exclusion Criteria*

The process of establishing inclusion and exclusion criteria for selecting studies to use in research is a standard practice that helps determine the scope and validity of systematic review results (Meline, 2006). It sets the boundaries for the systematic review and determines the characteristics that must be included or excluded from the study. In this chapter, the inclusion criteria were set from both two- and four-year institution perspectives, peer-reviewed journals, and book chapters published between 2005 and 2020, so as to best address current issues and interventions for undergraduate college students with respect to academic advising approaches with the use of technology. Given the focus on academic advising serving undergraduate students, literature that concentrated on K-12, master, and doctoral students were excluded.

Several education research databases were used, including, Education Source, ERIC, Educational Administration Abstracts, and Oxford Bibliographies Online to narrow down scholarly articles (see Table 14.1). Additional open access, peer-reviewed, academic mega journal databases, such as SAGE, Web of Science, Scopus, and Springer, were selected. Additionally, we accessed NACADA academic advising professional network (NACADA, 2017; Pasquini & Eaton, 2019) to navigate peer-review journals relating to the topic. Lastly, Google Scholar search engine was used with the same keywords to capture relevant research articles that might have been missed in the previous research database. The keywords that included "humanizing advising", "academic advising", "humanizing technology", and

*Table 14.1* Search Engines, Databases, Academic Articles and Books, and Keywords Used to Synthesize Literature

| Database | Library weblink | Date of access | Keywords | Number of articles/books |
|---|---|---|---|---|
| Education Source | https://www.ebsco.com/products/research-databases/education-source | 10/14/2020 (last access) | academic advising in higher education or academic advising or advising or advisor AND online advising | 178 articles |
| ERIC Institute of Education Sciences | https://eric.ed.gov/ | 10/14/2020 (last access) | academic advising in higher education or academic advising or advising or advisor AND online advising | 376 articles (academic journals; books) |
| Educational Administration Abstracts | https://www.ebsco.com/products/research-databases/educational-administration-abstracts | 10/14/2020 (last access) | academic advising in higher education or academic advising or advising or advisor AND online advising | 7 articles |

"COVID-19 remote learning" helped saturate the literature database. To maintain focus on this integrative literature review, each peer-review journal that was germane to this topic was screened in alignment with the inclusion and exclusion criteria.

A thorough examination of empirical studies scholarly journals (see Table 14.2) revealed three main and common themes, namely, humanized advising, technological engagement, and online community. All three themes structurally demonstrate coherence around the interrelated challenge to humanize the use of technology in academic advising settings. We begin by showing how literature engages with each theme, subthemes, and the various issues or arguments surrounding each one. We then demonstrate gaps in the

*Table 14.2* Categorization of Reviewed Interventions Involving Technology for Academic Advising

| *Nature of methodology, study, or report* | *Article(s) involving this form of methodology* |
| --- | --- |
| Book/ Book Review | (Frost, 2000; Glass et al., 2021; Knight, 2008; McDonald, 2008; Nutt, 2000; Pentland, 2010) |
| Case Study | (Amador & Amador, 2014; Neuwirth et al., 2020; Steele, 2016) |
| Conceptual Framework | (Chang & Gomes, 2017) |
| Secondary Data Analysis/ Archival Study | (Gutiérrez et al., 2020; Hayes, 1841; He & Hutson, 2016; Kimble-Hill et al., 2020; Lester & Perini, 2010; Mastrodicasa & Metellus, 2013; Michigan Department of Health and Human Services, 2020) |
| Literature Review | (Cass & Hammond, 2015; Castañeda & Selwyn, 2018; Kimball & Campbell, 2013; Kuhn et al., 2006; McClellan, 2007; Narita, 2018; Shahjahan, 2019; Williamson et al., 2020) |
| Mixed Methods | (Gray et al., 2010; Sobaih et al., 2020) |
| Population Study | (Hu, 2020) |
| Qualitative Study | (Feghali et al., 2011; Gyamera & Burke, 2018; Kalamkarian & Karp, 2017; McGill, 2018; Museus & Ravello, 2010; Pasquini & Eaton, 2019; Zhang, 2016) |
| Quantitative Study | (Ahlquist, 2020; Bickle & Rucker, 2018; Gemmill & Peterson, 2006; Joosten et al., 2013; Junco et al., 2016; Loucif et al., 2020; Pasquini & Steele, 2016; Schwebel et al., 2012; Thompson & Prieto, 2013) |
| Systematic Review | (Catalano, 2013; Chan et al., 2019) |
| Committee/ Conference Report | (NACADA, 2017; Stanoevska-Slabeva & Schmid, 2001) |
| News Report | (Beckstein, 2020; Durrani, 2020; Flaherty, 2020; West, 2020) |

Note: This table does not delineate the specific form of data collection and types of evidence collected in the methodology.

literature by rhetorically asking whether the theme is in congruent with the overarching claim.

## Findings

### *Humanize Advising*

Humanizing is a constant process of being our authentic self. A number of studies have recently conceptualized that humanizing is becoming more conscious in the interconnectedness of visible and invisible nature of being (Narita, 2018; Shahjahan, 2019). In the context of US higher education, humanizing academic advising matters because the academic advising professional competencies value student engagement and purposeful communication through technology (NACADA, 2017). To conceptualize,

Kuhn et al. (2006) describes humanized advising as the advisor helping the advisee by levelling themselves empathically, in which, advising actualizes the advisee's developmental process through authentic caring. In the discussion of academic advising, Kuhn et al. (2006) claimed that the academic advisor must meet the needs of the student as part of the humanizing experience. On one hand, Chan et al. (2019) argued that the concept of academic advising varies across different academic disciplines. On the other, others have maintained that humanizing academic advising signifies its multifaceted role within the institution that includes relationship practice (Amador & Amador, 2014; Junco et al., 2016; Mastrodicasa & Metellus, 2013), student outreach (Pasquini & Steele, 2016; Schwebel et al., 2012), and student support (Gutiérrez et al., 2020; McDonald, 2008; Steele, 2016). Needless to say, most researchers have a shared understanding that the role of academic advisors is vital to support college students (Chan et al., 2019; Kuhn et al., 2006). In essence, the core philosophy of humanizing academic advising is centering on student caring (NACADA, 2017). Our own view is that students will relate to and respect advisors who are genuine and caring.

Hence, academic advisors need to make a conscious effort to use technology as part of the humanizing experience for all students based on their capacity. The theme of humanized advising leads to the second theme that academic advisors need to be purposeful while engaging with students through technology.

## Technological Engagement

To (re)imagine what technology is, in its purest form, we propose that technology is a way for humans to communicate or a bridge between the human-to-technology-to-human interaction. We observed that the consumption of online technology has become a top priority for many US higher education institutions. However, as briefly mentioned in the previous section, excessive technology usage causes disruption and negative impact to student support by inducing stress to students (Gemmill & Peterson, 2006). Using a 71-item survey to 299 undergraduate students, Gemmill and Peterson (2006) found that excessive attachment to technology creates high stress among college students. Consequently, Steele (2016) asserts that academic advisors play a pivotal part in helping students to balance their experiences and relieve their stress through the intentional use of technology. Both studies shed insight that advisors play an important role to help students find balance and intervene with care.

### General Challenges

We are currently in an unprecedented situation with COVID-19 and in this new crisis, limited research exists on the pandemic's impact on higher education. However, there is a palpable understanding that it has awakened higher education institutions to the critical role academic advisors play in sustaining student engagement and learning through technology (Hu, 2020; Loucif et al., 2020). This pandemic gives new life to the conversation surrounding the discussion of in-person advising and that of remote or distant advising that utilizes technology.

Kalamkarian and Karp (2017) and Neuwirth et al. (2020) suggest that significant challenges accompany the use of technology in that the subtlety of humanistic connection, such as the ability to read body language, listen to speaker's tone and voice, and watch for minutiae facial reactions, may be lost. We argue that this is especially visible during the COVID-19 pandemic and with online classes, students will become more used to technology than human interaction. Additionally, students have had to make the shift abruptly and may not welcome this sudden technological pivot. Kalamkarian and Karp (2017) find, using focus group interview data from 69 students at six colleges, that students "preferred in-person interaction with an advisor" (p. 14). Furthermore, students "prefer in-person support for more complex undertakings, such as planning courses and refining their academic and career goals" (Kalamkarian & Karp, 2017). The essence of Kalamkarian and Karp's (2017) argument is that academic advising in a virtual space loses the humanistic people-to-people connection and that technology may not necessarily create a supportive environment for students.

On the other hand, Amador and Amador (2014) take on the critiques offered by Kalamkarian and Karp to envision how academic advisors befriend students by humanizing whole personhood into the technological virtual space. They argue that focusing on communicating clear expectations increases student's help-seeking behavior, deepens their college experiences, and strengthens the student-advisor relationship. Having a clear technological boundary between the student-to-advisor spheres will advance their relationship and trust to account for student's academic progression and therefore be aligned with the humanized approach.

In the end, we agree with researchers' conclusions that to actualize academic advisor's roles to serve in the best interests of students, technology must be viewed and used as a bridge and as a point of connection (Amador & Amador, 2014; Hu, 2020; Kalamkarian & Karp, 2017; Loucif et al., 2020; Neuwirth et al., 2020).

Indeed, Mastrodicasa and Metellus (2013) confirmed in their secondary data analysis that "[m]ost college students come to campus with multiple technology devices, using their devices for reasons both academic and personal" (p. 21). Both Lester and Perini (2010) and Mastrodicasa and Metellus (2013) support each other's claim that the 21st and the 22nd generation of college students have the technological capacity (i.e. smart devices) to be engaged in virtual spaces.

However, literature also shows that not all students are alike, and engagement looks different for different people and needs (Museus & Ravello, 2010; Thompson & Prieto, 2013). By employing a qualitative study, Museus and Ravello (2010) reified that purposeful engagement is a multifaceted approach in serving the student's need because "problems are rarely isolated to one aspect of their college experience" (p.54). The essence of Museus and Ravello's (2010) argument is that when students—especially Students of color—have an academic strain or difficulty in their coursework, their situation is often compound with financial strains, accessibility to technology strains, and much more. Thompson and Prieto (2013) also affirmed, after surveying 121 college students from a historically Black university located in the South, that students who have financial strains have strong correlation to technological strain and that in turn resulted in a lack of motivation to engage with academic advisors. To be explicit, literature suggests that purposeful engagement is not one size fits all, in which academic advisors are not all-knowing how technological engagement looks like for all students and their capacity to engage. Thus, for advisors to engage students with a clear purpose, higher education institutions also need to make conscious effort to meet the needs of the student when students do not have the technology capacity. Especially in the ongoing COVID-19 pandemic, research clearly reveals the significant minoritized students do not have the necessary technology to remote learning (Kimble-Hill et al., 2020).

*Positive Outcomes*

Research shows that the virtual technological connection enhances academic advisors to communicate with students (Junco et al., 2016). Junco et al. (2016) also found that alternative forms of communication such as email, texting, and social media have a positive impact on student's college experience.

In the discussion of positive impact in the use of technology, one controversial issue has been purposeful technological engagement. Literature claims that the advancement of technology accelerated the accuracy of students' academic performance data on demand (Feghali et al., 2011; Loucif et al., 2020; Williamson et al., 2020) and advisors' capacity to provide just-in-time student outreach (Amador & Amador, 2014; Thompson & Prieto, 2013; Zhang, 2016). That said, technology can also increase the accessibility for students and advisors and enhance relationship-building and individualized student learning (Cass & Hammond, 2015; Hu, 2020; Zhang, 2016). Lester and Perini (2010) even maintain that higher education institutions first need a paradigm shift to see what engagement should look like for college students because they grew up socialized, plugged in with technology and continuously connected in virtual spaces. Through a quantitative study, Ahlquist (2020) further complicates that technological purposeful engagement is for higher education institutions to exert efforts to engage with students because doing so establishes a meaningful sense of belonging to the university. Our view is that technology should be a tool to enhance the advising experience for students. Put plainly, technology is one bridge to the advisor-student advising experience and relationship-building.

## Online Community

When it comes to the topic of online community, most scholars agree that it is a form of support. Where this agreement usually varies, however, is on the question of typology. Whereas some attention is on technological online platforms (Stanoevska-Slabeva & Schmid, 2001), others maintain that social interactions and interpersonal relationships of human beings should be the center of discussions (Bickle & Rucker, 2018). While some emphasis should be put on the technicalities of online platforms, we should be careful not to overlook the affective qualities (e.g., a shared sense of inter-being) of human beings (Shahjahan, 2019). Ultimately, what is at stake is whether online communities build connection and support mechanisms for students.

Although Sobaih et al. (2020) found that students use technology to support each other by "building an online community and connection" (p. 14), McClellan (2007) maintains that an online community is to "love and the capacity to grow and develop as human beings are nurtured through community" (p. 43). Accordingly, the academic advising profession values that a strong community will "[c]reate rapport and build academic advising relationships" with students (NACADA, 2017). Nevertheless, the COVID-19 pandemic has created uncertainties and changes in student needs—lack of access to technology and other digital devices—that academic advisors continue to find alternative academic advising modalities w hen there are issues of technological shortcomings (Hu, 2020). Finding alternate modalities matters because advisors may not always have the capacity to ensure that all students' needs are met. Of course, many will probably disagree with the assertion of limited advisor capacity because academic advising may look differently in various academic disciplines at different institutions.

One implication of capacity building via online community, as literature emphasizes, is that technology has the ability to scaffold in a generalized group academic advising setting and to sustain a community environment of support and caring (Amador & Amador, 2014; Cass & Hammond, 2015; Zhang, 2016). For example, Cass and Hammond (2015) found that virtual community among student veterans "allow students to very quickly find the right community member who holds the expertise they need, when they need it … [similar mindset as] soldiers to go to war as a team; there are no singular acts in the military" (Cass & Hammond, 2015). Zhang (2016) also found among the international students instances in which international students feel supported when advisors serve as a mentor "via virtual communities that provide an online social space for individuals to communicate and interact with each other" (p. 167). Overall, literature claims that having a strong online community increases the support with one another (Sobaih et al., 2020). The theme of technological engagement with students leads to opportunities to integrate technology in a humanized way.

## Opportunities for Integrating Humanized Technology in Academic Advising

The COVID-19 pandemic highlights some important gaps in research on humanizing technology usage in advising. We assert that technology was largely utilized as a supplemental tool (i.e., email follow up after the advising session) and has moved in the social distancing reality to be the main mode of advising (i.e., real-time virtual advising via Zoom). There is also an opportunity in this pandemic season to be thoughtful about the deep stress and exhaustion that technology might impose post COVID-19 era. Second, no literature thus far provides deep insights on whether students' deep stress and exhaustion with technology in the post-COVID-19 era requires us to seek alternative advising methods—micro check ins or flip advising where the student takes the lead in the advising session to meet the specific student needs—to shorten the traditionally long advising session. Especially in the time of COVID-19, students may be overly exhausted with technology (i.e., Zoom fatigue) compounded with familial obligations (e.g., caring for the elderly or purchasing food) to merit additional exploration.

Thirdly and most importantly, students who commonly need the most help are those who do not seek help (Museus & Ravello, 2010), which merits further investigation and analysis whether academic advising through technological integration helps in closing (or widening) the graduation gap for certain student social identities or demographics (Feghali et al., 2011). Data shows that not all students have the technological capacity to be connected to the internet during the COVID-19 pandemic (Neuwirth et al., 2020), let alone engage with academic advisors through technology. So far, few scholars have contended to "equalized technology-mediated advising structure" (Hu, 2020) and "create a more equitable environment" (Kimble-Hill et al., 2020). We contend that there is a significant gap and data in the existing literature showing student's technological ability to be constantly connected to the internet. Consequently, in the post-COVID-19 era, higher education should think of new ways to engage and to help students through the lens of technological equity.

Lastly, literature urges that there are a myriad factors to ensure the safety and security of online communities between academic advisors and students. Lester and Perini (2010) cautioned of privacy concerns and risk of "transmitting personal information in an online environment" (p. 73). In a quantitative study, Joosten et al. (2013) warned that the use of online community platforms such as Facebook or Twitter must protect student's education records and should neither be publicly shared without the informed written consent of the individual student. While we believe in security assurance, we also believe online communities must also comply with the Family Educational Rights and Privacy Act (FERPA) (20 U.S.C. § 1232g; 34 CFR Part 99). Joosten et al. (2013) further argues that advisors can find ways to build a trusted community support with students within the legal boundaries so that public information can be shared timely and effectively. For example, using the online community as part of the general university announcements or calendar of events. Linking theory with intentional practice, Kimball and Campbell (2013) indicate that community-building is a complex and challenging process,  so academic advisors must critically reflect on the fact that students' needs are different, student demographics are different, and safely and securely support students should be individualized and highly cared for because situation is unique for different people.

In the same vein, research also shows that integrating humanized technology in humanized advising must be deployed strategically and timely (Amador & Amador, 2014; Cass & Hammond, 2015; McClellan, 2007; Zhang, 2016). For instance, academic advisors need to reflect student engagement critically and strategically in the lens of the student (Joosten et al., 2013; Kimball & Campbell, 2013; Lester & Perini, 2010). By connecting from the lens of a student to advisors, many scholars argue that technology such as learning analytics will both advance and accelerate the accuracy of student data collection in a secured fashion (Gutiérrez et al., 2020; Loucif et al., 2020; Pasquini & Eaton, 2019) and enhance the capacity of academic advising to reach students in virtual community spaces (Amador & Amador, 2014). We agree that learning analytics will assist academic advisors to see both micro and macro patterns of students' academic performance because my academic advising experience confirms it. We would caveat that community members need to respect community norms and not disclose private information without consent. Likewise, technology will significantly increase institutional ability to record online videos and modules for students to review the basic academic information (i.e., course selection) and will also develop a deeper philosophical discussion (i.e., major exploration) through group advising (He & Hutson, 2016).

## Discussion

Findings from this systematic review offer a few considerations to higher education educators, administrators, and policy makers for incorporating new institutional strategies, practices, and interventions that support the academic advising experience for students. These considerations are not meant to be generalizable. Rather, they introduce a basis for further discussion and study.

Putting theory into practice, higher education institutions can explore whether there are sufficient technological resources for academic advisors and all students. Second, institutions may need to elicit students' voices that are underserved and underrepresented to learn how to best care for their academic advising needs with technology support. Namely, when decisions are made fast, that is when institutions are not checking out biases and including the people in the conversations who need to be included. For example, many universities that went online may not understand fully about the needs of low-income students who did not have access to technology/internet or Black students who would soon experience significantly higher positivity rates of COVID-19 (Michigan Department of Health and Human Services, 2020). In other words, to humanize the academic advising experience the human or student must be put in the center of advising as well as institutional decision-making. For the students who can be technologically connected, how will higher education institutions ensure students' voices and messages are heard or seen in an equitable way?

## *Recommendations for Practice*

- Examine synchronous and asynchronous class schedules to ensure that students remain engaged with the university (i.e. providing a peer-mentoring program for students to build relationships and connection to campus).
- Adopt a systematic assessment of campus climate for diversity, equity, and inclusion to understand how students are feeling during remote learning with technology such as social isolation and classroom experience.
- Evaluate student learning outcomes in relation with institutional retention, persistence, and graduation rate to allow for meaningful opportunities for students to reflect on their experiences (inside and outside the classroom).
- Introduce a multifaceted approach to target different student populations (demographics, class level, SES, etc.) for understanding different degree of access to technology for institutional investment.
- Examine instructional processes to maintain high quality teaching and learning and provide short-, mid-, and long-view to improve course instructions that can be executed through multiple modalities concurrently and sustainably.
- Ensure institutional investment in technological resources (i.e., laptops, webcams, headsets) to achieve educational equity for student learning. The effective delivery of academic advising services online may require additional funding for enhanced technology and software licensing, therefore strategic investment or reinvestment in resources and programs to support students, especially at a time of crisis, must be prioritized by institutions.
- Provide space for intercultural communication and dialogues to promote a deeper understanding of challenges in remote learning environment, and shed light on reducing implicit bias, microaggression, marginalization, discrimination, and educational and technological inequities.
- Offer accessible courses in technology literacy or incentivize courses related to technological learning as part of a student's graduation requirement. For example, all students must be expected to obtain technology literacy before graduation.

## *Future Research*

This integrative review widens the discussion on humanizing academic advising with technology in higher education and offers a baseline for future research on the topic. First, academic advising in different disciplines within different institutions in the context of various countries could be considered. Second, future research may delineate student demographics within the context of student persistence and retention rate. More specifically, whether minoritized students remain stagnant or become less persistent and retentive because of the institutions' lack of support in providing sufficient technology capacity and resources. Third, literature also shows due to pre- and post-COVID-19 challenges, academic advisors are already shouldering a heavy load to find alternative advising modalities from in-person to on-line to ensure that students are effectively continuously to engage in learning (Hu, 2020; Kimball & Campbell, 2013; Thompson & Prieto, 2013). The COVID-19 pandemic is expected to change students' paradigms about advising as new students will only be accustomed to online advising. Hence, future research should explore whether overuse of technology causes academic advisors' overwhelming workload and stress, and whether this may lead to negative affect to the advising experience for students in the technological era. Fourth, researchers should further explore the institutional value in the work of academic advising as there is a significant disconnect in the literature between advisors' overextensive labor and institutional leaders' cost-cutting fait accompli strategies amid COVID-19. Lastly, and perhaps most importantly, as our student population are growing more diverse, fluid, and transient, we may need to see beyond western advising philosophies to best meet the needs of our student community. To be specific, we propose that future research must look beyond the western national container and expand into the Eastern and Indigenous philosophies that interconnect the visibility of technology with the invisibility of inter-being (Shahjahan, 2019). In other words, the meaning and utility of technology may contextualize differently in different parts of the world, so it behooves us to acknowledge where our epistemology comes from in relation to the rest of the world.

## Conclusion

In this chapter, we demonstrate how humanizing academic advising with technology impacts student interaction, engagement, and community-building with academic advisors. The overarching claim suggests that academic advising needs to focus on putting the human in the center of the student experience (i.e., technology-to-human-to-human-to-technology), and not technology (Castañeda & Selwyn, 2018; Selwyn, 2016). It identified humanized advising, student engagement, and community-building as three overarching themes emerged in this integrative literature review. It further discussed various issues or arguments in each theme, strengths, and weaknesses in the literature, and gaps for future research.

While literature was thoroughly examined, it was somewhat surprising that no literature interrogated the effects of minoritized students in academic advising due to the lack of capacity and access to technology. Outside of the higher education journals, there is evidence that minoritized students (i.e., Students of color) have the greatest need for online engagement and the largest disproportion accessing technology (Kimble-Hill et al., 2020). Kimble-Hill et al. (2020) concluded that the disparate impact of technological inaccessibility will be "the loss of income, skill development, and professional networking opportunities gained during a summer internship could irreparably disrupt and even permanently derail educational journeys for thousands of marginalized students" (p. 3393). Sadly, racial and ethnic minority (non-White) students are often overlooked and marginalized (Museus & Ravello, 2010). Worse, there is neither data nor mentioned for the Native Indigenous students in the literature relating to their academic advising experiences with technology.

We argue that humanizing academic advising with technology is even more important to less privileged students because humanizing is closely tied to the important issues of diversity, equity, and inclusion that higher education institutions embrace in an increasingly globalized and technologized world. So, in full circle we ask: how can we design technology that humanizes academic advising, and how can we measure the humanizing academic advising experience for *all* students?

## References

Abumalloh, R. A., Alghamdi, A. I., Azzam, N., & Abdulraheem, A. R. Al. (2021). Management of academic advising in higher educational institutions during COVID-19 pandemic. *Management Science Letters, 11*(5), 1659–1666. https://doi.org/10.5267/j.msl.2020.12.006

Ahlquist, J. (2020). *Digital leadership in higher education: Purposeful social media in a connected world.* Stylus Publishing.

Amador, P., & Amador, J. (2014). Academic advising via Facebook: Examining student help seeking. *The Internet and Higher Education, 21,* 9–16. https://doi.org/10.1016/j.iheduc.2013.10.003

Bearman, M., Smith, C. D., Carbone, A., Slade, S., Baik, C., Hughes-Warrington, M., & Neumann, D. L. (2012). Systematic review methodology in higher education. *Higher Education Research & Development, 31*(5), 625–640. https://doi.org/10.1080/07294360.2012.702735.

Beckstein, A. (2020). How are international students coping with the Covid-19 pandemic? Retrieved January 23, 2021, from Times Higher Education website: https://www.timeshighereducation.com/student/blogs/how-are-international-students-coping-covid-19-pandemic

Bickle, M. C., & Rucker, R. (2018). Student-to-student interaction humanizing the online classroom using technology and group assignments. *Quarterly Review of Distance Education, 19*(803), 1–11.

Cass, D., & Hammond, S. (2015). Bridging the gap: Technology and veteran academic success. *Journal of Asynchronous Learning Network, 19*(1), 83–91. https://doi.org/10.24059/olj.v19i1.517

Castañeda, L., & Selwyn, N. (2018). More than tools? Making sense of the ongoing digitizations of higher education. *International Journal of Educational Technology in Higher Education, 15*(1), 22. https://doi.org/10.1186/s41239-018-0109-y

Catalano, A. (2013). Patterns of graduate students' information seeking behavior: A meta-synthesis of the literature. *Journal of Documentation, 69*(2), 243–274. https://doi.org/10.1108/00220411311300066

Chan, Z. C. Y., Chan, H. Y., Chow, H. C. J., Choy, S. N., Ng, K. Y., Wong, K. Y., & Yu, P. K. (2019). Academic advising in undergraduate education: A systematic review. *Nurse Education Today, 75*(October 2018), 58–74. https://doi.org/10.1016/j.nedt.2019.01.009

Chang, S., & Gomes, C. (2017). Digital journeys: A perspective on understanding the digital experiences of international students. *Journal of International Students, 7*(2). https://doi.org/10.32674/jis.v7i2.385

Durrani, A. (2020). Ways U.S. colleges support international students during Coronavirus. Retrieved January 21, 2021, from U.S. News & World Report website: https://www.usnews.com/education/best-colleges/articles/ways-us-colleges-support-international-students-during-coronavirus

Feghali, T., Zbib, I., Hallal, S., Feghali, T., Zbib, I., & Hallal, S. (2011). A Web-based decision support tool for academic advising. *Journal of Educational Technology & Society, 14*(1), 82–94.

Flaherty, C. (2020). Study: The ABCs of advising are listen, respect, care. *Insider Higher Ed,* 1–7. https://www.insidehighered.com/news/2020/12/14/study-abcs-advising-are-listen-respect-care

Fried, M., & McDaniel, C. (2020, July 30). Academic advising technologies in the era of COVID-19 and beyond. Retrieved April 28, 2021, from Ithaka S+R website: https://sr.ithaka.org/blog/academic-advising-technologies-in-the-era-of-covid-19-and-beyond/

Frost, S. H. (2000). Historical and philosophical foundations for academic advising. In V. N. Gordon & W. R. Habley (Eds.), *Academic Advising: A comprehensive handbook* (1st ed., pp. 3–17). San Francisco: Jossey-Bass Inc.

Gemmill, E. L., & Peterson, M. (2006). Technology use among college students: Implications for student affairs professionals. *Journal of Student Affairs Research and Practice, 43*(2). https://doi.org/10.2202/1949-6605.1640

Glass, C. R., Godwin, K. A., & Helms, R. M. (2021). *Toward greater inclusion and Success: A new compact for international students.* Washington, DC.

Gray, K., Chang, S., & Kennedy, G. (2010). Use of social web technologies by international and domestic undergraduate students: Implications for internationalising learning and teaching in Australian universities. *Technology, Pedagogy and Education, 19*(1), 31–46. https://doi.org/10.1080/14759390903579208

Gutiérrez, F., Seipp, K., Ochoa, X., Chiluiza, K., De Laet, T., & Verbert, K. (2020). LADA: A learning analytics dashboard for academic advising. *Computers in Human Behavior, 107*(December 2018), 105826. https://doi.org/10.1016/j.chb.2018.12.004

Gyamera, G. O., & Burke, P. J. (2018). Neoliberalism and curriculum in higher education: a post-colonial analyses. *Teaching in Higher Education, 23*(4), 450–467. https://doi.org/10.1080/13562517.2017.1414782

Hayes, R. B. (1841). At Kenyon college, 1840–1841--Junior year. In *In Diary and letters of Rutherford B. Hayes* (Vol. I; pp. 53–54). https://resources.ohiohistory.org/hayes/browse/chapteriv.html

He, Y., & Hutson, B. (2016). Appreciative assessment in academic advising. *The Review of Higher Education, 39*(2), 213–240. https://doi.org/10.1353/rhe.2016.0003

Hu, X. (2020). Building an equalized technology-mediated advising structure: Academic advising at community colleges in the post-COVID-19 era. *Community College Journal of Research and Practice, 44*(10–12), 914–920. https://doi.org/10.1080/10668926.2020.1798304

Iatrellis, O., Kameas, A., & Fitsilis, P. (2017). Academic advising systems: A systematic literature review of empirical evidence. *Education Sciences.*https://doi.org/10.3390/educsci7040090

Joosten, T., Pasquini, L. A., & Harness, L. (2013). Guiding social media at our institutions. *Planning for Higher Education Journal, 41*(2), 1–11.

Junco, R., Mastrodicasa, J. M., Aguiar, A. V., Longnecker, E. M., & Rokkum, J. N. (2016). Impact of technology-mediated communication on student evaluations of advising. *NACADA Journal, 36*(2), 54–66. https://doi.org/10.12930/NACADA-16-014

Kalamkarian, H. S., & Karp, M. M. (2017). Student attitudes toward technology-mediated advising systems. *Online Learning Journal, 21*(2). https://doi.org/10.24059/olj.v21i2.918

Kimball, E., & Campbell, S. M. (2013). Advising strategies to support student learning success. In J. K. Drake, P. Jordan, & and M. A. Miller (Eds.), *Academic advising approaches: Strategies that teach students to make the most of college* (1st ed., pp. 3–16). John Wiley & Sons, Incorporated.

Kimble-Hill, A. C., Rivera-Figueroa, A., Chan, B. C., Lawal, W. A., Gonzalez, S., Adams, M. R., … Fiore-Walker, B. (2020). Insights gained into marginalized students access challenges during the COVID-19 academic response. *Journal of Chemical Education, 97*(9), 3391–3395. https://doi.org/10.1021/acs.jchemed.0c00774

Knight, J. (2008). *Higher education in turmoil: The changing world of internationalization.* Sense Publishers.

Kuhn, T., Gordon, V. N., & Webber, J. (2006). The advising and counseling continuum: Triggers for referral. *NACADA Journal, 26*(1), 24–31. https://doi.org/10.12930/0271-9517-26.1.24

LaPadula, M. (2003). A comprehensive look at online student support services for distance learners. *International Journal of Phytoremediation, 21*(1). https://doi.org/10.1207/S15389286AJDE1702_4

Larson, J., Johnson, A., Aiken-Wisniewski, S. A., & Barkemeyer, J. (2018). What is academic advising? An application of analytic induction. *NACADA Journal, 38*(2), 81–93. https://doi.org/10.12930/0271-9517-38.2.81

Leask, B. (2004). Internationalisation outcomes for all students using Information and Communication Technologies (ICTs). *Journal of Studies in International Education, 8*(4). https://doi.org/10.1177/1028315303261778

Lester, J., & Perini, M. (2010). Potential of social networking sites for distance education student engagement. *New Directions for Community Colleges, 2010*(150), 67–77. https://doi.org/10.1002/cc.406

Liu, X., Liu, S., Lee, S. H., & Magjuka, R. J. (2010). Cultural differences in online learning: International student perceptions. *Educational Technology and Society, 13*(3).

Loucif, S., Gassoumi, L., & Negreiros, J. (2020). Considering students' abilities in the academic advising process. *Education Sciences, 10*(9), 254. https://doi.org/10.3390/educsci10090254

Mastrodicasa, J., & Metellus, P. (2013). The impact of social media on college students. *Journal of College and Character, 14*(1), 21–30. https://doi.org/10.1515/jcc-2013-0004

McClellan, J. L. (2007). The advisor as servant: The theoretical and philosophical relevance of servant leadership to academic advising. *NACADA Journal, 27*(2), 41–49. https://doi.org/10.12930/0271-9517-27.2.41

McDonald, S. J. (2008). Review of "connecting to the net.generation: What higher education professionals need to know about today's students." *Journal of Student Affairs Research and Practice, 45*(2), 315–319. https://doi.org/10.2202/1949-6605.1953

McGill, C. M. (2018). Leaders' perceptions of the professionalization of academic advising: A phenomenography. *NACADA Journal, 38*(1), 88–102. https://doi.org/10.12930/NACADA-17-041

Meline, T. (2006). Selecting studies for systematic review: Inclusion and exclusion criteria. *Contemporary Issues in Communication Science and Disorders, 33*(Spring). https://doi.org/10.1044/cicsd_33_s_21

Michigan Department of Health and Human Services. (2020). The State of Michigan COVID-19 Dashboard.

Murphy, M. P. A. (2020). COVID-19 and emergency eLearning: Consequences of the securitization of higher education for post-pandemic pedagogy. *Contemporary Security Policy, 41*(3). https://doi.org/10.1080/13523260.2020.1761749

Museus, S. D., & Ravello, J. N. (2010). Characteristics of academic advising that contribute to racial and ethnic minority student success at predominantly white institutions. *NACADA Journal, 30*(1), 47–58. https://doi.org/10.12930/0271-9517-30.1.47

NACADA. (2017). NACADA academic advising core competencies model.

Narita, F. M. (2018). Informal learning practices in distance music teacher education: Technology (De)humanizing interactions. *Action, Criticism, and Theory for Music Education, 17*(3), 57–78. https://doi.org/10.22176/act17.3.57

Neuwirth, L. S., Jović, S., & Mukherji, B. R. (2020). Reimagining higher education during and post-COVID-19: Challenges and opportunities. *Journal of Adult and Continuing Education*, (2059), 147797142094773. https://doi.org/10.1177/1477971420947738

Nutt, C. L. (2000). One-to-one advising. In V. N. Gordon & W. R. Habley (Eds.), *Academic Advising: A comprehensive handbook* (1st ed., pp. 220–227). San Francisco: Jossey-Bass Inc.

Pasquini, L. A., & Eaton, P. W. (2019). The #acadv community: Networked practices, professional development, and ongoing knowledge sharing in advising. *NACADA Journal, 39*(1), 101–115. https://doi.org/10.12930/NACADA-18-031

Pasquini, L. A., & Steele, G. E. (2016). Technology in academic advising: Perceptions and practices in higher education. *NACADA Technology in Advising Commission*, 1–20. https://doi.org/https://dx.doi.org/10.6084/m9.figshare.3053569.v1

Pentland, A. (2010). *Honest signals: How they shape our world.* The MIT Press.

Peters, M. A., Wang, H., Ogunniran, M. O., Huang, Y., Green, B., Chunga, J. O., ... Hayes, S. (2020). China's Internationalized Higher Education During Covid-19: Collective Student Autoethnography. *Postdigital Science and Education.* https://doi.org/10.1007/s42438-020-00128-1

Schwebel, D. C., Walburn, N. C., Klyce, K., & Jerrolds, K. L. (2012). Efficacy of advising outreach on student retention, academic progress and achievement, and frequency of advising contacts: A longitudinal randomized trial. *NACADA Journal, 32*(2), 36–43. https://doi.org/10.12930/0271-9517-32.2.36

Selwyn, N. (2016). Minding our language: why education and technology is full of bullshit ... and what might be done about it. *Learning, Media and Technology, 41*(3), 437–443. https://doi.org/10.1080/17439884.2015.1012523

Shahjahan, R. A. (2019). From 'Geopolitics of Being' towards Inter-being: Envisioning the 'In/visibles' in the Globalization of Higher Education. *Youth and Globalization, 1*(2), 282–306. https://doi.org/10.1163/25895745-00102005

Sobaih, A. E. E., Hasanein, A. M., & Abu Elnasr, A. E. (2020). Responses to COVID-19 in Higher Education: Social Media Usage for Sustaining Formal Academic Communication in Developing Countries. *Sustainability, 12*(16), 6520. https://doi.org/10.3390/su12166520

Stanoevska-Slabeva, K., & Schmid, B. F. (2001). A typology of online communities and community supporting platforms. *Proceedings of the 34th Annual Hawaii International Conference on System Sciences,* (February), 10. https://doi.org/10.1109/HICSS.2001.927041

Steele, G. E. (2016). Technology and academic advising. In T. J. Grites, M. A. Miller, & J. G. Voler (Eds.), *Beyond foundations: Developing as a master academic advisor* (pp. 305–326). John Wiley & Sons, Incorporated.

Storrie, K., Ahern, K., & Tuckett, A. (2010). A systematic review: Students with mental health problems-A growing problem. *International Journal of Nursing Practice, 16*(1). https://doi.org/10.1111/j.1440-172X.2009.01813.x

Thompson, L., & Prieto, L. (2013). Improving retention among college students: Investigating the utilization of virtualized advising. *Academy of Educational Leadership Journal, 17*(4), 13.

West, C. (2020). Supporting international students during COVID-19. Retrieved January 21, 2021, from NAFSA website: https://www.nafsa.org/ie-magazine/2020/5/6/supporting-international-students-during-covid-19

Williamson, B., Bayne, S., & Shay, S. (2020). The datafication of teaching in Higher Education: critical issues and perspectives. *Teaching in Higher Education, 25*(4), 351–365. https://doi.org/10.1080/13562517.2020.1748811

Zhang, Y. (Leaf). (2016). An overlooked population in community college. *Community College Review, 44*(2), 153–170. https://doi.org/10.1177/0091552116633293

## Bios

**Charles Liu, JD,** is an advising director with the Neighborhood Student Success Collaborative at Michigan State University. He is also a PhD student in the Higher, Adult, and Lifelong Education (HALE) program in the College of Education at Michigan State University. His research interests include academic advising policies and practices that affect student success initiatives. Email: charlie7@msu.edu

**Ravichandran Ammigan, PhD,** is the associate deputy provost for international programs and an assistant professor of Education at the University of Delaware. His current research focuses on international higher education, with a particular emphasis on the student experience and institutional support services. Email: rammigan@udel.edu

# Index